Botticelli Blue Skies

Botticelli Blue Skies

AN AMERICAN IN FLORENCE

Merrill Joan Gerber

The University of Wisconsin Press

The University of Wisconsin Press
1930 Monroe Street
Madison, Wisconsin 53711

www.wisc.edu/wisconsinpress/
3 Henrietta Street
London WC2E 8LU, England

5   4   3   2   1

Printed in the United States of America

Library of Congress Cataloging-in-Publication Data

Gerber, Merrill Joan.
Botticelli blue skies: an American in Florence / Merrill Joan Gerber.
p. cm.
ISBN 0-299-18020-4 (alk. paper)
1. Gerber, Merrill Joan—Journeys—Italy—Florence.   2. Florence (Italy)—
Description and travel.   3. Authors, American—20th century—Journeys—
Italy—Florence.   I. Title.
DG734.23.G47 2002
914.5′510493—dc21

2002002833

For Jenijoy La Belle

Author's Note

My gratitude and affection to Professor Mario Materassi and his wife, Millicent Lim, who read this book in manuscript and made many valuable suggestions about Italian matters and language. For whatever errors remain, I am solely responsible.

For guidance, support, and friendship, I thank Katerine Gaja, Riccardo and Angela Martelli, Renata Ceramelli, and Emanuela De Carlo. My gratitude also to Phyllis Mael for creating the Pasadena City College study-abroad program.

The events described in this book took place in the fall of 1996.

Though this memoir is factual, in some cases names have been changed.

Contents

1.	I Can't Go to Italy	1
2.	I'm Going to Italy	4
3.	*Gli Studenti*	6
4.	A Flat Full of Sun	9
5.	*Siamo Arrivati!*	11
6.	Via Visconti Venosta	16
7.	All Florence and Fiesole	19
8.	Postcards and E-Mail (One)	24
9.	Mosquitoes *(Zanzare)*	27
10.	First Lessons	30
11.	Reserved for the Mutilated	34
12.	A Piece of Laundry *(Un Pezzo del Bucato)*	41
13.	Jewish New Year (Rosh Hashonah)	45
14.	In the Bosom of My People	50
15.	Florentine Hospitality	56
16.	The Mystery of Marriage	60
17.	Fiesole and the Etruscan Sigh	64
18.	Postcards and E-Mail (Two)	70
19.	Italian Trains, Italian Men	73
20.	Seashells from the Adriatic and Roast Sardines	77
21.	The Fire, the Wedding, the Gondoliers	84
22.	The Jewish Ghetto in Venice, Losses, and Other Thefts	90
23.	The Movie Sets of Venice and Florence	99
24.	Botticelli Women, Italian Wives	103

Contents

25. Sciopero! *(Strike!)* 107
26. The Five-Hundred-Year-Old Farmhouse 111
27. Losing My Way, Discovering Treasures 116
28. Cinderella in Drag, a Night at the Ballet 123
29. "Rita, You Are the Girl I Have Loved . . ." 128
30. The Incorrupt Body 134
31. The Altar of the Virgin of Siena 138
32. *La Bocca della Verità* (The Mouth of Truth) 145
33. The British Institute Library, Jane Eyre, *il Porcellino* 154
34. The Uffizi, the Spanish Chapel, and *Madame Butterfly* 161
35. Halloween in Tuscany 169
36. Gypsies *(Zingari)* 178
37. "A Pistol That Shoots a Big Nail in Front of the Animal" 182
38. A Farm Feast, Colle Val D'Elsa, Bongo Drums for the Bishop 189
39. Picasso in the Dustbin, Windmills on the Wall 195
40. "Tabu" 200
41. Daughters of Florence 204
42. Massimo's Lizard-Skin Keychains, Riccardo's Castagna 208
43. No Coins in the Fountain 215
44. A Roman Ruin, I, the Sistine Chapel, and Judgment Day 225
45. St. Peter's Basilica and the Pope's Fishing Cap 230
46. The Spanish Steps, Desperation at the Tiber River 236
47. The Mosaics and Karaoke Bars of Ostia Antica 244
48. Thanksgiving *Tacchino Arrosto,* Elvis in Sequins 251
49. The Olive-Picking 259
50. The Artist, Her Villa, the Bombs of World War II 264
51. The Christmas Mystery, Two Big Macs 274
52. *L'Ultimo Addio,* Last Views of the Ponte Vecchio 281

Botticelli Blue Skies

1

I Can't Go to Italy

There is no possibility on earth that I can go to Italy with my husband in the fall. I am too firmly rooted in my California life to pick up and move to a different continent, though he promises me we will have a fine adventure. "I can't tell you exactly what will happen, but something will. And it will all be new and interesting."

I explain to him patiently that Italy is irrelevant to the center of my life, which—as he knows—is my mother's endless dying. I can't be across the world when she dies.

Joe points out that my mother has been dying for an extremely long time, more than five years. We are moving along ourselves—if we want to travel, the time for us is now. To each of my arguments he offers a solution. My sister will be here to look after my mother. Our daughters are grown and independent; perhaps one or all three of them can come to visit us in Italy. The cat? We will hire someone to feed him. My writing? I can do my work in Italy as well as here; we'll take along my laptop computer. He points out the many virtues of this opportunity for him to teach a group of students in Florence for next year's fall term. "We'll have three months in Tuscany, with an apartment provided and my regular salary to live on. How else could we ever afford to live in

Italy for three months! I think we should definitely do this," he says. "It's our chance."

The next day I go to my mother's bedside at the nursing home, where she lies paralyzed and on a feeding tube. I ask her what she thinks about my going to Italy for three months.

"You can't wait for me, I could live to be a hundred. Go and do what you have to do. I'll just be here. And if something happens . . . don't come back."

"Meaning?"

"Meaning if I die, don't come back."

Even with her permission, I am resistant. Do I really want to leave my friends, my comfortable life, my familiar surroundings? Do I want to leave my kitchen appliances, my computer, my down comforter?

Each evening at dinner, as the deadline for Joe's decision approaches, he and I debate at the kitchen table, he using words like "adventure" and "travel" and "new things to think about" while I counter with "comfort, obligations, our life here." Who will water the plants? Who will take care of the house? I remind him of the scene in Virginia Woolf's *To the Lighthouse,* where—after the mother dies and the family abandons the summer house—the place is invaded by the elements, by wind and rain, by rats and mice, and goes to ruin. Joe seems incredulous that I am worried about the grass in the yard, and a few scraggly houseplants. The problem is, he's not a worrier. He doesn't have my highly developed skill of being able to imagine catastrophes.

In secret I invent private, infantile arguments I can't bring myself to say to his face: "*I'll just be a tag-along teacher's wife. I'll be a third wheel. You and the Italian teacher will be a team, and I'll have nothing to do. The students won't be interested in me; you'll be too busy to pay attention to me. I'll be bored.*" Bored in Italy? I'd have to be in a coma, I assure myself. One day I am talking to the clerk at the Post Office and remark: "I may have to go to Italy for three months." He replies: "My heart is breaking for you. You really have my sympathy." He hands me a roll of stamps. "Could I come and carry your bags?"

"Okay," I tell my husband at dinnertime one night. "Okay, I'll go to Italy." My tone of voice suggests I have been coerced, have no choice, that I must give in, go to this foreign country and possibly lose my mind there, maybe even my life.

"Good," Joe says cheerfully. "I'll tell the director of the study-abroad program that we accept the offer." He gets up from his chair and kisses the top of my head. "Thank you," he adds.

With the trip still months away, I begin making my "Trip List." Errands to do, items to take, bills to pay in advance, things to be sure not to forget. I will have to interview candidates to feed my cat. I will have to ask my doctor for medicines for every possible disease. (I check the Merck Manual and begin to make lists of what diseases might befall us in Italy.) I will have to buy walking shoes, reinforced and padded, to prepare for the cobblestones of Florence. I will have to get travelers' checks, put my checking account in order, exchange dollars for lire. I start looking through my wardrobe and find it totally lacking. I do not own one article of clothing I could take on a trip. I am exhausted already.

In the meantime, Joe gets busy improving his Italian.

"*Buona sera, signora,*" says the tape player at breakfast. "*Dov'è il gabinetto? Quanto costa un biglietto turistico? Vorrei una birra.*"

"Don't you want to practice?" Joe asks me.

"And learn to talk like a two-year-old? No, thank you. *Arrivederci. Ciao.*"

2

I'm Going to Italy

When you have a major shock in life, the kind you first refuse, then resist, then deny, you must finally take it in and make a space for it.

I am going to Italy in September, and that is that.

What will I do there? I don't know yet. I hold in my mind, as a kind of mantra, what Joe said to me: "I can't tell you exactly what will happen, but something will."

Taking this trip will be a matter of faith. What is the game children play in school to help them learn to trust others? They fall backward and let others catch them. So I must fall backward into the arms of Italy and hope to be embraced and treated gently. Still, should the arms of Italy be slightly out of position when I land, I have to make some preparations for my being dropped there for three months.

Will I go to the famous museums? Of course, but not too many. Will I go to the great churches? Of course, but not every day. Like a newborn, I will discover life and language at my own pace in this new world.

For the past year or two, my three daughters have communicated with me daily from their various places in the world by e-mail. If I can continue to connect to them from Italy, I will be happy. However, no computer expert to whom I turn for advice seems quite sure how this will work or whether it will work; I am cautioned by everyone that Italy is famous for how nothing works as expected. The Italian phone lines are different, equipment from the United States may not recognize Italian dial tones. But slowly I put together a plan: I buy a modem, a voltage regulator, an Italian phone jack, plug adapters, surge protectors, even a portable printer. I subscribe to an internet server that promises a connection in Florence but cautions me: there are no guarantees. The moment of truth will come the day I try to log on.

I begin to hear from friends who learn of my travel plans: one will give me the address of a woman she knew in Rome thirty years ago and who now lives in Florence in a five-hundred-year-old farmhouse. Another will put me in touch with a professor at the University of Florence. I might look into the Jewish Community Center, or the American Church.

The more I do in preparation, the more confident I feel. My spirit is lighter, my heart happier. When I find a neighbor boy to feed my cat and discover that they actually enjoy each other's company, I am filled with relief and pleasure.

I attack my desk with zeal: I pay $200 in advance to every service I can think of: the phone company, the gas and electric companies, the water department, the Department of Motor Vehicles, the car and home owners' insurance company, the gardener, even the plumber—in case a pipe bursts. I pay estimated taxes up to the next century, it seems. I arrange for my sister to take care of our mail. I plot to use up all my perishable food before we leave.

My blood is up. An adventure lies ahead. At my time of life, this is no small matter!

3

Gli Studenti

Today, Nicoletta, the Italian teacher who will be teaching with Joe, is holding a reception for the "Semester in Florence" students at her home, a mixer where they will get to know one another better and choose roommates for the stay in Italy. Nicoletta and Joe have interviewed and accepted thirty-eight students for the trip; each one has been told of the rigors of travel and warned of the culture shock they will face. A special admonition is offered about the quantity of wine that is available in Italy—and how everyone is counting on their good sense in dealing with it.

The course of study is settled: Joe will teach humanities and history, Nicoletta will teach Italian language. That Nicoletta resembles Sophia Loren is of no small interest to me, though Joe has protested that he hadn't noticed. Nicoletta has an easy laugh, a happy nature; I can tell at once that she is counting the moments till she is in Italy. She was born in Rome and is anxious to demonstrate its beauties and glories to the students. I admire her energy, her large dark eyes, her sensual Italian mouth. (Well, it is a good thing I have decided to go along, isn't it?) Her husband, an American, is a handsome, cheery fellow and is busy setting out refreshments for the students when we arrive. He won't be with us on the trip—he has his business to attend to at home.

The students arrive one by one. Joe has prepared me for some of them: Marta, the cabaret singer who wears great dangling music-note earrings; Robin, the boy with the silver stud in the middle of his tongue; Rosanna, the tall blonde young woman who is a hairdresser and has offered to bring her scissors to Italy in order to serve as official haircutter for the students. There will be thirty-two young women going, and only six men. (Or are they girls and boys? For the most part, they are in their early twenties—except for Mrs. Pedrini, the seventy-two-year-old student.)

Even as I am wondering which of these young women will want to room with a seventy-two-year-old, the woman in question enters Nicoletta's front door. With short dark hair and elegantly applied makeup, Mrs. Pedrini sails in, wearing a glittery skirt and backless lucite high heels. A silver beret perches on her head. She is carrying a basket full of colored wool pompoms and sets out at once distributing them to all of us—students and teachers alike. She says we must attach them to our suitcases—since then they will be easier to identify at the airport. She is all bounce, energy, and good will.

Many of the students are from Hispanic backgrounds. They think their knowledge of Spanish will make it simple to use the Italian language. Also, since Italy is the home of the Pope, their families are thrilled for them to have this opportunity. Most students will be getting financial aid and loans from the college to make this trip.

Nicoletta makes her prepared announcements—that everyone should pack warm pajamas since the heat is not turned on in Italy—legally—till November 1. That we should all bring towels, since they are not provided in the apartments. That we must remember we will have no TVs, no VCRs, no microwaves, and no luxuries. That living in Italy is *expensive*. That we will all have to learn to get around the city by bus, learn to use the currency, to buy food, and to live among Italians. That the buildings are very old, that those in *centro* generally have no elevators. Some of the apartments may be four or five flights up. "It may be tough at first," Nicoletta tells us all. "But be flexible and creative. And, remember, this is only for three months, it isn't your Life."

I suffer a little pang of terror at that moment. It seems to me it *will* be my life. What if we get a tenth-floor walkup, without a shower, with beds made of concrete? My knees feel weak—what if we end up living in a dungeon?

But Mrs. Pedrini is passing around a tray of pizza slices and presses us each to take a piece.

"Molto delizioso!" she says as the scent of basil and oregano swirls through the air. She urges us to breathe in—deeply—the aroma of Italy.

"I'm already packed!" she assures us all. "I can't wait to set foot in Bella Italia!"

4

A Flat Full of Sun

E-MAIL FROM CENTRO LINGUISTICO ITALIANO DANTE ALIGHIERI:
Signora, herewith we give you the address of your apartment,
which is Via Visconti Venosta, 66, 50136 Firenze, ITALIA
This flat that we have reserved for you and the Professor is
very nice it is on the fourth floor and is composed of: two bed-
rooms, one with two beds (for married couple), and a smaller
room with just one bed. This small room is with a terrace,
there is also an other terrace on the kitchen overlooking the
Arno River, from where you can see Florentine hills. Then a
big kitchen with washing machine, a bathroom with shower
and bath, and very spacious living room. There is also a roof
terrace from which you can really see all Florence and Fiesole.
I repeat that the apt is really nice, maybe one of the biggest
that we have, there is a lift, but the flat is not close to school.
It is 45 minute nice walking along the river, but there is also a
good bus no. 14 which in 10/15 minutes takes you to the cen-
tre. It's a flat full of sun, and in a very nice residential area,
with a lot of good shops, an alimentari and supermarket, not
far from a swimming pool and near a big green area. IT HAS A

PHONE PLUG TOO—*for E-mail connection. If you want to find the street on a normal map, it is difficult but follow the river towards the right side, and it is after the last bridge, Ponte Verrazzano, and the area is called Bellariva. We look forward to meeting you and the Professor and to welcome you to Italy.*

5

Siamo Arrivati!

We fly to Rome on TWA Flight 801, shortly after TWA Flight 800 to Paris blows up in midair just outside New York and 230 people are lost in the ocean. I have brought along my laptop computer and entertain myself with Tripeaks, Golf, Tetris, Free Cell, and Tut's Tomb until my battery blinks a warning and quits. Joe is continuing to study Italian verbs, having the ability to concentrate in situations where I can barely stay in my seat. My friend Jenijoy said to me before we left, "Let's see if your fairy tale marriage can survive a trip like this. Three months with no one to talk to but your husband!"

It's true that—even as we cross the mighty ocean—all my safety nets are being removed: my family (not counting Joe, who is, in fact, not even my blood relative), my language, my environment, and all my appliances that run on 120 volts. Mrs. Pedrini was kind enough to pass out to everyone a lire-equivalent list, with 1,500 lire to the dollar being the base of her calculations. Just imagining that a ten-dollar item will cost 15,000 lire makes my heart skip a beat. I have already packed away in my carry-on luggage my brown leather American-money wallet, with its green bills, and taken out my pink cloth Italian-money wallet (with Velcro closures), full of pastel-colored lire. The 1,000-lire note has a kind-looking older woman on one side and on the other a sweet family scene of a boy and girl doing homework at a table in a room with blue and pink wallpaper. The 5,000-lire note shows a foppish, curly-haired man on one side and what seems to be the statue of a woman in the woods, singing an operatic aria, on the other. The 10,000-lire note offers a Napoleon look-alike on one side and a state building on the other. I have two more bills to examine: the 50,000-lire note displays a handsome Errol Flynn type on one side and a warrior on a rearing horse on the back. Finally, the 100,000-lire note (I feel I am holding gold bouillon now) shows a man and a woman touching hands, with the added face of Caravaggio (labeled) on one side and an elegantly arranged bowl of fruit in a woven basket on the other. This bank note alone, according to Mrs. Pedrini, is worth $66.66.

The students going with us do not seem to be considering their new money. Those that I can see, since they are scattered randomly around the plane, are generally sleeping, or watching the complimentary movie. Two of them are huddled, heads together, in the very back of the plane: Robin, the boy with the pierced body parts, and a long- and curly-haired buddy of his. Nicoletta has somehow gotten a seat in Business Class, and I see—as I glance through the partition on my way to the lavatory—that she is peacefully sleeping, stretched out in the large space. When I return to my seat, Joe tells me that 120 students from various colleges in California are on this same flight with us and will also attend classes in the Scuola Dante Alighieri where Joe will be teaching his students. He has met a couple of the other teachers who will be sharing classroom space in the school with Nicoletta and him.

I check my watch—it's still on Los Angeles time. When do I set it to Italian time? It's nine hours later in Italy—that means—no, better not to know. Better just to get there and join into life as I find it. We left our house at 3 A.M. this morning—we're due to arrive in Rome at 9 A.M. Roman time. In the meantime, I should be watching the complimentary movie about people being blown through the cosmos by tornadoes. Sooner or later the airline attendants will come along, singing their menu: "Chicken or beef." After that I will inflate my neck pillow and try to imagine I am not in a silver sardine can speeding through the cosmos. And, somehow, eventually, if Fate is good to us, we will land in Italy.

Three tour buses wait at the Rome Fiumicino airport to take the 120 American students to Florence. There seems to be a problem. Each student has brought the maximum luggage allowance—two large suitcases and one carry-on. There are lots of extras, too, from what I can see in the pile on the tarmac—a guitar, pillows, stuffed animals, tennis rackets. (Do Italians play tennis?) The problem is that there's no room for all the suitcases. These are touring buses, and the tourists they serve are usually on vacation for a week or two—and have one suitcase apiece. It becomes clear that we will not be able to load everything on these three buses. Much arguing is taking place between Nicoletta and the bus drivers—my introduction to the Italian language in-the-flesh. Shouting, gesticulating, pushing forth of lips, chins, fists. The debaters address the heavens with their open palms. I'm terribly impressed with how real Italian life is unfolding before me.

Just then I happen to look down at my feet—and gasp. I have elephant legs! My ankles are as thick as hitching posts. I look at Nicoletta's feet—they seem as shapely as they were in California. Thirteen hours of flying time with a two-hour layover in New York has done this to me. I should be grateful to have arrived with only this damage, but I am appalled at these sausages sticking out of my shoes.

Joe—whose recently acquired Italian can't quite bring him to comprehension—is looking for a hint as to what is going on. Nicoletta informs him finally that they will have to hire a van—otherwise we can't get all the students and their suitcases to Florence. And the van? When will it arrive? Nicoletta shrugs. "Who knows," she says. "You know how Italians are."

We have been in Italy three hours, it is now noon, and we are all—120 students and their teachers alike—leaning on our luggage carts and fending off postcard salesmen. The men rush up to us and display photos of the treasures we have just recently seen in a video of Italy that Nicoletta showed at one of the orientation meetings. There is the Colosseum, the Arch of Titus, the Trevi Fountain, the Baths of Caracalla—we've seen it all. Why not just take the next plane home so we can have some food, find a bathroom, and get some sleep!

Still, the price seems cheap. I buy a packet of postcards, sit down on the cement right there where some of the other students are already sprawled on their jackets, and start writing postcards to my three daughters. *Siamo Arrivati!* I tell them. *Daddy and I are safely arrived in Roma, the Eternal City.*

After two hours on the road—the hired van, overflowing with suitcases, is following the buses—the caravan of vehicles make a stop along the autostrada. Our bus driver, speaking into the microphone, announces: "Pee-pee stop."

A ripple of laughter comes from the amused students. We all pour out and find our way into a food and rest building where in a downstairs area the girls and I rush into the ladies' room. And there sits a lady, with a plate of coins on a little table. Apparently we have to pay her to use the toilet. However, none of us have Italian coins. I take from my fanny pack my pink wallet and pull out my smallest bill, 1,000 lire. A thousand anything seems a lot to pay for what we are all here to do. Still, at this point, I would pay a king's ransom. I hand the woman my 1,000-lire bill, and she gives me back a two-color coin—silver in the center, gold around the rim. Mrs. Pedrini is close behind me and informs us that it's costing us 500 lire—about thirty-three cents—to pee. A bargain, we agree, at any price.

Upstairs, our students are having their first go at Italian cuisine— panini: sandwiches with cheese and tomato, or cheese and prosciutto. Or sliced melanzina—eggplant slices swimming in olive oil. I can't imagine that my stomach will accept anything of that nature just now. What I want is comfort food, what I want is . . . mashed potatoes!

Three hours later, our drivers deposit us all on the bank of the Arno River where the lungarno, the street that runs along the Arno River, meets the bridge called Ponte Alle Grazie. The time in Italy is 5 P.M. Two secretaries from the Scuola Dante Alighieri are there to arrange for the 120 students to be identified, given keys to their apartments, and taken to them. Several taxis are waiting at the curb to begin the transfers. They can take a couple of students at a time with their luggage. I understand that they will come and go, come and go till all of us are deposited in the far and distant reaches of the city.

It looks like we will be here all night. We are the "teachers"—we have to stay here till the last students are safely delivered to their apartments. My bladder is full again—it cannot wait, my hungry stomach cannot wait, my elephantine legs cannot stand, I never wanted to come to Italy in the first place, and my husband looks extremely foreign and unattractive to me. I begin to cry, silent, unadult tears of exhaustion, misery, and frustration. It has been thirty-three hours since we rose from our comfortable bed to come to this . . . to this movie set! Through my tears, I can see the blurry, gaudy orange dome of the Duomo, the towering tower of the Palazzo Vecchio, and the muddy waters of the Arno down which a lone kayaker strokes his way against the current. In the distance are the arcs of the famous bridges, the Ponte Vecchio, the Ponte Santa Trinitá, and the Ponte Alle Carraia.

I am not ready to appreciate beauty, I refuse to appreciate beauty, I hate beauty. Beauty is an illusion; life is all pain and suffering. I am more than willing to embroider variations on this theme, but, against my will, my tears of misery begin to dry in the mellow rays of golden light from the setting sun. I lean against the lungarno wall and watch the river moving beneath me. A thought taps at another dimension of my mind, pointing out a tower of high white clouds that float in great snowy swoops, one above the other, at the east end of the river. The Florentine hills are emerald green in the distance. Stands of cypress trees decorate the hillsides like the points of small crowns. I lean back, resting my elbows on the river wall, and breathe deeply. A soothing breeze blowing over the Arno seems to catch my pain in an invisible net and lift it up to the top of the Duomo. I see it land—and dissipate—atop the golden glowing ball of the Duomo's lantern.

Joe comes up behind me and puts his arm around my shoulder. "Just one more round of kids to go—and then we'll get to our place. Hang in there."

6

Via Visconti Venosta

We stumble through the three fortress-like doorways of our new home on Via Visconti Venosta, dragging our four enormous suitcases and two roll-ons. We stop at each barrier to figure out how to use the three keys given us at the lungarno: front metal gate, front glass door of building, and wooden apartment door. We ride up in the *ascensore* to the fifth floor . . . and find heaven. A bed, a toilet, a kitchen—what more could anyone ask? The bed (*letto matrimoniale*) is a soft, square basket with a foam base, two single mattresses laid within, and an edging all around of cloth-covered foam. At once I lay myself inside it, on the dull green cloth that matches the edging, fully dressed, arms crossed over my chest like a saint in a display case. It doesn't take long for Joe to join me on the other side. Our bodies crave the horizontal position. We breathe with relief, staring at the ceiling: our new Italian ceiling. Further exploration and discovery must wait. First we must have this healing moment, a pause in which we absorb rest like a balm. Joe's hand inches over to cover mine, but even that is almost too much sensation. He takes his hand away. We need total absence of stimulation. We need only to breathe and to close our eyes.

An hour later we crawl out of the basket of our bed and look around. We have two windows in our bedroom, both armored with slatted wood shutters; we have a wardrobe closet, as well—a splintery, nailed-together box with a few wooden drawers at the bottom and a rod for clothing (a couple of hangers are provided) at the top. We notice two bedside tables, and two lamps upon them. Good . . . wonderful, in fact. They've thought of everything, those mystery persons who are our landlords.

The taxi that took us here drove a long route—we know our apartment is far beyond the old city of Florence—but the advantage of distance is modernity. There is, for one thing, the elevator, and now I see the lovely bathroom: big (Italian!) tub, stall shower, and the inevitable bidet, which sits face to face with the toilet and next to the sink.

Joe and I, in a kind of euphoria, wander about the apartment, calling out to each other what we've discovered. He, the living room! He guides me into it, and I see furniture covered with flowered sheets. Matching sheets, it must be acknowledged, but under the sheets I find ancient leather furniture, scarred and torn, but once (in its day) elegant. I sit and find the couch comfortable. Joe tries one of the two chairs. He declares, "Not bad." All right! We can live here!

The decorations around the room are composed mainly of stones and rocks. A tin pot of gray and white stones stands on a table in the corner. And on the coffee table (made of painted black and white wooden squares) is a small wooden bowl . . . filled with little, smooth-edged rocks! Well, it's clear our landlords are not taking any chances by having valuables in the apartment. The artworks on the walls are paper posters of Florentine churches.

In the kitchen I find what I feared having to deal with: a gas stove that must be lit with matches, a scratched porcelain sink (with red rubber mats on each side), and a refrigerator three feet high with a freezer big enough only for two narrow ice-cube trays. (Already they are coated with a thick layer of frost.)

I knew I would not find a kitchen like the one at home, with microwave, dishwasher, convection oven, and seamless white countertop. But I hope I am a woman of character; I hope I can stand up to what I find in the cupboards. I count two blackened frying pans and two aluminum pasta pots, dented and with broken Bakelite handles. The drawers reveal a few dull knives with red plastic handles, some forks, six *cucchiaini caffè*—tiny spoons to be used with espresso. There's no peeler, no can opener, no corkscrew . . . but Joe says there must be a corkscrew. This is Italy. And he is right—there is a corkscrew . . . but no wine glasses. The drinking vessels consist of two very large mugs, several espresso cups, and a few juice glasses.

In the middle of the kitchen is a round table, covered with green oil-cloth pinched to the table rim with silver clips. And in the middle of the table stands a bag of provisions; Joe guesses they were left there by the staff of the Scuola Dante Alighieri. A box (!) of milk, a package of "toast" (dried, hard bread squares), two oranges, and a small packet of espresso coffee.

"Italians think Americans like toast," Joe says. "That's nice of them."

"Very nice," I agree. "Could we go to bed now? My knees are buckling."

"Should we eat something?" Joe suggests.

I saw into one of the oranges with a dull knife. We each eat a piece of the crumbly toast and share the orange. I see the coffee maker on a high shelf and take it down; it's a two-tiered thing with octagonal sides, parts that unscrew into two pieces, a strainer in one, a little chimney in the other. Making coffee now would be far too difficult an undertaking. Besides, how would I light the stove? There isn't a single match in the apartment.

It's dark out, we can't see much from the windows but the headlights of cars. We don't even unlock our suitcases but peel off our clothes and drop them where they fall. Joe sleeps in his undershirt and I in the shirt I wore on the plane. I almost forgive him for making me come to this new land. We kiss goodnight in Italy, pull up the rough woolen blanket, fall instantly asleep.

7

All Florence and Fiesole

In the morning, the Italian sun brings us both to the windows. From the kitchen we see the promised Arno River (or, rather, we see the depression beyond the trees that would be the river) as well as the *autostrada,* whose entrance is directly across the road from our building. Beyond both the river and the highway are the graceful arcs of the Florentine hills, punctuated by stands of cypress trees. From the "small room with terrace" we can see the hills of Fiesole, as well as the terraces of the neighbors who live in the surrounding apartment houses. Already, at this early hour, women on several of the terraces are hanging out clothes. They seem expert at this, shaking out workshirts and lining them up with colorful clothespins like an array of hanging men. When one of the women looks up and sees us, I smile, but she looks away quickly. I get a clear message that this is not a social arena; she's in her bathrobe, she's doing personal chores, she is not interested in a visit. One floor below, an old man is on his terrace, talking to a canary in a cage. A dog is at his feet, tail swishing. The old man smells a flower in a pot, takes a pair of clippers from an outdoor storage cabinet, and gently trims a few leaves from his plant.

Joe reminds me we have a washing machine in the apartment. We do? He says it's the small white object with a glass window next to the

A flat full of sun

refrigerator. In my dazed state the night before, I had not even seen such a machine. Now I rush to the kitchen to check and instead find that I am in the living room. There's something about the geography of these four small rooms that confuses me—perhaps it has something to do with the red spiral staircase that stands just inside the front door, giving the appearance of a spinning top from all the rooms around it.

"Let's climb up the staircase," I beg Joe, who has come in from the terrace. I go first up the twisting flight, holding onto the rails. There's a tinny clanking sound as I reach to the darkness at the top. "There's a door here, but the doorknob doesn't turn," I report.

"Here, let me try." I move back to let him squeeze past me, hear him manipulating metal against metal, hear the turn of a key, and suddenly our faces are flooded with light. The roof terrace is dazzled with sunlight; before us is a white expanse of pebbled asphalt as large as the apartment beneath, with a breathtaking, circular view of the city of Florence. I step into the light, and there in the distance is the dome of the Duomo, as majestic from afar as it was from the edge of Ponte alle Grazie. Below us is the hidden river, the *autostrada,* the cypress trees, while behind us are the hills of Fiesole. I spin on my heel in the dizzying beauty of it all. I understand that this view is mine, or mine for the next three months, which for now seems almost as good as forever.

Food is the next requirement. Where are these "good shops and supermarkets" we were promised? We will have to find them ourselves. There is only one way to walk, away from the river (unless we wish to cross the autostrada bridge that goes over the Arno and heads south), so we carefully lock the door of our flat, take our many keys with us, and set out to explore.

Rounding the corner, we see that a Fiat body shop is situated just below our bedroom windows. (How strange that in the midst of a densely populated residential area there should be a car repair business. Even as we pass it by, we hear the sound of a pneumatic drill loud enough to rattle the windows.)

A *pasticceria* is on the corner, its display resplendent with tortes, cream puffs, lemon tarts, and delicacies whose names I don't know yet.

Though bread is number one on my shopping list, there is no bread in the shop. We walk on and pass the local bar—several men are standing up at the counter, drinking coffee from tiny white cups. Next are the *macelleria,* where meat is sold, then the *fruttivendolo,* where a great variety of fruits and vegetables are displayed outside the store.

I think I could manage to ask for *due banane* or *tre pomodori*—but more than that could be beyond my skills. What are the Italian words for garlic, for onion, for celery? I should have studied more of the language, I should have practiced.

But across the street, I discover, there is a supermarket. "Conad" says the sign above the door, and below are grocery carts, lined up and inviting us to take one. Crossing the street to get there is no easy matter—a line of motor scooters is roaring along the road. Joe and I pause, waiting for them to pass; several are driven by young women wearing dress suits, heels, jewelry, with leather purses down on the floorboards by their feet. Their faces express a certain aloof dignity, even as they accelerate and zoom past us. I think of my own daughters riding such vehicles, bodies vulnerable and open to accident and injury. But I see no Italian mothers wringing their hands in the street. In fact, there are a few women my age blithely zipping along on their motor scooters, as well.

In the parking lot, I find that I can't take a grocery cart; each one is chained to the next.

"I think you have to pay," Joe says. "There's a slot for money."

The only coin I have is the change I got from my 1,000-lire note in the ladies' room on the autostrada—I try it in the slot, and the cart comes free. With our rented cart, we pass a young black man selling cigarette lighters, socks, and other items on a blanket he's spread out near the entrance. Once in the store, we hear, coming over the PA system, the voice of Cher singing "Babe, I got you Babe. . . ."

We encounter surprises at every step. Before I can select fruits and vegetables, apparently I must—for hygienic reasons—put on plastic gloves. Only then am I permitted to squeeze and poke the tomatoes to my satisfaction. Once selected and dropped in a plastic bag, the fruit must be weighed on a scale. This is done by pressing the drawing that best corresponds to my purchase. I push the "tomato" button and out comes a sticker, displaying the name of the product, the price per kilogram, the actual weight of my tomatoes, and the price I am to pay. This bag is 1430 lire. Almost a dollar, using Mrs. Pedrini's scale of exchange. Joe is ahead of me now at the meat counter. The chickens come in two versions, with and without heads and feet. An Italian chicken costs four times as much as a California chicken. I choose one minus its head, then pick up speed and select other items we need to begin our cooking life: eggs and juice and milk (milk comes fresh in a carton or unrefrigerated, sealed in a box), yogurt and margarine and olive oil, boxes of pasta, jars of tomato sauce, cans of olives. ·

Because we have been advised to drink bottled water, I buy two liters of *acqua minerale sorgente*—whatever *sorgente* means—and add a couple of bottles of Chianti Classico, as well.

When we check out at the counter (they do have bar codes in Italy, and the process is swift), I open my pink wallet filled with lire notes and explain to the checker the first rendition of what I know I will have to say every day in Italy: *"Non parlo Italiano, sono Americana."* I trust the young woman to choose the bills she needs, while Joe stands by watching. She gives me back a handful of bills and change, asking if I want to buy *sacchetti* (she holds up a plastic bag). Apparently I do— since what will we carry the food in otherwise? She takes some additional coins from my hand to pay for the bags. Then she turns to the next customer, our indication that her job is done, that the persons who buy the food are the persons who have to bag it. Joe and I load our purchases into six bags—and then realize, with another little shock, that the persons who bag the food have to carry it home in their bare hands.

8

Postcards and E-Mail (One)

Peaceful Hills Convalescent Hospital, Room 123:
Dearest Mother—
We arrived safely in "Bella Italia"—we have a comfortable apartment with a view of the Arno River. I have to light the gas stove with a match ("fiammifero" is the word for match. And the word for flaming is "fiammeggiante"—isn't the language beautiful and amazing?) I am hoping a nurse will read this to you if you can't hold it yourself. All my love, M.

Dearest Girls—
This is the "acid test"—to see if all my preparations for sending e-mail will work. If you get this letter, we can communicate across the continents! We tried to make our first pot of pasta tonight but couldn't get the burners to light. Dad saw an electric wire with a plug on the end coming out of the stove and thought there might be an electric broiler inside the stove. As soon as he plugged it in, all the lights in the flat blew out. Thinking a neighbor might be able to tell us what to do next,

I knocked on doors in the building till a woman one flight be-
low us opened her door and—thank heavens!—could speak
English. She rents her bedroom and provides meals to two
young women students, about your ages, mid- to late twenties
(one is from Kansas, studying sculpture, and one is from
Brazil, studying Italian language). The girls offered to come
up at once and show us where the fuse box was located. A
push of the button and the lights were on again, but the girls
warned us never to plug in the stove at the same time the wa-
ter heater switch was lit. Today we don't have to worry, since
there's no water in the building at all. Luckily we bought
bottled water to drink. I had no idea what the word "sor-
gente" meant on the bottle, but I have since found out it
means "to rise, to surge" and also that it is spring water. So
we have surging, carbonated water spring. Acqua minerale, al
gas. I learn a fact a minute here.

The girls from downstairs advised us to buy an "accendi-
gas," a device that lights the gas via a spark from a flint, a
safer way than from a match. (Remember those toys you had
as children, rainbow-colored wheels that spun and sparked as
you pressed the handle?) The reason we couldn't light the
gas—even with a match—was that we never turned on the
gas safety valve (on the wall behind the stove), which has to
be in the upright position for gas to flow. The accendigas,
however, will not light the oven, which requires that a match
be put in the hole to ignite the broiler flame beneath. After all
this education, Dad and I are too hungry to try to cook, so
we're going down the street to the Grande Mondo Ristorante
Cinese. Love, Mom

E-MAIL TO MY SISTER:

Dearest B—
We've had our first Italian dinner, and I fear I must admit it
was Chinese. The Grande Mondo has a great goldfish tank in
the window, populated by ordinary goldfish as well as by eels.

*When we admired them, the Chinese waiter said, smiling,
"Mangiare?"—meaning did we want to eat them? I definitely
declined, and we ordered Dragon chips, Zuppa Wan Tan, and
Primavera something-or-other, which last two I guessed might
be won ton soup and spring rolls, which they were! The
"Dragon chips" were shrimp-flavored dragon morsels, I suppose. They didn't serve tea but did serve little ruby colored
glasses of sweet wine with the meal. We had "gelato fritto"
for dessert, fried ice cream. Just as we finished dinner, a group
of Italian young men and women came in and were seated.
The women immediately stuck the chopsticks into their hair
(for entertainment), and the young men lit up cigarettes. In no
time the room was filled with a fog of smoke. I see that Italy
hasn't figured out yet that smoking will kill you. These young
people seemed so happy, though—laughing and talking
loudly. Italians seem to have a talent for happiness—perhaps
it's their religion that keeps them inwardly peaceful.*

*Another thing: I haven't seen a single overweight person in
Florence. Florentines are thin and stylish—even if they do eat
fried ice cream. As we left the "ristorante," we saw a group of
young Chinese girls, apparently related to the owners, sitting
at a round table with a mountain of bean sprouts before
them. They were patiently and lovingly picking the green
husks off the tips of the sprouts, all the while talking animatedly in Italian. Dinner was not expensive—38,000 lire, which
sounds like a lot but was really only about $21 for the two of
us. And did I mention that the restaurant has a glass floor,
with lights beneath, under which there is water, and probably
goldfish (or eels), though I didn't actually see any. Love, M*

9

Mosquitoes (*Zanzare*)

All night they attack like kamikaze planes, these filaments of torture—squadrons of Italian mosquitoes. In our innocence we have opened windows during the evening and now our bedroom is a bombardiers' haven.

"Do you hear one?" I say in the deep of night, and Joe, beside me, says, "I hear ten."

We listen; they are right above our faces.

"Turn on the light fast," he says.

The minute I turn on the light, it is silent. The minute I turn it off, they are back at our ears. Nature's mistake was to give them a buzz, and thus give their prey warning. This seems only to prevent us from sleeping. Eventually they bite us anyway.

We try to sleep again. I cover my head with the heavy wool blanket but feel I am suffocating. Even with just the sheet over my face, I have a sense of myself immobilized, corpse-like.

Joe isn't getting any closer to sleep either. "Turn on the light again," he suggests, and, though I do, the light cast from the 40-watt bulb doesn't do much to illuminate the room. There is no bulb in the entire apartment that emits a light bright enough to read by. Our good fortune under the circumstances is that the walls of the room are painted white; the only decorations are a pair of Rorschach-type prints opposite the bed. We each take a shoe in hand and tiptoe around the room, Joe in his T-shirt, and I in mine.

"Could that be him?" he calls softly, and I look up to see a three dimensional thread near the ceiling above the bed. "I think that's him," I say, "but doesn't it have to be a her?"

Joe stands on the spongy mattress and aims. He throws the shoe—and the creature vanishes.

"You blew him away! Let me try if it lands again."

Though we peer and stalk and tiptoe around for another five minutes, no bug appears. I'm tired. Joe is tired. We discuss the hopelessness of getting back into bed. It's then that I see a landing take place low down on the blank wall, near the wardrobe. It's so delicate, so invisible; it could be a filament of spider web, a molecule of dust. I use the palm of my hand, moving it very slowly, like a T'ai Chi master, toward the three-pointed shadow. I lunge and smash it.

Blood is on the wall in the shape of a little red flag. It's my blood, or Joe's—but there it is, evidence of violence done to us. I hear a sharp smack from across the room, and Joe cries, "Got it!" We are on the warpath. Blood is everywhere.

"I'm sorry—I can't live in Italy," I tell Joe. "No one warned me about this—that we'd have to live here three months without sleeping. I think I have to go home. They didn't mention this in the travel books."

"Maybe there's a fly swatter somewhere in the apartment."

"Don't be silly, that would be an admission that life in Italy is not heaven on earth."

In the morning, we make another foray to the Conad supermarket and see an entire shelf dedicated to the murdering of mosquitoes: *"Tutta la notte senza zanzare," "Antizanzare elettronico! Protezione costante per tutta la notte."* In case this method fails, there is another product called "StopPick"—apparently for use after the bites drive you crazy. Which to buy? There is the spiral filament you light with a match and burn all night, incense-like. There is the plug-in glass ball filled with green fluid that emits a constant vapor. And there is the *Vape Mat con 10 pi-*

astrine insetticida—a machine with little lozenges of poison that dissolve through the night and possibly poison you along with the mosquitoes.

We buy a fly swatter for 1,500 lire: red plastic. Thus armed, and ecologically responsible, we venture home again.

Nicoletta phones as we come in the door. She tells Joe that tonight there is a festival at the Duomo to commemorate the 500th year of its completion. There will be candles lit all over the church's facade and processions and parades. It's also the Day of the Madonna—an occasion called *Rificolona* is celebrated that recalls the past when peasants came into town to worship, lighting their way with funny-looking lanterns so that the city-folk made fun of them. Now, children carry lanterns shaped like stars or moons or puppets, with candles inside them. They walk in a procession along the River Arno to Piazza Santissima Annunziata—where the children try to break each other's lanterns with pebbles shot from elastic slingshots.

"We'll try to get there," Joe tells her—and we spend the afternoon poring over the ATAF Autobus schedule *della zona di Firenze centro*. It looks like nothing so much as a bowl of multi-colored pasta squiggles, intertwining and twisting in a game of untangle-these-strands. If one of these brightly-colored lines is a bus from our neighborhood to the Duomo, we can't fathom which one it is.

"We'll figure it out," Joe says, the first of his many such pronouncements. But as evening approaches, we fall down into our basket-bed near senseless with jet lag and sleep deprivation from the previous night's "Festival of the Mosquitoes." Bless the Duomo and its birthday, and bless the little children and their lanterns. We can't make it to this party.

10

First Lessons

On Sunday morning, the girls from downstairs tap politely at our door. They understand that to ring the doorbell would throw me into a frenzy—I've already learned, by experience, that the buzz requires immediate action through the intercom. Someone is either standing outside the front gate and wants to be buzzed in, or is outside the main door to the building, or is standing just outside my door—which is most alarming, since it requires a verbal exchange in a language unknown to me. The bell-ringer might just be the mailwoman who needs to collect money before she can hand over an envelope addressed from home. (This is a very mysterious Italian tax—1,000 or 2,000 lire charged for a small parcel that is sent, fully paid, from the United States.)

The mailwoman (she's about twenty years old) rides up to the gate on a bicycle with a big leather pouch on the front and props the bike against the fence. Then she apparently buzzes someone (or everyone) in order to get into the building. To all buzzes one must reply *"Prego!"* or *"Sì!"* followed by *"Un momento, scendo,"* which means someone is coming down (with money!).

The neighbor girls (in truth they are young women, but to me they seem like girls) come in and seat themselves (in their blue jeans and snug T-shirts) on the flowered sheets that cover the torn couch and chairs in our living room. Patty, who first introduced herself as a "corn-fed farm girl," does look beautifully healthy, with her fair skin, pink cheeks, and red hair put up in a swirl with a barrette. Maria has a dark-skinned South American beauty; she looks at us out of her large dark eyes and swings her long black hair out of her face. Neither of them wears makeup. Neither, just now, is wearing shoes.

They want to know whether they can help us in any way, and the truth is they also have a favor to ask. Could they please, later today "borrow our roof terrace" to study? Paola, from whom they rent their room, is at home today. She chain-smokes and has three cats, and, though she's very nice to them, they are desperate for some space and air. Paola supplements her work as a night clerk in a hotel by renting her one bedroom to foreign students during the school season. During that time, she sleeps on her living room couch. Though she usually works at night and sleeps all day, on Sundays she likes to do cleaning and listen to opera.

Patty says, "Paola is so good to us, she cooks us the most immense meals, every single night! There's always the *primo,* a huge bowl of pasta, and then the *secondo,* some fried cutlet or sausage or pork chop, and mashed potatoes with butter, and peas, always peas. I've gained a ton since I'm here. I mean, my regular diet used to be grains and fruit and salad—and here it's all cheese and olive oil."

Maria smiles softly, eyes downcast. "You don't have to eat it all," she reminds Patty.

"Oh, but then Paola gets insulted. 'You don't like my cooking?' she asks."

"Are you bothered by the mosquitoes?" I inquire.

"Oh, you just ignore them," Patty says. "They don't like me, anyway."

"They eat me up alive," Maria confesses. "But Paola lights the poison every night and leaves the windows open."

Joe spreads the city map on the table map and asks the girls whether they can show us how to get into town. Maria and Patty, using a red pen, outline the route Joe will take to the school, showing him where he must catch the #14 bus on Via Aretina, just near the Conad supermarket, and where, on Via Ghibellina, he must wait to take it home again. Anytime we are in the city, we can always get our bus at the Santa Maria Novella train station or at the Duomo—being sure that it goes toward Bellariva, which is our neighborhood. They trace a line from the stop where Joe must get off the bus (just after it turns off Via dell'Agnolo), to where he must walk south toward the river, passing Santa Croce on the left, crossing the river at Ponte alle Grazie, walking a block to Via dei Bardi where he will come to the Scuola Dante Alighieri.

This seems a bit much to take in all at once. The girls also make us a "must-see" list: La Specola, the museum where there are full-size wax forms of humans featuring medical abnormalities; the Browning house, where Elizabeth wrote her poetry (but open only on Wednesday and Friday afternoons, after 3 P.M.); the Uffizi, where the great Botticellis reside; the *Mercato Centrale*, which has the greatest food displays in all of Firenze; and of course we must not miss the Baptistry doors, the Medici Chapels, the Bargello, the Accademia, the Buonarroti House with Michelangelo's sculptures . . . and then there are the best places to eat . . . pesto, pizza, gelato.

Joe laughs and holds up his hand. "I think that's all we can remember for now."

In the afternoon, the girls knock on the door again, this time wearing sunglasses and shorts and bearing beach chairs, Walkman radios, books, and paper. They clank and bang their way up the spiral staircase, laughing at the weird music the chair legs make on the metal railings.

We wish them happy studying, and then Joe and I leave to go for a walk along the river.

The Arno is muddy in color, but, as it flows from the east and cascades toward the city, it glitters silvery in the sun. We gaze toward the Duomo from the bridge where the *autostrada* to the south begins, and just be-

Sunday fishermen along the Arno

low us we see a rainbow of weekend fishermen lining both sides of the riverbank below the road where they have parked their cars. There must be a hundred of them, men in bright T-shirts sitting on plastic stools under red and blue umbrellas. They seem to be using segmented bamboo fishing poles perhaps twenty feet long. As we stand and watch, one fisherman pulls in a catch—a large, convulsing fish—which he dumps triumphantly into a plastic tub filled with water. The men nearby look on with envy.

Descending some steps from the bridge, Joe and I walk along the river's edge, past a sign that reads *"Orto del Cigno"* (Garden of the Swan) that displays a menu, for both the trattoria and the pizzeria.

"We'll come here for dinner one night," Joe says. He squeezes my hand, and we walk along, eyes open to the newness of it all, taking in each sight like children let loose in a new place. Somewhere on the path, out of sight of the fisherman on the bank below us, we stop in the middle of the road and kiss. I am gratified that not only the young can be in love in Italy.

11

Reserved for the Mutilated

We screw our courage to the sticking point and strike out for the bus stop, each armed with a *biglietto, Valido 60 minuti*, which we have bought for 1,400 lire each at the *tabacchaio*. With instructions from Maria and Patty, we find the bus stop opposite the recreational vehicle lot on Via Aretina. We wait, looking into the window of a shop that sells hair dryers, toasters, irons, and other electrical appliances. (If my calculations are correct and the tag on the toaster that reads "112,500" is the price, then a toaster costs $75 in Italy. Likewise, a hairdryer costs $45 here.)

The day is warm, full of white clouds in a blue sky. I am wearing what I think of as my "Clementine cloppers" ("and her shoes were number nine, herring boxes, without topses, sandals were for Clementine"). Having been warned about the rough roads and the miles we would be walking, I had bought at home a pair of strange looking hi-top oxfords of white suede with thick soles. I'm also wearing my fanny pack—recommended for carrying keys, wallet, and keeping my hands free while at the same time protecting my valuables from potential purse snatchers. I feel practical, unglamorous, and rugged. The women who pass on the street look me up and down and do not appear to admire what they see. Every Italian housewife walking by with carry-bags from the Coop or the Conad is clearly fashion-wise, wearing matching shoes and handbag, carrying herself proudly in a good-looking suit or skirt and blouse. Not one seems to worry about the flagstones: heels and stockings seem to be the rule in this neighborhood.

In the distance, we see the square orange face of a bus approaching. Joe steps into the rectangle drawn on the street and raises his arm. The bus stops for us. All three of its doors open. We get on at the front end. The driver takes no notice of us—he's enclosed in a glass booth. We have tickets—but no one takes them. There are very few seats on the bus. A line of single seats on each side faces the front of the bus, and a few sideways seats hold two or three people. I sit in a single seat and indicate to Joe that he should sit behind me. Beside me, on the metal wall of the bus, is a sign that says "*POSTO RISERVATO AI MUTILATI E IN-VALIDI CIVILI, DI GUERRA E DEL LAVORO*." As far as I can understand, it means that the seat is reserved for invalids, the disabled, the mutilated, and veterans of war.

Since I see no one of this definition around me, I stay seated, although Joe seems loyal to the idea that a healthy male should not take a seat and remains standing above me, hanging onto a loop suspended from the horizontal bar above. We speed along past shops whose names fly by before I can attempt to translate them. As others get on the bus, I discern a pattern: those getting on enter either at the back or front door, while those getting off exit though the middle door. There's a puzzling fact I also notice: some passengers who get on hold a ticket identical to ours and thrust it briefly into a small orange box, wait for a clicking sound, then retrieve it and put it in pocket or purse. However, many riders get on, hold no tickets at all, and simply take a seat or stand. What does this mean? Is there a "free ride" in Italy?

As we pass through the city streets, the bus begins to fill up. An older man gets on, holding a cane. He comes down the aisle, stops directly beside my seat, and knocks at my feet with his cane. I look up at him, and he hits me harder. I jump up. He sits down in my seat. My heart is pumping with insult and surprise. He stares out the window, his jaw set.

By now, the bus has turned into a street so narrow that the doors of the buildings are within arm's reach on either side. It's as if we are driving through a dark canyon. We can peer into the windows of apartments if their shutters are open. Joe pulls the bus route map of Florence from his pocket and seems to reach a conclusion. He pushes a red button, and a sign begins to flash at the top of the bus. It says *"fermata prenotata."* When the bus stops, Joe takes my hand, leads me toward the middle door and pulls me down the steps fast before the door closes on me. Just as I step out, I throw an angry glance at the old man who knocked me out of my seat.

No matter where we look, in every direction, there are narrow streets and tall buildings. We pass a bakery whose cookies gleam with powdered sugar, a leather shop whose hanging black jackets seem aggressive and seductive, a *verduraio* where mushrooms are piled high in boxes on the street. The sidewalk is so narrow that we have to walk single file; if we encounter someone coming toward us, one of us has to step into the street. Joe stops at every corner, checking his map and then peering up at the cornerstone of the building where the street name is engraved in the stone block high above our heads.

He gestures with a pointing finger (this is his new mode of communication—he points, I follow). We are supposed to meet Nicoletta and the students for our first formal tour of the city, given by a professional hired guide. Joe thinks we are now walking toward the river, though no river is in sight, no riverbank, no bridges, just the narrow sidewalks and inches away the roaring traffic of the motor scooters. From time to time, we encounter total blockage—one or another of the many tour groups, all of which are hurrying after their leader, who holds up an umbrella or a flag to mark the way.

"Are you sure this is the right direction?"

Joe takes me by the arm, we step down a curb, and suddenly, to the left, a great piazza opens before us. There, like a king on a throne, sits the church of Santa Croce, with its blue, six-pointed star at its top. To the left of the church, on a pedestal, is a towering statue of the poet Dante, stern and beautiful.

There's a shock about this, the suddenness of the space opening out of the tangle of dark buildings, the awesome architecture of the enormous church appearing before us like an apparition.

Joe is staring, too. It's as if we have unearthed this treasure ourselves, personally, like archeologists in the field uncovering a hidden tomb. I don't want to leave, to be pulled back into the dark and narrow streets. But Joe checks his watch, pulls me along. We make our way over the flagstones, hurry up and down curbs, follow the map till we are once again let into light, this time at the river's edge, where across the Arno we see hills and cypress trees and where, to the west, the rows of bridges, like mountain ranges, arc one behind the other into the infinite distance.

Ponte Alle Grazie, Ponte Vecchio, Ponte Santa Trinita, Ponte Alla Carraia, Ponte Amerigo Vespucci—I read the names of the bridges on the map, and the words seem to be part of a song. The vision of all of them, one after another, crossing the flowing tube of water, makes me stare with wonder. Others must be feeling this as well; at every convenient stopping place, people are poised with their cameras, trying to capture this image. I do the same—so that when I am home again and miles from Italy, the feeling of standing here above the swirl of the river will come back to me like perfume that wafts up from old stationery.

It is in this state of mind that I reencounter our students, massed on the lungarno at the place where only days before we were all collapsed in exhaustion and misery. Nicoletta and Mrs. Pedrini are talking to the tour guide (identifiable by her red umbrella held aloft, even on this clear and sunny day.) The students stand in clusters, talking animatedly with one another. Joe joins Nicoletta, and they confer with the guide, who, from the sound of her loud voice, is likely to be American, and very perky. I already don't like her. I hear snatches of the students' remarks:

"Our apartment is five flights up. . . ."

"We can see the Duomo from our window!"

"But not even a washing machine! Can you imagine wringing out blue jeans by hand?"

The Ponte Vecchio

"My bed broke the first minute I got into it. . . ."

"And we had no running water, and then, when we got it, the sink overflowed. . . ."

"I already used two rolls of film, and I only brought six with me. . . . Do you know how expensive film is here?"

"Have you tasted Italian bread yet? It's like sawdust—there's no salt in it. I'll die if I can't get a bagel for the next three months."

The students are all so young! Except for Mrs. Pedrini. But she looks like a starlet among them, wearing a jaunty hat and her huge Hollywood sunglasses, generously passing out chocolates to everyone. We seem to have survived the worst of our jet lag, managed to find food, to sleep, and to navigate the city well enough to gather here, all alive, all together, and all awaiting further adventures.

I can't listen to the tour guide. We dutifully follow her along the river's edge, we cross the Ponte Vecchio, where she stops to lecture about the history of the bridge, the only one not blown up in World War II because Hitler had an affection for it. I turn away to look over the water.

I don't want Hitler in my mind when I already have a happy association to this bridge: my daughter, Becky, played violin in the high school performance of "Kiss Me, Kate." She was impressed by the fact that Cole Porter had used her name in the song in which the hero, remembering his old loves, sings: "Where is Rebecca? My Becky-Wecchio— could she still be cruising that amusing Ponte Vecchio?" Thus, humming the tune to myself, I gaze around at the jewelry shops, at the hawkers and the sidewalk artists, at the tourists and the natives. I see two nuns, both dressed in blue habits—one in a wheelchair and one pushing the wheelchair. They are both eating ice cream cones and holding their faces up to the sun.

A bust of someone (the tour guide might know who he is, but I don't want to ask) faces west over the river, and around the statue is a low black iron fence. Hundreds of padlocks decorate the fence's spikes, locked on the rails, locked upon one another, locks locked onto locks, and on every lock is scratched or engraved or painted in nail polish a name, or names. "Jess and Will." "Lynn and Darrell." "Jack M. 1994." "Bonnie." "Maria Elena." "Mary Ann and Jim."

Crossing to the other side of the bridge, I see another tree of locks hanging from a metal rod extending from the wall of a shop. No one has the keys to these locks, locks that lock their owners into the history of Florence, that seal their names together with the musical words *Ponte Vecchio*—the old bridge. Some of the locks must be from trunks and suitcases, some are American made, others are from all parts of the world. I wish I had a lock to lock onto these. I want to be part of this bridge, also.

I tag along behind our students as they follow the guide. I can hear, coming back to me on the breeze, the canned speech presented for our benefit; there's a singsong tone to it, there's a deadness to it. I have never been able to stand still in a foreign country and let someone instruct me—no matter how cute the anecdotes or how peppy the presentation. I remember how, on a trip we took to Israel in one summer, the guide always stopped in full sunlight and lectured for twenty minutes, marking time in place while the rest of us swooned in the burning heat.

I want to look around by myself, to think about what I see. The rest

39

I can find in books. At the statue of Neptune in the Piazza della Signoria, the guide is reciting: ". . . the Roman sea god surrounded by water nymphs commemorating Tuscan naval victories . . . ," while what I see is something beyond that—the overt and aggressive sexuality of the god, his cocked head, his easy grace and superiority. All around him, beyond the fountain and the nymphs and the horses, are the earnest tourists, buying postcards and posters and key chains and plastic trays and belts and scarves and models of Michelangelo's *David*. A horse and carriage are pulled to the side of the piazza; the driver loops a bag of feed over the horse's ears, and, as the animal dips his muzzle to feed, the driver himself pulls an onion focaccia (I am close enough to smell it) from a paper sack and enjoys his snack in the sunshine with his horse.

The guide takes us toward the Palazzo Vecchio ("Here the history of Florence was forged, here her bitter internal struggles were fought, and here she affirmed her power and glory . . . ," she intones.) The students are looking elsewhere while Joe and Nicoletta politely pay attention. I will not be getting a grade for this trip. I will come back here myself in the weeks ahead, with or without my guidebook. With my own eyes, I will see for myself the Baptistry doors and the Basilica and the Bargello and the Brunelleschi dome and the Botticellis—but in my own time and in my own way. And the voice in my head will be mine.

12

A Piece of Laundry
(*Un Pezzo del Bucato*)

The design of Italian washing machines seems to express the cherished idea that in Italy the simplest activities of life are an art form. I spend three hours watching my laundry in the process of cleansing while at the same time, at the kitchen table, I cut and wash mushrooms for the risotto I will make for dinner.

Unlike my American washing machine, which agitates in pit-bull furor, shaking the dirt out of the clothes, then spinning them wildly as if wringing their necks in revenge, this Italian version gives our clothes a gentle half-turn and then pauses for what seems three minutes before it gently shimmies them about again for a few seconds. A cluster of soap bubbles appears in the round glass window and then vanishes while the clothes rest or gather strength for the next little jiggle. At this rate, the sun will have set before I can even hang them outside.

The September sunlight streams into the apartment, while below, at the Fiat body shop, a chorus of pneumatic screwdrivers punctuates the quiet morning with its roar. This is clearly a laundry day in my neighborhood—from every rear terrace hangs a load of wash blowing brightly in the breeze. On the terrace opposite mine, a woman, wearing what looks like pajamas, cigarette hanging from her mouth, is ironing men's shirts; she's fierce and fast about this. From time to time, a dog wanders outside and gets tangled between her legs; she barks an order, and he goes back inside.

On the terrace below hers, the old man I have seen before is out with his pruning shears, delicately clipping a leaf or two from his potted plant. Beside the plant, on a little table, his canary is singing. Its notes echo across the courtyard and hang in the bright air.

I count my clothespins. Clearly, I am short. I will have to buy some at the Conad next time I shop. For now, I'll have to double up, hang two socks on one pin. I seem to be short of everything here. We have only a few pots, a few dishes, and just one set of sheets. This means I will have to wash the sheets early on a sunny day and hope they will dry by nightfall. The sheets are made of the kind of thick cotton that doesn't dry fast, even in sun and wind. Today I am washing only Joe's underwear and my own, plus our two bath towels and two dish towels—all that we have been entrusted with.

On the terrace just below mine, someone has set out a large wooden crate filled with grapes. Beside them is another crate of root vegetables of a sort I can't identify. Again, I understand that space on a terrace is simply an extension of the family home—and what's on it is not my business. When I go inside to check the clothes, they are still in a peaceful limbo; not finished, not washed, not wrung out. Just hovering there in a bath of soapy water.

I turn my attention to the mushrooms. They are still fused at the root, two at a time, with clumps of dirt clinging to them. They're beautiful, large, and white—twice as fresh as can be found at home and half the price. My receipt from the Conad says *"Funghi Champignon 2360 lire"*—which computes to $1.57 for two pounds. The *pomodori maturi* I bought—ripe tomatoes still attached to vine and leaves—cost 515 lire, about thirty-four cents for a cluster of heavy, fragrant delicious tomatoes, nothing like the cardboard-tasting ones we so often get in California.

The washing machine is now producing a notably different purring sound that is followed by the draining sound of water running through the pipes. This must be the spin cycle. I peer into the glass window and see that a gentle whirling has begun, slow and languorous, a sleepy, delicate spin. It stops after a few seconds. Shuts down. Rests again. Begins to whir and drain once more. I wait and daydream in my Italian kitchen. My mushrooms are washed clean, my onions and garlic ready for the knife before Joe gets home for dinner, the rice ready to be cooked in a liter of water (uncovered, not as we cook it at home), and now, at last, the light goes off on the washer, signaling that my clothes are ready for the line.

When I open the round glass door, a cup of water spills onto the floor. I pull the knotted and twisted clothing out and let it fall into a shallow yellow basket provided by my landlady. The clothing feels heavy with water, if not exactly soaking wet. I make two trips to the terrace with my clean laundry and begin attaching it to the line with the brightly colored plastic clothespins. This hanging out of clothes on the line is a new skill I must learn—at home everything goes into the dryer.

We are five stories up here. Below me are four lines of laundry, already hung out and drying. From the water dripping at my feet through the grids of the basket, it's clear that my clean clothes are going to drip upon the lines below. This is very tricky business—holding and pulling taut the garment with one hand, quickly putting on the clothespin with the other. As I try it, a pair of my underpants falls from my hand, flies through the air, and lands—a purple cotton clump—square on the clothesline below. What do I do now? The line below billows with men's work pants, with bed sheets of pink floral cotton, with delicate, lacy underwear. And there, on top of something pink and silky, are my purple underpants.

When Joe gets home, I tell him how one's entire wardrobe of underwear can fly away and land on the lines below, or, worse, in the dirt of someone's garden, which is not accessible from anywhere but from that person's apartment. What is to be done?

Joe says we must write a note. We sit down at the table, and he dictates to me, looking up a word or two in the dictionary.

"*Per favore—Mi dispiace, un pezzo del bucato è caduto. Può restituirlo al apartamento al quarto piano. Grazie.*" I sign my name and, under it, add, at Joe's instruction, "al quarto piano."

Joe takes this opportunity to suggest I should learn more Italian. This is only the first of many emergencies during which I will need it. Yet he is kind enough to translate the note for me: "Forgive me, a piece of washing has fallen. Kindly return it to the fourth floor apartment."

And, lo and behold, the next morning, the pair of underpants arrives, without fanfare, by an invisible messenger, at my front door. It is left neatly folded on the floor. To my dismay, when I retrieve it, I see it has a hole in it. What will the Italians think of me? Look what shame I have brought upon my country.

13

Jewish New Year (Rosh Hashonah)

I receive an invitation to celebrate the Jewish New Year with an Italian family. A woman calls, introduces herself as Ruth Ianello, and says that she and Doctor Ianello would be honored to have me share Rosh Hashonah dinner with them and their family at their home after services at the synagogue. She is proud of her yearly tradition of opening her home to Jewish travelers far from family and friends—and would my husband and I join them? She got my name from one of the letters I wrote from the United States to the Jewish Community Center in Florence.

"How kind of you to ask us. We'd love to come."

She gives me instructions: I am to take the #14 bus to Via dei Macci and walk from there to the synagogue—I shouldn't have too much trouble, I can ask directions along the way and I will easily see the large green dome of the shul as I approach it. After the services, I am to look for her daughter, Rachel ("a heavy-set girl with long, curly hair—everyone knows who she is"), and then I am to come home with Dr. Ianello, their son, and her daughter. Ruth won't be at services herself. She'll be cooking.

When I tell Joe we are invited to join an Italian family for the Jewish New Year, he reminds me that Friday is the day he and Nicoletta are

45

taking the class for an all-day trip to Pisa and Lucca: Pisa to see the Leaning Tower, and Lucca to see the ritual procession of the *Volto Santo*—a festival in which the entire community turns out to follow the carved wooden statue of Christ through the town.

"I don't want to miss Pisa!"

"Then come with the class."

"But I don't want to miss Jewish New Year services or the dinner!"

"It's up to you," Joe says. "Just decide."

Just decide. This is one of the recurring ordeals of my life. Sometimes I wish I were a puppet on strings controlled by someone wiser than I am, more knowing, and more certain of what is "good for me." In other words, I want someone to tell me what to do.

My general technique for making decisions is to propose scenarios for myself for each of the issues in question. (Later I always find out how completely wrong they are, that I didn't come even halfway close to guessing what the experience would be like.) But that never stops me from trying. This time I imagine myself in a state of total anxiety—how will I know where to get off the bus? How will I find my way to the *sinagoga israelitca*, as the *shul* is designated on the map? Once there, how will I find the "heavy-set girl with dark, curly hair"—and how on earth will I ask anyone where she is if I can't speak Italian? (*Dov'è Rachel Ianello?* Will that be enough to have someone lead me to her?) On the other screen of my mind, I project the Leaning Tower, the bus trip to Pisa through the glorious countryside (if I don't go, Joe will sit on the bus with Nicoletta, and who knows what could happen?) Then there will be the movie-like procession (I think of the movie *We're No Angels*), the archetypal Christ-on-the-cross being carried through the city, the magnificence, the pomp and circumstance!

But I already know I will choose the dinner with real people, to hear about real life in Italy and to see it with my own eyes. Ruth Ianello is an archetype herself, one of thousands (she told me this on the phone) of American girls who come to Florence as students, fall in love with Italians, and marry and spend their lives here.

"I'll go to the synagogue," I tell Joe. "I've already seen the Leaning

Tower in the movies. In fact, we have a little plastic model of it somewhere at home. We also have a Pisa drinking glass that tips over."

"I remember," Joe says. "Your iced tea spills into your lap."

I call Ruth Ianello and tell her my husband has another commitment.
Can I bring anything to the dinner?

"Nothing at all. Everything is accounted for. But perhaps, since
you're a writer, you could bring me one of your books."

"I'd be delighted," I tell her.

What I don't account for in my imaginings is that Joe will leave the
apartment at 7 A.M. on the designated day and that I will be here alone
till 6:30 at night, at which time I will strike out on my own for my adventure. It's only 8 A.M., and I am already lonely. I packed Joe a sandwich of prosciutto, lettuce, tomato, *senape* (mustard), and *maionese,*
along with a plastic jar of *succo di pera* and the closest thing I could
find to potato chips. When I kissed him good-bye, I said, "Try not to
come home and tell me it was the most wonderful thing you ever saw,
that you had the best time you ever had in your life."

"You could still come," he reminded me.

Now, to compound my doubts, a jackhammer begins shaking the walls
of the building. I can feel the vibrations in my very teeth. The noise is
too loud for the Fiat body shop, and too close to my skull. I go out on
the small back terrace and see that workmen are carrying into the back
yard of one of the apartments below me an entire bathroom: toilet,
bidet, bathtub, sink. A remodel is beginning. I assume it will go on for
months.

I close the glass doors to the terrace and climb into my bed with the
Walkman radio. I tune it till I find the Beatles singing "It's A Hard Day's
Night"—but not loud enough to drown the commotion from below.

By late afternoon I have gone up and down to the roof terrace three
times, I have taken a long bath in the long bathtub, and I have ridden
the *ascensore* down to the ground floor to check the mailbox. I decide

47

to cut my hair, which is something I have done over the years to get my-self through a crisis. There is not much to cut, since it is already short and curly. But it's something to do. Then I take another bath, wash my hair, blow it dry with my dual-voltage hair dryer, choose my outfit for the evening, and actually get ready to leave the apartment. But I feel too hot in the dress I'm wearing. I change to another outfit, and then an-other. Now I'm hungry, because in America it's dinner time. But I'm not even close to a meal for hours. I eat a few tangerines and set out—fi-nally—for the *sinagoga israelitica*.

On the bus I witness an archetypal ritual of a different sort than Joe will find tonight in Lucca. I am seated opposite two handsome Italians, young men with the three-day-beard-stubble-look that so many young Italian men cultivate. At the next stop, a young and gorgeous woman gets on the bus, very tall, very blonde, very exotic. She stands (there are no seats, and the young men surely do not offer her one of theirs) be-tween the men, holding onto the loop handle hanging from the bar above her head. She's wearing extremely tight black pants of a silken, stretchy fabric, so tight in fact that at the top of her legs the seam seems to dissect her body in two. Her shoes are high black clogs, raising her already tall form to a formidable height. She stands between the two young men and with her free hand keeps brushing her long blonde curls from her eyes. The men look up at her, look her up and down, look at each other . . . and smile. The smiles they exchange are thrilling, conspiratorial, and lascivious. The bus speeds along, the young woman swings and sways on her handle, oblivious, or so she ap-pears, to the reaction she is causing. The young men can't look at her enough and can't smile at each other too much.

It's lovely, but it makes me a little sad. No Italians are going to smile this way at me these days.

But Via dei Macci has just passed, we are already—I fear—at Via Guiseppi Verdi if my map is correct. I push the red button, make my way to the middle door, and get out. I have my usual encumbrances with me: sweater, fanny pack, backpack (with camera), water bottle, and the book of my short stories for my hostess. In the street I consult my map, with no idea at all in what direction to walk.

"Can I help you?" and there beside me is the gorgeous young woman in the tight black pants speaking in a charming, accented English. I am somehow astonished that she speaks at all—I thought she was just an angel tempting men and inciting them to lust. But here she is, bending over my map with me, pointing this way and that to the direction of the synagogue.

"Where are you from?" I ask.

"Yugoslavia. I am a student of art."

Ah, yes, I think . . . but there is more beauty and art in the young women of Florence than in all its museums.

14

In the Bosom of My People

I am lost. When I reach the Arno River, I know that I have walked in the absolutely wrong direction. There is something about the swirls of the map, the way street names change at every corner, the nongeometric layout of the city of Florence, and my own shortcomings that make it impossible for me to form a plan with the map as guide and to walk straight to my destination.

Joe has written out for me an emergency script, which goes from simple request to desperate plea. For directions from strangers I am to say: *"Dov'è la sinagoga?"* If I ever get there and eventually locate the heavy-set Rachel Ianello of the dark, curly hair, I am to say: *"Sua madre mi ha invitato a cena."* (Your mother invited me to dinner.) If I never find her and have no idea how to get home, I am to say to any stranger: *"Come si fa per ottenere un tassí?"* (How can I find a taxi?) or *"Ho bisogno di un tassí."* (I need a taxi.) When and if I get a taxi, I am to say to the driver: *"Abita al vicino a Via Aretina,"* or *"Abita al vicino al supermercato Conad in Via Aretina. La mia casa è in Via Venosta."* If all fails and I find no taxi at all, I can always say to any passerby: *"Dov'è la stazione?"* or *"Dov'è le fermata d'autobus per la stazione?"* Once at the station, I am certain to find the #14 bus, which goes to our neighborhood in Bellariva.

I pray I never get to this moment—for, once I get the on bus heading home, how will I know where to get off it? If I do get off in the wrong neighborhood (and if Joe is likely to be back from Pisa), my instructions are to find a public phone and ask anyone: *"Come si fa per usare questo telefono?"*

This exercise in "what if" catastrophes is giving me a massive headache. I look ahead and see a nice looking stranger approaching me. I hold out my map to the young man, posing my shortest question: *"Dov'è il sinagoga?"*

He points ahead, to the right, to the left, and then makes a little swirl with his fingers. A half hour later, I wander into a bakery. Two women behind the counter, seeing me come at them with a map in hand, turn their backs and continue their conversation. I wait—politely—as they ignore me—rudely.

Finally, drenched in sweat and exhausted, I pause in front of a store whose sign reads *"ANTICHITA—Fratelli Faini."* Two enormous stone lions grace the window. A man toward the back of the shop, handsomely suited and with a kind round face, beckons me inside. I step over the threshold and see all manner of antiques—towering wardrobes, carved tables, china lamps bright with pink and gold cherubs, bronze urns with ear-shaped handles. I know this world; my father had an antique shop in every place we ever lived.

"Per favore" (I remember this from the lost laundry episode), *"dov'è il sinagoga?"*

"Aah!" the gentleman cries, running forward toward me. *"La sinagoga! Shalom! Shalom!"* He grasps my two hands in his and says *"Lansman!"* which in Yiddish means "countryman." Indeed, we hold onto each other, happy to have discovered we are relatives in this land of Popedom and Christendom.

A conversation ensues of which I understand little, but I say at some point, *"Sono* Californian," and he answers, *"Aah, ricchi, eh?"*

"No," I say emphatically, "I am *not* rich," but add, *"Mio padre, anche antiquario."*

So we have another round of handshakes to celebrate this miracle of connection. He bows and gestures to the back of the shop—does he want to show me his wares, or has he more romantic notions in mind? He may be Jewish, but he's also Italian. I indicate my wrist watch—"I must get *to il sinagoga,*" and he understands: my religion calls. He bids me farewell (I think he invites me to come again soon)—and again I'm on the street, walking in the direction he pointed out to me. I see the same bakery I passed before. After a while, I stop one more woman; she is eating a gelato and seems to be in good enough spirits to be interrupted.

"Scusi, dov'è il sinagoga?"

She steps back and points skyward. There above our heads rises the majestic green dome for which I have been searching.

"Grazie! Grazie!"

I keep my eye on the dome and round the corner. There I see a military tank and armed guards at the gate waiting to welcome me to the house of worship.

There's a line waiting to pass through the open gate. "Let me see your ID," a woman barks at me as I approach her. When I open the zipper of my backpack and dig inside, my camera comes into view. The woman thrusts her face at me. "A camera! You are Jewish? And you bring a camera to the synagogue? What kind of mother raised you?"

"I'm sorry. I always have it with me. I'm going somewhere later where I'll need to have it."

"You Americans," she sneers. "You'll have to leave your camera outside." She gestures to a bare wooden shelf near some bushes. It's clear that, once services begin, no one will be out here to protect my camera.

"I can't," I say. I hardly think it needs an explanation. Would I leave my wallet unguarded on that shelf? My infant child? Why would I put at risk my new, expensive camera that already contains irreplaceable pictures of Florence, my apartment, my kitchen, my bed? It doesn't matter that we are here among celebrants of a religious holiday, or even that they are Jewish. Religious thieves exist, and so do Jewish ones.

"If you don't leave it, then you can't go in." She pushes me out of the way and gets ready to interrogate the next foreign visitor to the synagogue.

The synagogue in Florence

"*Sono americana,*" I say, meaning that I come from a free country, that no one can dictate to me in this way, that I will not be treated like a criminal. My back to the machine guns, I push past her—camera and all—into the house of worship, where I feel fully entitled to be.

The women are required to go upstairs to the balcony, whereas the men, of course, enter the downstairs sanctuary, as is usual in an orthodox congregation. I am aware of the great ceiling, the hanging lanterns, the marble floors and pillars, the intricate designs of this awesome structure, but my state of mind is such that I am not in the tourist mode of admiration.

As I take a seat in the high balcony, what I do respond to—and not with appreciation—are the wrought iron bars that rise from just in front of the first row of seats, making it seem as if the other women and I are enclosed in a cage. Some of the women go to stand at the bars in order to look below. I follow to see what I can see—but, whatever the men are doing down there, chanting and praying, handling the Torah, they are out of the range of our vision. So I see nothing, and what I hear

53

Rosh Hashonah services

is as good as nothing, since the sounds rising from below are totally unlike the prayer sounds I recall from the synagogue of my childhood.

The women around me seem frankly indifferent. They are not reading from prayer books or sitting silently with respect and humility. In
fact, several are shielding their eyes from the badly aimed lights that are
designed to illuminate the sacred area below but are blinding to those
sitting in the balcony. A few at a time, women migrate out to the hall,
where I can see them standing around with their children, talking
pleasantly to one another. This event seems not so much a religious holiday as a pleasant social occasion to which they can wear their best
clothes and exchange news and gossip.

For some reason, tears rise to my eyes, surprising me. In the place
where I thought I would be welcome, I feel most alienated. Anger and
disappointment surge through me as I feel again, like a slap, the sense
of humiliation I felt at the gate, the meanness of the guard, her fascist
orders, her intent to make me feel worthless and criminal.

I might as well fulfill her expectations. Very quietly I unzip my
backpack and take out my camera. Moving forward toward the rails,

holding the camera low and hidden, knowing this is against all tradition, all good manners, all fair behavior, and surely against my better
judgment should I later reflect on this act, I open the shutter, point, and
unreligiously photograph the bars that—on this important night—
keep the women isolated from the men, who below us are invited to
pray to God while their women chatter and admire each other's jewelry.

When I find Rachel Ianello at the close of the services, she is not the
"heavy-set girl" her mother described to me but a gorgeous, volup-
tuous Italian beauty who looks like the young opera star sharing her
same lush radiance and beauty. My *"Dov'è Rachel Ianello?"* brings instant results. I am led to her by a kind woman. Rachel greets me with
open arms and a hug for the new year, telling me she has been waiting
to find me. She and her brother, the handsome Pietro, and their father,
the even more handsome Doctor Ianello, escort me to their car and
drive us all to the celebratory dinner. At last, after being lost so long, I
am found.

15

Florentine Hospitality

The doctor's home is in one of Firenze's ancient stone buildings, fortified by iron gates, a twenty-foot carved wooden door (with brass
knockers that resemble hands), and doorbells that require that one be
buzzed in. The doctor and his son and daughter lead me through these
various barriers into their bright and spacious apartment. Though
dinner is not yet on the table, the family's beautiful china, silver, and
crystal are out, laid on an elaborate lace tablecloth. The Ianellos' living
room is furnished with white leather couches and chairs, a soft white
carpet, mahogany tables, and tall brass lamps.

Ruth, the doctor's wife, welcomes me warmly and introduces me to
some of the guests. There's a young Jewish sculptor from New York, a
lawyer and her husband, a pair of traveling college girls, and a friend
of Ruth's named Sara Pushkin, who is busy bringing things to the table.
The sculptor (who wears a beret) confesses that he must get the 11 P.M.
train back to Carrara, where he lives and carves marble, and at once
the party is thrown into an uproar. The hostess reports that dinner will
surely not be done by 11, even though the train station is only one
block away. (This news is a comfort to me in case I have to take the bus
home from there.) The young man, embarrassed, says he will call a
friend and see if he can stay the night in Florence. We all wait in awk-

ward silence while he uses the phone in the living room. His disappointed response means he can't get the accommodation for which he hoped. Now Ruth and the doctor confer in Italian—where will the boy sleep? He is a stranger to them, apparently, so it seems they are not willing to offer one of their white couches for the night. The doctor suggests a local hotel that he says is relatively inexpensive; Rachel at the same time thinks of a friend she can call who might put the visitor up for the night. The doctor gets on the phone again, and Rachel brings in a cell phone from somewhere in the house. Everyone is dialing and calling.

The dinner guests are paralyzed by this small emergency—we cannot socialize until the crisis has passed. We all wait and stare around the room.

On the walls of the dining room and living room are many framed pictures and paintings, most of them having to do with Jewish life and ritual in some way. The college girls and I go and stand before them, studying them as if in a museum. But finally the doctor has apparently had success in calling a hotel that is nearby and has a room for the night—"Can you afford 80,000 lire?" he asks the young man.

"Sure, that's okay," he says, but he looks a little pale to me.

"Fine," the doctor says. "Why don't we all sit down now and have our dinner?"

As it turns out, the doctor is head of gynecology at the hospital in Prato, and the young woman lawyer in her thirties is going to have a baby. The conversation centers upon theories of childbirth as Ruth and Sara bring in the first course: chicken soup with pasta stars in each bowl. The bread is passed around. We each tear off a piece from the soft challah (so different from the coarse Italian bread) and listen as the doctor says the blessing over bread, which prayer I actually recognize.

Then comes the second course of cold poached salmon. The enormous fish, head and all, reclines regally on a beautiful oval platter. When it has been passed around and is transformed into head, tail, and skeleton, a steaming platter of boiled chicken is placed before us, and, finally, a baked dish of eggplant, tomatoes, and pine nuts. Rachel reminds her mother to tell us the name of the dish. Ruth says, smiling, "It's called 'And the Priest Fainted.' The story goes that this is a Turkish dish. When it was served to the priest, he found it so delicious that he passed out." We taste it, the wonderful blend of *melanzane* and *pomodori*—all concur that we too are close to fainting.

After our wine glasses are refilled, the pregnant woman admits to the doctor, "My first choice is to have a Cesarean birth. I want to wake up holding a perfectly beautiful, round-headed baby in my arms, not having suffered a minute. And my second choice is to give birth to my baby in a pool of warm water."

The doctor looks directly at her. His English is accented but very pure. "Nature did not design women to be cut open, nor to have their babies under water. Maybe baby whales, yes, not little human babies. And although a Cesarean birth is convenient for both the mother and the doctor, do you know how many complications can arise from this surgery?"

"No, and I don't really want to know," she says. She adds: "And I hope you won't be on duty when I come in!"

Ruth passes around a dish of apples and honey for sweetness in the New Year. The pregnant woman says to the doctor, "You've been delivering babies for so long . . . are you tired of it?"

"Oh, no," he says, touching his wine glass gently. "To the contrary. Each arrival, I believe, is a sacred moment. Just at that moment before birth, I try to ensure that it is very quiet in the room, that the lights are dim, and that everyone is serious and still."

For a moment we are all serious and still, considering life and birth and all matters great and mysterious.

Sara sets at each of our places the last course, raspberry torte and apple cake. Tea and coffee are poured. A rosy glow settles around the table. We are happily fed, calmed by wine and good company, grateful to be alive in this new year.

When we adjourn to the living room, I ask the doctor and his wife whether I may photograph them, their children, their guests, their house—even the bones of the poached salmon, which still repose in the serving dish in the kitchen. They are happy to cooperate.

The hour is very late. The two young girls must get back to their rooms, the pregnant woman and her husband have a long drive back to Prato (she tells the doctor she has decided she will give up the idea of a Cesarean birth), the sculptor must get to his hotel. Sara offers—most kindly—to drive me home. I give Ruth and the doctor a copy of one of my books of short stories. They ask me to autograph it. We wish one another a happy and healthy new year. The guests shake hands and say they hope to meet again. Ruth hugs all of us. I do indeed feel, at this moment, in the bosom of my people.

Driving with expert ease, Sara finds Via Venosta with no trouble at all. We say goodnight; she reaches to clasp my hand and promises to be in touch with me.

I use my three keys to gain entrance to gate, building, and apartment. There I find Joe sitting in the darkened living room.

"I just got home five minutes ago," he says. "Did you have a good time?"

"Wonderful. I'll tell you all about it. And you? How was the Tower of Pisa?"

"It was leaning," he says.

We laugh, both too tired to say more, and get ready for bed.

16

The Mystery of Marriage

Sunday morning: the secular world in Italy is closed, the gates in front of the shops are locked tight. If you are out of food, you are out of luck. Joe suggests we walk to the newsstand to buy the *International Herald Tribune* or *Newsday*—we have had no news of home since we left. If the United States were at war, we'd hardly know it.

We walk the now-familiar walk: out the gate, right on Via Venosta to Via Filippo Turati, right again to Via Aretina, and then left past the gas station, the pastry shop, the tobacco shop, till we come in view of the Coop, which is the supermarket in competition with the Conad. At the newspaper shop, a steady stream of neighborhood people marches in and out. Each one buys two newspapers (to which the shopkeeper adds what looks like a comic book for the children in the family). Joe observes that newspaper delivery would be impossible in this city, with every apartment behind gates, walls, and locked doors. Italians, now as in the past, continue to make a literal fortress of each home.

Our search turns up no English-language newspapers here. Joe thinks they're likelier to be available in the city center, where tourists circulate in greater numbers.

We decide to walk the couple of blocks down to the river. Sunday strollers are out: old couples walking slowly arm in arm, men with their dogs, fathers with their children. Down toward the bridge, the river-banks are dotted with the colored umbrellas of the weekend fishermen, their long bamboo rods hanging far out over the water. Several groups of older men are walking together, walking and arguing, debating, talking with the confidence of old friendship in which liberties may be taken. And then there are the ever-present grandparents with their grandchildren. (We have seen—from our own apartment window—how, early on workday mornings, one parent or another will deliver their children to the grandparents and leave them for the day.)

"Look at all the devoted old couples," I say to Joe.

"How do you know they're devoted?" he asks. "I don't see a little sign on them saying 'Devoted Couple'—do you?"

"They don't see one on us, either, " I remind him, squeezing his arm.

The sun is sparkling on the Arno; small families of ducks are sailing along in erratic formations, and there are a few towering white clouds in the sky. Joe suggests we go back to the apartment, have some lunch, and take the bus to Fiesole in the afternoon. The idea of such an outing seems fine. In fact, I am exceptionally happy at this moment, which is why, a moment later, I am amazed at how angry I become.

As we walk along toward home, I see a pile of discarded newspapers and magazines in a bag on a doorstep. In a movement not so much a decision as a simple reflex, I bend down and begin to pull out a couple of magazines and a handful of newspapers. (I am aware of some neighborhood people standing on the curb nearby, talking.) But my thought, if I even have a thought, is this: I need some newspapers for putting on the sink when I trim my hair. And I'd like to leaf through some Italian magazines—look at the ads, the pictures, the recipes—since I'm here to learn.

But then Joe says, "Leave them there and let's go."

"But I want them," I protest.

"Put them back."

"Why? I *need* these," and suddenly I am sure I need them desperately.

"Just listen to me," he says very quietly, almost ominously.

"No, I want them." And I take my loot, now precious to me, even if the old Italians on the sidewalk are watching me with disapproval on their faces. And, in truth, they are; their expressions are quite ugly. Joe and I walk along fast, without speaking, separately, each of us in a cocoon of hostility. What has just happened, so fast, so fatally? Finally, I ask him. "What *is* it?"

He says, "That wasn't a good idea."

"But what was so bad about it? All I did was take something someone was throwing away!"

"When I tell you to do something," Joe says, "do it and ask questions later."

"Well, did you think it was dangerous? That those old guys were Mafia?"

"It doesn't matter," Joe insists. "Just trust me when I'm sure something is not a good idea."

"I don't understand." And I really don't. Is he ashamed of me? That I rummaged in the trash? Does he fear that—because of me—all Italians will now have a low opinion of Americans?

His jaw is set. Maybe he doesn't know why he feels the way he does. But the day has gone dark. I feel mean as a snake. The papers and magazines I clutch feel like burning coals in my hand.

When we get to our building, we ride up silently in the elevator. We go at once to separate rooms of the apartment. We don't talk for an hour. When we do, all I say is, "There's some lunch on the table." My husband comes into the kitchen and we silently eat packaged ravioli I have boiled on the stove. We are locked in this black misery, whose swift appearance has mystified and alarmed us both.

After lunch, I lie down in my bed with one of the magazines I stole. *Sorrisi e Canzoni TV* is the name of it; so as far as I can tell, it's called *Smiles and Songs TV*—and seems to be something like the American *TV Guide*. Displayed on the cover is the great Italian tenor Luciano Pavarotti, dressed in a red-flowered Hawaiian shirt with his arm around a young woman, Nicoletta Mantovani, a beautiful creature wearing a low-cut yellow sleeveless dress adorned with large pink flowers. The caption beneath them says *"Acuto d'Amore."* Since I'm in the room with the Italian dictionary, and my estranged husband is in the kitchen with the bag of *cantuccini alla mandorla* (almond cookies), I make my way without his help through the Italian-language article by guesswork and the art of deduction. One thing is clear. Nicoletta Montovani was born in Bologna on November 23, 1969, and Luciano Pavarotti was born in Modena on October 12, 1935. Even without my calculator, I can figure out that this smashing girl is thirty-four years younger than Pavarotti. In the interview, he says how much he admires her "mind and her abilities," and she says how much she admires his "imagination." On the next page, she's wearing a striped leopard evening gown, and the great opera star is in a suit and red tie. They are exchanging kisses and embraces, so much in the throes of passionate love that they hardly notice the camera that will present them in full color to the readers of *Smiles and Songs TV*.

All I can think of is the poor original Signora Pavarotti, who, like me (and who is probably about my age), one day picked up a magazine from a trash can on the street, annoyed her husband—and that was that! Luciano—disgusted with her low moral values—went looking for someone with a better mind and abilities, not to mention long flowing hair, red lips, and a flashing smile.

I realize that not only has my husband dragged me to this distant foreign country, separating me from my children, my cat, my mother, and my friends; he will soon be out cruising the night spots of Florence to find a new wife. I drop the magazine to the floor on the side of the bed, pull the covers up, and begin to cry.

After a while, Joe comes looking for me. Wordlessly, he lies on the bed beside me, and, after a long moment, reaches for my hand. I gasp with relief, but say nothing. We both stare up at the ceiling dappled with the corpses of mosquitoes. In the drowsy, dreamy, afternoon light, without the jackhammers going (on Sunday they rest), we finally relinquish our banners of war and find that a truce is possible.

Joe squeezes my hand under the covers. I squeeze back. After a while, Joe says it's not too late to take the bus to Fiesole. Shall we go?

17

Fiesole and the Etruscan Sigh

On the #7 bus to Fiesole, which we board at the *stazione,* two lovers—the ages of Romeo and Juliet—travel up the mountain with us. They sit in facing seats, profiles stamped against the passing slopes of Mount Ceceri, their eyes locked, with each breath inhaling the image of the other. Such a pure and perfect love touches my injured heart. Since my camera is in my lap, ready to memorialize the scenery, I take apparent aim at the vista beyond the bus window, focus my lens upon their yearning faces, and capture this icon of young love.

Italy is exploding with lovers, all of them energized, I suspect, by the great erotic statues that fill the city squares, gardens, and museums. A copy of Michelangelo's *David,* naked but for his sling in the Piazza della Signoria, towers above the onlooker in such a way that the eye is drawn naturally to the heavy bulbous parcel between his legs. The bodybuilding Neptune, bursting upright like a lord of his fountain, is a pillar of sex. Even the horses lurching from the fountain seem to have their veins engorged with passionate blood. (I think of how, in the movie *A Room with a View,* E. M. Forster's heroine Lucy Honeychurch faints in view of these statues while resisting the attentions of George Emerson, with whom she falls in love against her will.)

The young lovers in my camera's viewfinder hold hands and stare into each other's eyes; if the bus went over the edge of the cliff, I doubt their gaze would waver. I look to my husband's face. Where is his gaze focused? Not upon me, of course, and not upon the lovers, but out the window, at the scenery.

The Teatro Romano—a short distance from Fiesole's main square, where the bus lets us off—is a ruin; everything in Italy takes on an awesome quality when the word "ruin" is attached to it. Or "Roman." If you put them together—"Roman ruin"—you have your heart's desire, all that Italy can offer. We pay our entry fee and make our way into the stone theater, where, it is said, unlike the bloody events at the Colosseum, kinder spectacles went on. They are going on now, in fact. We see young and old visitors alike sitting peacefully on the stones or lying back against the sloping grass, their faces turned gratefully to the sun. There is not much to see, but just to be here may be quite enough. Being here is the single overwhelming attraction of Italy—to be able to say to oneself: *I am in Italy. This is Italian grass, above us is Italian sky, the quality of light is Italian.* (We all know what masterpieces that light inspired!) Soon, in fact, we will be hungry, and the food we eat will be—above all—Italian food.

We walk the edges of the arena; we stand and observe the nearby hills, in which the long span of the San Francesco monastery, whose arches resemble that of an aqueduct, stretches out like a train on its way to heaven.

In the small museum, we examine unremarkable broken objects, shards, chips of statues, pottery slivers, stone lions and miniature horses but, even so, feel we are in the major presence of history, art, and beauty. Everything we see today is a balm. Looking outward together helps us begin the process of healing ourselves from the morning's astonishing conflict. If we can't understand it, we recognize that it is best simply to leave it behind.

As we walk down a long sloping road and find ourselves coming toward a wooded area, we see, at the same moment, a nun, all in white, stepping into the tangle of trees and undergrowth. Her habit is a sheen of brightness against the dark. Like an apparition, she begins to disappear into the woods. I aim my camera and catch her just as she bends to collect something—mushrooms, perhaps. Or truffles.

I have seen for sale in the windows of shops the black fungus *(tartufo nero)* famous for being an aphrodisiac and for its exquisite taste. These tubers (*un tubero d'oro,* the Italians call it) are discovered deep in the woods, by pigs (and perhaps by nuns?). Just this morning I saw a photo of a truffle gracing a recipe in my stolen magazine. The truffle's dark, ridged outer skin, its spherical nature, gave it the appearance of a human scrotal sac.

Joe and I stand under a great cluster of trees whose dropped nuts are hard and bumpy beneath our feet. Picking one up, I tell Joe I think it must be a chestnut because of its shiny brown cover and dark nipple. Further down the road we see a young couple tossing the nuts beyond the trees and down upon the hillside below. The young man, before each toss, seems to take the stance of a discus thrower.

"I'd like to take some home and roast them," I say tentatively, looking toward Joe for some signal. (Is this a mistake, also?) But he seems quite agreeable, in fact begins to help me gather the nuts by the handful, filling the pockets of my jacket and letting me fill his. We are laughing now. His pockets are puffed out like a chipmunk's cheeks.

"Are you hungry?" he asks.

"What shall we eat?"

"Anything you like."

We bypass the trattoria in the city square, deciding instead on a little outdoor stand where a tray of panini is on display: the choices include sandwiches of focaccia, mozzarella cheese and tomato, or focaccia, mozzarella, and prosciutto or a *primo piatto,* a simple bowl of pasta and cheese. Joe and I each order the buffalo cheese and prosciutto. The young woman behind the counter takes the sandwiches off the tray, whisks them between two silver flatirons that hiss as they heat the food and melt the cheese. In half a minute we are seated at a little outdoor table, eating our meal. We devour our sandwiches in three bites.

The nun in the woods

"Fiesole," I say. "The word sounds like the wind sighing in the trees."

"This place is famous for something more like a choking sound," Joe says.

Then he explains, like the history professor he is, that, in this earliest of Etruscan cities, the language is famous for a certain sound—a guttural sigh—a "huch" sound instead of a hard "k" sound, as in the word "casa."

"They still speak that way now, with a catch deep in the throat." Joe demonstrates, as if he is clearing his throat.

I tell my husband that it's a privilege to have my own private history professor as my guide. He seems pleased, so I press my advantage. Could we buy some dessert at the gelato place in the main square?

The display is impressive; an artist's palette of colors in the gelateria's silver trays. On the counter is a vast display of cones—plain wafer cones, sugar cones, extra-tall cones, cones dipped in chocolate, cones dipped in chocolate and nuts. (Then there are the paper cups: small, 2,000 lire, medium, 4,000 lire, large, 5,000 lire, and the glass parfait dish on a little pedestal, 7,000 lire.)

How can we possibly choose? Each bin has been dipped into deeply; great scoops have been dug from them and in their wake are ridged invitations to the tongue. I want to taste them all.

The flavors are described on hand-printed signs, which I read aloud to Joe, softly. When I'm not sure of a word, Joe translates for me: *cioccolato* (chocolate), *crema* (cream), *nocciola* (hazelnut), *noce* (walnut), *pistacchio* (pistachio), *vaniglia* (vanilla), *torrone* (nougat), *riso* (rice!) Then there are the fruit flavors: *pesca* (peach), *albicocca* (apricot), *lampone* (raspberry), *mora* (blackberry), *banana, fragola* (strawberry), *melone* (melon), *frutti di bosco* (berries of the woods), *petali di rosa* (rose petals), and *cioccomenta* (chocolate mint). There are two we ask the salesgirl to explain: *bacio* (which means "kiss" but is really hazelnut-flavored chocolate with nuts), and buontalenti (which means, she says simply, "very Florentine").

"I'll have them all, " I tell Joe. I select two tiny plastic spoons (shaped like shovels) from the bowl on the counter: one bright yellow, one chartreuse.

He says to the girl, "I'll have the *buontalenti*. And my wife will have . . . ?" He looks at me.

"*Bacio,*" I say.

She points to the cones, to the cups, to the glass parfait dish. "*Quale?*"

"*Grande,*" Joe says and indicates the glass—and for that extravagance we learn we are entitled to take our bowls of talents and kisses and sit (for no extra charge) at one of the small tables on the square; to savor our own and each other's luscious, smooth cream; to watch the passing crowds, and to breathe the country air of Fiesole.

18

Postcards and E-Mail (Two)

Peaceful Hills Convalescent Hospital:
Dearest Mother—
*On the other side of this card is the famous "Duomo"—the
great cathedral of Florence that can be seen for miles in every
direction. Next week we are going with all the students to
Venice, the city of canals, but no streets (and no cars!). Maybe
I can get Joe to take me for a gondola ride! I think of you
every day and love you.*

Dearest B—
*I have finally met my landlady, the Countess Rina Masotti.
She is a beautiful, fashionable, intelligent, and interesting
woman who used to work in the fashion industry and speaks
excellent English. Rina is about my age, has an old mother
about the age of ours, children about the ages of ours, and is
married to a Count! How do I know? She left us a bottle of
Chianti Classico wine from their farm in northern Tuscany,
and on the label it says* "IMBOTTIGLIATO ALL'ORIGINE DAI

70

CONTI MASOTTI PROPRIETARI VITICOLTORI IN COLLE VAL D'ELSA"—*Colle Val d'Elsa is where their farm (or "fattoria") is—not far from Siena. They grow wine for grapes, raise pigs and rabbits and turkeys, and also rent rooms to summer tourists who want to be in the "agriturismo" environment (that is, to vacation on a working farm). The farm has been in Rina's husband's family for seven hundred years, and the original palazzo on the property is now rented to a hotel agency, which made it into a luxury hotel. The outbuildings on the farm (pigeon coop, barn, farmer's cottage) have been transformed into the apartments they rent in order to keep the farm in the family. She said she hopes we will come to visit them at the farm some weekend. (They also own another apartment in Florence where they live part of the year.) Our present apartment was where they first lived when their children were small and before there was a freeway entrance (the one we see from our kitchen window) just across the road. In those years only the river was there, and lovely fields full of flowers.*

She did ask whether we needed anything: I suggested we could use another pillow or two, though I would have liked to ask her for wine glasses and a pizza pan and a potato peeler and some pots that are not so dented (and whose handles aren't nearly burned off)—and even a vacuum cleaner. When I told her we can't clean the rug since there's no vacuum here, she said they don't generally use vacuum cleaners, but they sweep the rug with a broom! When she noticed the plastic umbrella stand was missing from the entryway, I had to show her where it was, upside-down in the shower where it holds my soap and shampoo.

We did of course conduct some business; she wanted a 100,000-lire deposit on the phone (did I tell you that every time we make a call, there's a counter attached to the phone that registers the number of "scatti" used—it clicks away at a slower rate for local calls, much faster for long distance. Each click costs about 200 lire). When I told her I was a writer, she said "Perhaps someday you will put us in one of your books." Perhaps, indeed.

Thank you for checking my mail, taking care of Mom, and seeing that Maxie is doing okay. I'm glad he likes the boy who comes to feed him. Poor little cat, he will probably never speak to me again. Love, M

19

Italian Trains, Italian Men

On the morning we leave for Venice, due at the *stazione* to meet the students and Nicoletta at 9 A.M. for a 9:18 departure, we find ourselves caught in the early morning crush of traffic. On the #14 bus, holding our wheel-on suitcases at our feet and hanging for dear life to the straps above, we vie for what little space there is with a hundred schoolchildren carrying neon-colored backpacks big as elephants. (Two preteen girls in the seats below are actually painting each other's nails with blue polish.) I hold to the thought that we will shortly be on the train to Venice, moving along the rails through the scenic countryside, sitting in—most important of all—*posti prenotati*—seats reserved for all our group.

Or so I think, till we find ourselves at *binario* 9 and board the train. The problem is that Italians without reserved seats have gotten on the train and are already sitting in our seats. All of us, Joe and Nicoletta, myself and the thirty-eight students (and all our luggage) have squeezed into the outer aisle of the train while Nicoletta goes to each compartment, waves her group ticket, and argues that these seats are *our* seats. There is much gesticulating, voices are raised. Nicoletta's knowledge of the language and of Italians (we are grateful to remember that she was born in Rome) keeps her grounded and firm. Eventually, one by one, or six by six, the passengers in each compartment grumblingly squeeze out

73

into the narrow corridor with their luggage, and we, six by six, kicking or pulling our luggage behind us, squeeze in.

Joe and I find ourselves in a compartment with Mrs. Pedrini and three of our female students, the singer Marta, and two of her friends, Noreen and Marcella. The girls immediately adjust the headphones on their Walkman players, turn on their music, and proceed to fall asleep. Mrs. Pedrini whispers to us that they've stayed up late at the discos last night, poor things. They're exhausted. It's hardly their fault, since the discos don't open till 11 P.M., so it's no wonder (since they are young and must have their fun) they are so tired. Mrs. Pedrini is dressed in one of her adorable outfits, a sweater embroidered with enormous flowers, matching slacks, cute little beret. She tells us, apropos of nothing special, that her heroine is Auntie Mame and that her highest aspiration is to emulate her. She immediately hands us some candies, an expensive brand, Perugina, wrapped in blue and silver foil, made of luscious chocolate layered around ground hazelnuts. We don't refuse. The chocolate melts instantly on my tongue and spreads immediately to my bloodstream, exquisite. Mrs. Pedrini confesses she always keeps a large supply of these on hand to smooth out the jagged edges or sad thoughts of those traveling with her.

"Aren't they darling?" she says of the three sleeping girls whose heads—directly opposite ours—are lolling to the rhythm of the train on the tracks. "They can't keep their eyes open." (Joe knows about this; he tells me how many of the students sleep through his class.) The girls look alike to me: dark hair, a kind of purplish lipstick that they all seem to favor, blue jeans, sweatshirts, tennis shoes, and the ubiquitous earphones. Two of them have leather jackets stuffed in the overhead rack. How can they not want to stay awake and see the Italian countryside? (I find this difficult to achieve myself, since it turns out I am sitting with my back facing the direction in which the train is traveling. As soon as I perceive some vista speeding past, the train thunders into an underground passage and the black walls of a tunnel appear before my eyes.)

To pass the time, Mrs. Pedrini undertakes to tell us the story of her life. Her dear husband died two years ago, and her children urged her to take this trip back to the Mother Country where he was born, and her ancestors, as well. She smiles and offers us each another chocolate candy. We both accept. She confides that life goes on, even if Mr. Pedrini can't go on with it. From the day they married, she never left his side; they worked together from the time she was eighteen till he was stricken. But she knows he would want her to live and enjoy what life (and money, which is quite a bit) is left to her.

Joe asks what kind of work they did together. Mrs. Pedrini smiles coyly. Would we believe she played drums and her husband accordion in a nightclub act? "My trademark was my hat; I always wore beautiful hats." She does have the mark of an entertainer about her—her bigger-than-life gestures, her glamorous makeup, and her coquettish smile. "Not so bad for seventy-two, am I?" she asks. "I used to sing quite a bit," she adds. Joe suggests that perhaps someday she will sing for the class. "After all, it's a humanities class—and music is surely part of the humanities." Mrs. Pedrini laughs—perhaps she will. She indicates that, if coaxed, she might be persuaded.

Halfway through the trip, the sleeping beauties awaken and stretch— they pass among themselves Italian versions of junk food: potato crisps, sugared corn cereal, crostatini (little fruit pies), and a variety of Italian gum labeled "Brooklyn."

The geography of a train compartment (especially when one knows the occupants) creates an enforced requirement of friendliness. One side is staring at the other, face to face (and, in fact, if the seats are slid forward slightly, one could easily rest her feet on the cushion opposite). Mrs. Pedrini passes around her chocolates. Joe says he hopes the tapes the girls are listening to are the tapes he distributed for his humanities course. I personally doubt this, since his tapes are Gregorian chants and operatic arias.

I say to the girls, "Those are nice leather jackets up on the rack. Did you get them in Italy?"

Two of the girls look at each other—their eyes offering a question to the other. Then they laugh at the same time.

"Shall we explain?" Marta asks Noreen.

"Why not?"

Mrs. Pedrini apparently already knows the story. Her eyes sparkle with the vicarious romance of what we are about to hear, which is this: the girls (Marta, Noreen, and Marcella) met three young men at the "Full-Up" disco on their second night in Florence. When the dance hall closed, the men invited the girls to their warehouse out in the country, where they said they had an import-export used clothing business. They told the girls (apparently this interchange took place in Italian, but the girls, with their Hispanic backgrounds, understood quite enough): "Come with us, and we'll give you all the clothes you want. We have a van, we can all fit in."

At this point in the story, it's Joe and I who exchange a look. "And you went with these strangers? In their van?" I ask.

Marta grins. "Yeah, we went. They were nice guys."

"And then?" I am sure there must be a terrible end to this story.

"And we got all the clothes we wanted. The guys gave us each a giant trash baggie and told us to take whatever we wanted. There were huge piles of clothes all over the place. So Noreen and I got these leather jackets . . ." (she points above her to the rack). "Aren't they great? And I got these blue jeans and this sweatshirt, and we all got dresses and sweaters. . . . I'll never be able to get all this stuff in my suitcase when we go back home."

"And you, Marcella, you didn't get a leather jacket?"

"I didn't like any of them," Marcella says, shrugging.

"Look, I have to ask you this. I have three daughters. It really alarms me that you just got in that van. Weren't you worried that these men might be dangerous?"

"No," Noreen says. She pushes forward her bag of potato crisps, and I decline. "They were really great guys. They introduced us to their parents the next day, and a few days later we went to their homes for dinner and met the whole family. In fact, they're taking us to Elba next weekend."

"Did it even occur to you that they might have taken you away in their van and you'd never be heard from, ever again?"

"Nope," Marta says. "And here we are . . . with these great jackets."

What more is there for me to say?

20

Seashells from the Adriatic and Roast Sardines

Venice is the fabled city. I know it from Shakespeare and from the movies. What will I see with my own eyes? Rain strikes my face as we disembark from the train. On the dock is an odd, slatted, wooden sculpture, triangular in shape—which I don't have time to consider since we immediately board a *traghetto* for the Lido, where our group has rooms reserved in a cheap hotel.

The students, who have all slept on the train, are in the mood to take photographs; they rush outside the glassed-in area to the bow of the boat and lean recklessly upon one another while their friends take pictures to document their arrival in the mythical city. They seem to take dozens of pictures of themselves at every historical site, using it mainly as backdrop for their mugging.

Nicoletta is busy counting heads; her general query is always the same: "Check for your roommates! Is everyone here?" Since no one speaks up, she assumes, fairly, that everyone is on the boat—till we are well out on the canal, when someone shouts, "Oh, Clarita isn't here!"

Her consternation is visible; she and Joe confer. What to do? Joe reminds Nicoletta that Clarita used to be in the Marines; Clarita will probably find her way to the hotel on the next *traghetto*. Though the students are all over eighteen, and in theory the teachers are not in loco parentis, both Nicoletta and Joe are concerned about the kids' safety.

I turn my attention to the waterway, prepared for the great scenes of the Grand Canal, the palazzi on the waterfront, the carved facades I have studied in my guidebook, *Venice and the Veneto.* Joe seems puzzled—we are in some kind of backwater place, passing unremarkable buildings, docks on which gas stations seem to be located, loading piers, industrial storage areas. He and Nicoletta confer again—"I think they're taking us on a back route to the Lido," she says. "It's probably shorter this way." She looks thoroughly frustrated. The students are still so busy making human pyramids and taking photos they haven't noticed that we aren't yet seeing the beauties of Venice. Oh, well. Joe and Nicoletta assure each other there will be plenty of opportunities for everyone to experience the Grand Canal in all its aspects.

The Hotel Euclid, at the Lido of Venice, has an *ascensore* only to the fourth floor; however, Joe and I have been assigned *una camera matrimoniale* on the fifth floor. We struggle up the narrow staircase, bumping our small suitcases behind us, and find ourselves in a room as small as a closet, damp and chilly on this rainy day, no heat in the pipes, and a bathroom that seems to serve in its entirety as a shower. The narrow *letto matrimoniale* is shoved against a wall; the mattress is rock hard. The towels in the bathroom are made of stiff, starched waffle squares that scratch my face when I dry it. When I look out the window, I see only a clothesline hung with large white sheets that flap in the wind and block whatever view may be out there. I feel my good will drifting away; childish emotions, easily aroused lately, are creeping up on me: I want to blame someone. Why didn't we get a good room? Why doesn't the elevator go to our floor? Why isn't the heat on? Why don't we have a view of something? Anything! (Why didn't I stay home? Not just home in Florence, but home at home, in California!)

Now that we have deposited our luggage, we are scheduled immediately to take a *traghetto* back to Venice. All this transporting of my body has begun to seem a major burden. (I remember one writer's arch comment about travel; his body, he said, was the "valet for his soul.")

A call to Nicoletta's room confirms that Clarita has indeed turned up safe at the hotel. In fact, she got here somehow before the rest of us. But there's another problem; Mai Jing, our Chinese student, neglected to bring any identification with her—neither visa nor passport nor credit card—and the hotel is forbidden to register anyone without proper ID. Nicoletta and Joe hurry back to the registration desk to argue that the girl is with our group, an authentic student, registered in the travel-abroad program. They plead for the clerk not to refuse her accommodation. He mumbles and grumbles but finally sees that to refuse is more trouble than it's worth to him.

The kids have been warned to drop their luggage and come right down to the lobby so that we can sail off again to Venice. They're not here, and Nicoletta has asked the desk to ring all of their rooms. While we mill around waiting, Marta says there's a beautiful beach a five minute walk from the hotel—facing the Adriatic Sea.

Never mind Venice, never mind the canals—I want to see an ocean. Don't we have ten minutes? I convince Joe to come with me, I guarantee they won't leave without him. I pull him along till we are running in the rain. The rain on my face, the wind in my hair feel like the return of blessed freedom I have lost. I want to see something *I* want to see. I want not to check in with the group, adhere to some schedule, do what was planned for everyone! (I'm here, and I have needs!) I need to dispel my sense of disappointment with our room, with the weather, with the weightiness of lugging myself around. What I want most now is to see the ocean! I want to hold a seashell in my hands.

And then we're there, at the edge of the Adriatic on this cold, gray day. Striped canvas dressing room-tents, closed up tight, flap quietly in the wind. A bird shivers at the end of a flattened-out wave, dips his beak into the receding foam. I breathe deeply of ocean smells, of salt spray. I let my eyes soak up the endless blue-gray of the water. After the crowds everywhere, the density of Florence, the intensity of being with forty other people for so many hours, this emptiness is a balm. I drink it in. I calm myself. I find a seashell on the beach, then another. I fill the pockets of my jacket with seashells, see that Joe, too, is gathering a few beautiful mussel shells, black on the outside, pearly within.

79

Okay. I've had this moment. I'm back in balance. Once I know I can speed along on my own track, if only briefly, I'm ready to clank and bang along once more with the freight train of the group.

I think that, because we prepare mentally for certain moments, fantasize about them in so many ways and for so long a time, when they finally come, we are bound to be overwhelmed with disappointment. Seeing the Grand Canal in Venice at long last, with its great palaces rising shoulder to shoulder from the greenish-muddy waters, is a blow to my imaginings. On this cold and rainy afternoon, the vista seems shabby, devoid of color, without variety or beauty. In California (I think without charity), they would have taken a wrecking ball to these old crumbling places and built modern condominiums in their places. The cracked stones and peeling paint offer an ominous lesson: those who built these ostentatious structures are long dead. Their money, their power, their distinction have been reduced to these last remnants fading beside the rank waterways.

By some queer twist of logic, this thought cheers me up. Those old guys are dead and gone, but look who's here! We are, a happy lot of tourists, souvenir vendors, shopkeepers, gondoliers, *traghetto* drivers, babies, dogs and cats, everyone with open eyes, alive and sensitive to experience. Looking at it this way, I decide it's quite thrilling to be here, now, in this movie set of Venice.

The living get hungry. We are all famished after our long train trip and many exertions. As soon as we arrive on the dock, we agree we must go in search of nourishment. Nicoletta calls the students together and gives a few instructions: "This is Venice. The shopkeepers and restaurants know what they have here and make you pay dearly for it. Be sure to budget your money for the weekend, and make sure you know in advance the cost of what you order in any of these local trattorias. We will meet at the Accademia, the museum, at 3 P.M. sharp, and I'll distribute your tickets for entrance into the museum at that time. Any of you who want to join us for lunch, please come along." (By "us" she means the grownups—the old folks—the two teachers and Mrs. Pedrini and me, who by default tend to travel together.)

Most of the students head out on in twos and threes; they have already formed strong attachments and created their own little groups. A romance has begun, in fact, between two of our students, Phil and Sara, and they form the core of a clique that tends to follow them around, out of envy, and support, and a need to tease and torment. Phil is a tall, good-looking kid with light brown hair, and Sara a dark-eyed, statuesque young woman with a black braid down her back. They, in some way, are playing out all of our private fantasies: to be young and in love in Italy.

There is no menu in Due Torri trattoria in Dorsoduro. What I see are six or seven tables in the long narrow shop; on the walls are photos of a soccer team and paintings of the holy virgin. Mai Jing, Marta, and Clarita have followed us inside. We choose two adjacent tables, and Mrs. Pedrini immediately orders *"vino per tutti."* Nicoletta asks the man wearing an apron what he is serving today, and a conversation ensues in Italian. "Roasted sardines," Nicoletta translates for us. "And pasta alla bolognese."

Joe and I are wondering what roasted sardines look like, how they are eaten. (We are familiar with sardines packed in a can the usual way—"like sardines.") The proprietor, a jovial, kind-faced man, indicates that you hold the sardines up to your mouth between two fingers, by head and tail, and eat them as you might play a harmonica. He pretends to play a tune on his mythical sardine.

Thus we all happily order roasted sardines—without a menu, without a price. We count on Nicoletta to guide us; this is her Italy.

The meal is delicious, though there is the problem of a thousand tiny bones, none of them soft enough to be edible. The *primo piatto*—a huge plate of pasta and meat sauce—has already filled me up, and Mrs. Pedrini's wine has clouded my perception, so, when I hear a cry from the next table, where three of our students sit, I think at first it

must be a cry of exuberance or laughter. But, no, Mai Jing is screaming something at Marta: it sounds like, "I have my rights. You mind
your own business. You don't know what you're saying!"

Nicoletta turns to the girls sternly; she will not stand for a scene.
"What's going on?"

Mai Jing continues to cry. Marta yells something in return. Clarita
tries to clarify the problem: Mai Jing asked the waiter for hot red pepper to put on her sardines, and Marta said, "Oh, you're so spoiled, you
always have to have things your way. This isn't China. In Venice they
don't put hot pepper on everything."

Nicoletta says fiercely, "That's enough."

But Mai Jing is beyond control. "I may be foreigner, I may be Chinese, but, still, I am human being. You—" she accuses Marta, "you are
lousy. You are lousy person." Mai Jing's sobs are heartbreaking. Her
whole body shakes. She is trembling and sobbing. I go over to her and
put my arms around her. "Of course you are a human being," I whisper in her ear.

"I want to go home," she cries to me.

"Home to China? Or to California?"

"Home to California. Here I do not have my regular foods. Everything is strange, I understand nothing, I didn't bring passport, they
don't want me in hotel." Her words dissolve into a new outbreak of
sobs.

"Oh—I know just how you feel!" I tell her. "I sometimes wish I
could go home, too. We're all in a strange country here, it's so mysterious and frightening." I say this with such feeling that I think I might cry
myself.

"Yes," she agrees, pressing her head against me. "It's terrible here.
No one likes me. No one wants to share my room at the hotel. The girl
who has to be with me says she will sleep in the lobby instead of be with
me. She doesn't like my clothes I wear, or the country where I come
from."

Mrs. Pedrini, who has joined us and is now standing with us, says,
"I'll be your roommate, darling girl. Don't you worry a bit." She fishes
in her purse for some chocolates. Nicoletta is frowning upon all of this.

She says something apologetic to the proprietor, who looks quite worried at the commotion.

Mrs. Pedrini tries to get Mai Jing to eat her plate of sardines, but they do look quite awful now, dead little fish with whitened eyes and greasy tails. Mai Jing pushes the plate away with disgust and bursts into a new round of tears.

Suddenly the proprietor appears with a plate in his hand. He sets it down in front of Mai Jing—a portion of fragrant, steaming fried potatoes. He beseeches her by getting on his knees in front of her, smiling his sweet warm smile. Fried potatoes, who can resist this wonderful food? Even I am overcome by the aroma. "Mai Jing, could I have one of your potatoes?" I ask. Still sniffling, she nods her head. She realizes we are all staring at this delicacy before her. She lifts the plate and offers it round, to Mrs. Pedrini, to Nicoletta, to Clarita . . . but not to Marta. "Not you," she says. Marta utters something that sounds like "Oh, fuck!" and gets up and leaves the restaurant. But then Mai Jing begins to calm herself. She eats one piece of fried potato. Then another. The owner comes over with a little jar of hot red pepper. Mai Jing smiles up at him. The man is an angel.

In a few moments he serves us all espresso coffees. His wife comes forth from behind the counter and delivers the bill. Heaven knows what all this will cost. But Nicoletta examines the *conto* and proclaims a very modest price for each of us.

"*Grazie, grazie,*" we all say as we leave the Due Torri. Mai Jing bows her head shyly, but there's a little smile on her face.

"*Molto benissimo,*" I add to the owners, who stand smiling, their arms linked. Though I'm not exactly sure of what I said, I know it conveys the right idea. My heart is flooded with love for Italians, and especially for this kind man and his wife.

I'm ready to take on the rest of Venice now.

21

The Fire, the Wedding, the Gondoliers

We are scheduled to meet at the museum, the Accademia—a huge, imposing structure guaranteed to be replete with treasures. But I can't go in. Why would I (just now) want to enter a dark museum when all about me is the life of Venice, the crowds, the canals, the pigeons, the gleaming ceramic masks in the windows of the shops?

Museums are an acquired taste. To step inside one, you must be willing to suspend the rhythm of travel, to interrupt the pace of adventure, to slow down to a crawl. You must be willing to walk solemnly and silently (whispering, if at all, as in a funeral home) along a directed pathway, be willing to pause and inspect (often without comprehension) objects of art that are so famous you are shamed into appreciation. There is far too much to see at once. Everything on display is out of its original context—but still you feel the obligation to be awed, or, if not, to consider yourself ignorant and insensitive. Today I am not up to that challenge: I elect to forgo my prepaid ticket. I tell Joe I will meet him outside the museum in a couple of hours.

The rain is coming down hard; I open my umbrella and merge with all the tourists who have opened theirs. In fact, an entire congregation of multicolored umbrellas is massed on the Rialto Bridge, where some-

Fire on the Grand Canal

thing is happening—perhaps something great. An emergency horn is blaring the Italian SOS—a bleating sound that could wake the dead. I hurry along behind the line of umbrella crowns moving up the stairs of the bridge and, peering between umbrella spokes, see a red fire boat ("Vigili del Fuoco" is written on the side) rushing along the Grand Canal to where a boat is noticeably on fire. The firemen—at least six of them— are dressed in red jackets and are poised for action on the speeding boat.

Smoke is issuing skyward in a black plume from another boat some distance away. All the tourists are frozen on the bridge like a great clump of colored mushrooms. We begin to talk to one another as people do during emergencies (as neighbors in California do after an earthquake). Here we speak in a great variety of languages; everyone is asking, "What happened?"—some in German, others in French, Italian, Hebrew—other languages, also. No one knows what happened; we simply look outward to where the smoke is being damped down to a spiral of gray . . . and then it's over.

The fireboat circles around and comes back in our direction, the

Wedding gondola on the Grand Canal

smoke settles over the water like a low-lying rain cloud, and the day is saved. A great cheer goes up from the crowd on the bridge—a cheer to the brave firemen as their boat passes beneath us.

As if this much real life has not been enough of a show, the crowd barely begins to move away from the edge of the bridge when a long black enamel gondola comes gliding toward us. A bride and groom sit in a carved and gilded throne-chair; flowers bedeck the gondola, and two handsome gondoliers stand on red velvet carpets, guiding their charges along what was a moment ago a river of fire but is now a river of love.

The bride and groom turn from side to side, waving like royalty to the onlookers on the bridge and all along the Grand Canal. The bride's veil blows in the wind, and her face gleams with raindrops. We all wave and cheer this wonderful tableau before us.

There—going in one direction—are the courageous firemen, and there—sailing off in the other—are the beaming newlyweds. The tourists still massed on the bridge look around; we smile at one another. We have somehow, in these few moments, become a family. Waving and murmuring good-byes, we slowly part from one another and go our separate ways. I am grieved to have to leave them.

I wander the city in the rain, savoring my time alone till I'm to meet Joe at the Accademia. At a vendor's stand, I examine figures of blown Venetian glass; for each of my daughters I buy a set of miniature glass cats—a mother cat and her kittens, all three a delicate gray, with black whiskers and orange noses.

My aunt, who collects cows, will get a little glass cow with white udders and black horns. For my mother and sister I consider various objects, but nothing seems appropriate. There is plenty of time ahead to shop for them in Italy.

When I rejoin Joe and Nicoletta and the tired band of students at the museum, I am full of the glories of Venice present, while they—exhausted and bleary-eyed—are full of the glories of Venice past.

This time when we get to the hotel on the Lido by *traghetto,* we find that our fifth floor room, tiny and cold and without a view, has been transformed. The heat is on: it's cozy and warm. The sheets beyond the window have been removed from the clothesline and there, across the water, is a clear view of Venice at night, lit and resplendent, as charmingly blurry in the continuing rain as an Impressionist painting. The tiny bed after such a long day is all the more enticing—we fall into it, exhausted and grateful. We fit together, like the sardines at Due Torri. Tomorrow's adventures are yet to be dreamed of.

For this last day in Venice, the rain stops and a scrim of fog hangs over the city. Our breakfast in the hotel is the traditional unheated hard roll, butter and jam, coffee or hot chocolate. The students, for the most part, are not to be seen yet—Mai Jing and Mrs. Pedrini are already breakfasting in the corner of the dining room with Nicoletta. Marta is sitting alone at a table, having a cigarette. Cigarette smoke is inescapable in Italy—it's a fact of life everywhere we go. Joe and I greet Marta who tells us that the band of the singer Diana Ross is staying at our hotel (but not Diana Ross. She's at a better hotel!). Where is everyone else? Well, of course—the students found a disco last night—they're all still sleeping.

"Where do we all have to go today?" Marta asks.

"It's a free day for everyone, " Joe tells her. "Just as long as everyone meets tomorrow morning in time for the train back to Florence."

We give up the idea at once of going into St. Mark's cathedral. The line of tourists is a thousand people long and five hundred deep. St. Mark's Square is a study in motion; a million figures, all forms of life (pigeons, dogs, babies, the young and the old) moving to some predetermined destination.

As we wander along, Joe points out to me the Bridge of Sighs, over which it is said prisoners crossed on their way to the dungeons of torture. (Why is there a legend that lovers who kiss beneath it will find true love forever?)

Joe and I move a bit off the beaten track, along the back streets and smaller canals. A water-taxi comes along, and on the prow of the boat is a dog, standing regally with two feet up on a box like a figurehead on a sailing vessel. The taxi driver smiles at us and waves. A young couple stops and asks us to take their picture together, posing against the picturesque backdrop of the canal. Then they offer to take a photo of us. We sit on a low wall, we smile, they click the shutter, and then we part, almost friends.

At the open fish market, Joe and I examine the octopus, shrimp, mussels, even a large blowfish, that are spread out on beds of ice. Can these fish possibly be from the muddy canals? We decide they must have been caught in the fresh waters of the Adriatic Sea.

This is lovely, being alone with Joe, free of the students and the restraints that our position puts upon us. Though we are, by definition, their chaperones, they have in fact been chaperoning us. Not only have we been circumspect in their presence, we have nearly been frozen by the rules of propriety. We hardly ever hold hands! Yet here we are in the world's most romantic city, I am full of romantic longings, and at heart I feel no older than the students.

Noting that now there is nothing to stop me from throwing my arms around my handsome husband and kissing him, I do, quite suddenly—on the four directions of his face, north, south, east, and west. I kiss my husband quite furiously and madly. It's my right and privilege. And, to his credit, he takes my attack like a man.

22

The Jewish Ghetto in Venice, Losses, and Other Thefts

When we reach the Jewish Ghetto by following the map, we turn somber. The square is small but contains the "skyscrapers of Italy," buildings as high as nine stories, with some floors having ceilings as low as six feet. These buildings were created over the years as more and more Jews were packed into a tiny area. Five synagogues are hidden in the upper floors of these buildings.

The small Jewish museum, in which are displays of sacred religious articles, tapestries, jewels, and prayer books, is for some unannounced reason (as often happens in Italy) closed. No announcement is made or excuses given. The door is merely locked.

We pass a small Jewish grocery store, with matzos and Jewish wine in the window, and a Jewish gift shop, in front of which a guard stands, holding his weapon. This sight causes my heart to skip; it is more shocking here, somehow, than the sight of the guards at the synagogue in Florence. Venice, which up to now has promised only beauty, entertainment, and pleasure, reminds us by this armed presence that there is history to be remembered and present danger here, as well. On a single wall on one of the buildings in the square of Campo del Ghetto Nuova are seven bronze sculptures memorializing the Holocaust. We pause in

Holocaust plaque in the Jewish Ghetto, Venice

front of these for a long time, taking in the scenes of Jews pouring from the boxcars, of Jews being hanged, shot, and shoveled into mass graves. The Venetian sky turns dark as we move along and see engraved on a wall the names of Jews killed in World War I:

GLI EBREI VENEZIANI
CADUTI IN GUERRA PER LA PATRIA
LA COMMUNITA
CON AMORE CON ORGOGLIO RICORDA
MCMXV — MCMXX
(THE VENETIAN JEWS
FALLEN IN WAR FOR THEIR COUNTRY
THE COMMUNITY
WITH LOVE WITH PRIDE REMEMBERS)
1915–1920

I am impelled, for some reason, to read aloud to Joe the list of their names, pronouncing them as best I can:

Aboaf, Umberto
Ancona, Paolo
Boralevi, Giorgio
Foa, Davide Guido
Grunwald, Beniamino
Levi Bianchini, Angelo
Levi Minzi, Guido
Levi Morenos, Alberto
Levis, Giuseppe Ernesto,
Nacamvilli, Mario
Navarro, Abramo
Padoa, Aldo
Pardo, Giorgio
Polacco, Abramo
Polacco, Sansone
Sarfatti, Roberto
Segre, Ippolito
Soave, Amedeo
Soave, Attilio
Sonino, Oliviero
Stecher, Bruno
Todesco, Marko
Vivante, Ferruccio
Finzi, Ruggero.

Too many share the same last names. Father and son? Brothers? In any case, it's nearly impossible to imagine these losses.

On an adjoining wall of the ghetto—carved on wooden planks and protected behind iron bars—are the names of Jews murdered in the Holocaust. A poem, on a bronze plaque, proclaims in Italian, with a translation in English beneath it:

MEN, WOMEN, CHILDREN, MASSES FOR THE GAS CHAMBERS,
ADVANCING TOWARD HORROR BENEATH THE WHIP OF THE EXECUTIONER,
YOUR SAD HOLOCAUST IS ENGRAVED IN HISTORY

AND NOTHING SHALL PURGE YOUR DEATHS FROM OUR MEMORIES
FOR OUR MEMORIES ARE YOUR ONLY GRAVE.
ANDRE TRONO—ANCIEN DES FORCES FRANCAISES COMBATTANTES

After we leave the Jewish Ghetto, we pass a small church from whose open door the sweetest sounds issue forth. Joe leads me inside, where we see a choir of women singing motets. The notes of their song echo in the vaulted dome of the church and seem to shimmer like tiny birds above our heads. Joe and I sit in the dimness, letting the music enter our souls. Peace descends upon me. It feels to me like a visitation or a benediction. From whom or for what I do not ask. I simply receive it.

My camera has taken so many sad photos, of the bronze Holocaust carvings, of the plaques memorializing the war dead, that I want to bring some lightness into my recording of our passage through Venice. We make our way back to the throngs of St. Mark's, where two competing orchestras are playing across the square from each other. Standing in front of the famous Caffè Florian, we watch the great panoramic scene before us: the musicians in formal attire playing "O sole mio" and "Volare," the thousands of tourists tempting the pigeons with handfuls of crackers and bread crusts in order to take a photo wild with the life of the square. There is more motion and color here than I have ever seen in any one spot in the universe. So many disparate souls pursuing their goals—fun, love, souvenirs, food, dance, religious ecstasy, the mere requirement to "travel and see the world." Babies are crying, lovers are embracing, old people are struggling along with their canes (some are being pushed in wheelchairs), hawkers are hawking, vendors are vending, and above us all are the spires and cupolas and domes and statues and bell towers of a civilization once great and grand.

Just as I glance to my left, a waiter, carrying a tray of delicacies, arrives at the door of the Caffè Florian; I lift my camera and aim. He stops in his tracks, flashes me a dazzling smile (he is black-haired and blue eyed, a man of surpassing sexual beauty) and poses long enough for me to take my photo and fall in love with him forever. He knows this and telegraphs it to me with his eyes. We collude in a farewell laugh, and I turn back to my innocent husband.

Now we are hungry. We order a pizza and a bottle of *acqua minerale* at a sidewalk cafe, take seats at an outdoor table, and gratefully rest our feet. When the pizza is served, it is inferior (the mushrooms are canned), and the large bottle of water is warm. Giant iced beers are served to the couple at the next table—at least a quart to a glass—and I feel a stab of envy. (Why didn't we order iced beer?) When we are rested and fed, Joe calls for *il conto*. His face darkens as he reads the bill. There must be some mistake—we have been charged about forty dollars. He calls the owner over, and they confer. The man has a crook's face, I decide. They debate; Joe points at the bill, the man points at the heavens. Finally, my husband stops arguing and hands the man 60,000 lire.

"Why is it so much?" I ask, knowing all too well the answer. This is Venice. Here a bottle of water costs twelve dollars. Here you pay for a table, a service charge, the view of the pigeons.

I try to swallow my outrage that Venice charges you for the air you breathe, for merely being alive.

"Think of it as our travel tax," Joe explains to me as we walk away. "Don't worry about it. We are here only once in a lifetime."

We walk, and we look at everything. We breathe deeply of the air of Venice. As evening falls we consult our map and head back toward the dock, toward the columns of San Teodordo and San Marco where a marble statue and a winged lion sit atop them. I have read in a guidebook that the designer of these columns was granted the right to set up gambling tables between them; also that superstitious Venetians will not walk between them because many criminals were executed on the spot. Today there is nothing so ominous taking place; in fact, a colorful throng of gondoliers is waiting there for customers—an army of handsome men in white middies, blue and white shirts, and straw hats bedecked with red ribbons.

And isn't that Mai Jing standing with a gondolier? And isn't his arm around her while Mrs. Pedrini takes a picture? Indeed, we come upon a group of our students, all of whom have just come back from a gondola ride—five of them dividing up the 100,000-lire price. As a bonus, the gondolier, whose name I am told is Giancarlo, will pose for photos with everyone. The man is six foot five, an exquisitely featured, sexy Italian, powerful and beautiful, grinning with the pleasure of all the women clamoring for his arm. Even Mrs. Pedrini takes shelter briefly in his muscled embrace for the camera's pleasure. I glance at Joe—I wonder if even I should be thus photographed for the sake of posterity. But there are limits to one's rank desires, and the feelings of others to be considered. I settle for a photo with my husband between the towers, with Mai Jing doing the honors for us.

In the morning, at the hotel, there is a serious problem as the students gather to leave. The concierge informs us that two towels are missing from one of the rooms. They must be paid for. Nicoletta appears exasperated: "Look," she addresses her students, "whoever took these for a souvenir, please—you have to put them back. This is not Las Vegas; you're not invited to take souvenirs."

The students look variously mystified, outraged, indifferent . . . and guilty.

"They are very serious about theft here," Nicoletta informs the students as they all stand in the lobby near the checkout desk. "We have our reputation to uphold—American students will not be welcome here if this is what they think Americans do."

Silence, no one knows anything. No one has the towels. No one has had anything to do with this. Joe and Nicoletta confer. We have a train to catch, we have to get the *traghetto* to the Venice *stazione*. Nicoletta returns to the desk.

"Do you know from which room they are missing?"

The clerk, a red-faced agitated soul, consults his records. Just then, Mrs. Pedrini comes up to Nicoletta and whispers something in her ear.

Motioning for the students to gather round her, Nicoletta says, "All right, Mrs. Pedrini tells me that last night two of you girls came in inebriated and throwing up and that she gave you two towels from her room to help you clean up."

The handsome gondolier with Mai Jing

After a moment's silence, one girl says, "Well, that's true, but then we threw the towels down the laundry chute at the end of the hall."

Nicoletta relays this information to the desk clerk. A housemaid is dispatched to check the laundry chute. She returns with the news that those towels were found and counted but that there are still two towels missing.

Nicoletta leans back against the desk, exasperated. She will wait. We will all wait. We will miss the train to Florence if necessary. In the background, we hear the television in the lobby advertising Italian chocolates. This is one time Mrs. Pedrini does not get out her purse and distribute hazelnut delights.

The students murmur among themselves, bringing pressure to bear on their friends. Finally, Robin, our flamboyant student (the one so proud of his body piercing) suddenly stands up in our midst. He's wearing a floor-length overcoat and flings it open, whereupon from his side pockets he extracts, like a magician, the two missing white waffle-squared hand towels. "Ta da!" he says. "What the hell, you can have them. They're crummy towels, anyway; they scratch your face. I just wanted a souvenir from Venice."

The rain begins to fall again as we wait for the *traghetto*. It's getting colder, and we are all very tired. Mrs. Pedrini and Marta break out into song: "Singing in the Rain" is first, and then a sexy song by Mrs. Pedrini, "La Vie en Rose." Her voice is strong, rising into the gray sky above us.

When we get on the train, we once again have to argue for every seat, forcing Italians to stand so that they can then hang over us, smoking, for this time Nicoletta has inadvertently reserved seats on a smoking car without compartments. A man is so close to me that his hip bangs into my head at every slight bump of the train.

Not long after, the electricity fails completely—so we have no lights or air circulation. The windows are locked shut and cannot be opened. "Call a conductor," someone cries, and another voice answers, "This is an Italian train. Good luck."

I have never had a panic attack, but I think I am having one now.

97

There is no possible way for me (or anyone else) to get into the aisle, to find a bathroom, to get to a window to inhale a breath of air.

When the lights come on again, Joe begins to write a postcard to his sister and suggests I write cards to our children and my mother. He sees the state into which I have worked myself, and I know he's trying to distract me. He pulls a folding packet of cards from his pocket and hands them to me to make my choices. He gives me a pen, too.

Then he offers to me the card he's just composed to his sister: "I am writing you this postcard from the train on which Merrill and I are re-turning with the students to Florence from Venice. Unfortunately, in Venice they do not sell postcards with photos of stifling train cars filled with smoke, and people leaning over you with wine-y breath, so I am sending you instead this peaceful scene of a gondola cruising down the Grand Canal."

23

The Movie Sets of Venice and Florence

Back from Venice, and walking again in the streets of Florence, I realize how thoroughly my mind is saturated with movie images. When I first saw the barbershop striped poles in front of the Doges' Palace on the Grand Canal, I thought at once of *Death in Venice* and of the death-colored man dressed in white who moons over the beautiful boy in the sailor suit.

During my first ride on the *traghetto,* I remembered the Daphne du Maurier thriller-movie *Don't Look Now,* in which Donald Sutherland tries to reclaim his grief-stricken wife from the thrall of the weird and ominous twin sisters, one of them blind and psychic. As the miasmic fog rose from the canal, I not only saw what passed before my eyes on that drizzly, damp day in Venice but added the remembered scenes from the movie: the dark and narrow streets, the sulfuric steaming canals—and always the flashing image of the dead child appearing and disappearing under the myriad, mysterious bridges.

Later, when Joe and I had lost our bearings somewhere near San Marco, I remembered *The Comfort of Strangers,* the movie from the novel by Ian McEwan, in which the honeymooning couple get lost in Venice and are seduced by the charismatic older man who finally—

after terrorizing them and stealing their clothes—murders the young husband.

When we stopped to buy the mediocre pizza at the sidewalk cafe, I watched the passing hordes and recalled the sunlit scenes from *Brideshead Revisited*—the days when Charles Ryder and Sebastian Flyte go to Venice to visit Sebastian's father (played by Laurence Olivier) and his mistress. No conversation I had with my husband that day (about how much we were overcharged for our pizza) could ever be remembered as thrillingly as I still recall the significant glances and innuendo that passed between Charles and Sebastian.

On a school day when Joe is on his way to teach his class at the school, I accompany him into *il centro* and part with him at the piazza of Santa Croce. As soon as I come into the airy piazza, I think of E. M. Forster's characters, Lucy Honeychurch and Miss Lavish, in *A Room with a View,* just as they come into a "piazza, large and dusty, on the further side of which rose a black-and-white facade of surpassing ugliness."

On the contrary, I find (when I enter this same piazza from a maze of dark narrow streets) a space full of light and wonder, and its treasure, Santa Croce, one of the most beautiful churches in Florence. In the square, a dog runs after the milling pigeons, and the birds swoop away in fluttering hordes against the sun. When they come down to earth again, several battle for a foothold on the head of the statue of Dante.

This morning, I see that great crowds of tourists have the same idea as I do. Busload after busload march across the square, each group following its tour guide, one holding up a red umbrella, one a rolled white poster, one hoisting an Italian flag above his head. Posted on the entrance to the church is a sign warning that pickpockets are a danger and that one should be on guard. An old gypsy woman seems to be sleeping beneath the sign, a white plate with a few coins in it at her side.

Inside, I take the opportunity to attach myself to a tour group whose guide is speaking English. She holds forth in that clipped, artificial way that guides use to address their groups, ready at every moment, in a perky and chipper tone, to tell a cute historical anecdote.

This woman, in her practical low heels, is standing before the monument to Michelangelo, who is buried in Santa Croce.

She tells us that the three sad ladies moping at his casket are the muses of Architecture, Sculpture, and Painting. We must be sure to note the cherubs flying above his carved bust. Michelangelo, the guide tells us, was first buried in Rome, but one of his students (or perhaps his nephew) spirited his body back to Florence. (At this juncture I recall Charlton Heston, in *The Agony and The Ecstasy*, lying on his back on flimsy scaffolding as he paints the Sistine Chapel ceiling.) However, the guide admits that no one really knows where the sculptor's body is, in which of the crypts beneath the church, since, in the Great Flood of 1966, all the bodies were tumbled from their crypts by the raging waters and were mixed up, bones and skulls, in a great mishmash. In fact, she adds, since the remains of Rossini and Galileo are also buried below, "we can think of them as a kind of Genius Combo mixed together down there."

The guide waits for a laugh. Her charges are already tired, listing and leaning against pillars where they can, shifting the weight of their guidebooks, backpacks, cameras. They are as restless as beasts of burden whose journey is summarily halted.

I take my leave of the tour group and stand to watch two American boys begging their mother to give them money to light candles. For a moment, as the boys hold the long white tapers in their hands, then light them by touching their wicks to another burning candle, their faces are illuminated, their fair pale skin shining as if lit from within like the skin of cherubim in the great paintings. Though I have no video camera, I feel that, if I had one, I could frame a scene as beautiful as any by Fellini. Everything I see in Italy passes by me as if on a movie screen.

I move along toward the frescos by Giotto. A soon as I reach the Peruzzi Chapel, I flash to my memory of it from the movie *A Room with a View*. Why, I wonder, do the movies hold so powerful a place in my memory that they often affect me more than the reality of the moment I am living in? Whenever I walk through the Piazza della Signoria and see the magnificent Neptune rising out of the water, I think of Helena

Bonham-Carter as Lucy Honeychurch, witnessing the fight between the two Italian men at the fountain, fainting at the sight of the bleeding man, and dropping her postcards in a pool of blood. When she swoons, she is caught in the arms of the beautiful George Emerson, who is falling in love with her. Their kiss in a field of flowers in Fiesole rates as one of the great romantic love scenes in cinema. However, whenever *I* wander in the Piazza della Signoria, nothing so dramatic happens to me. So, as I stand, in person, in Santa Croce, looking, in person, at the art of Giotto on the walls, I cannot see what is before me so much as I see what I once saw in the movies.

24

Botticelli Women, Italian Wives

On the benches along the Arno, their heads tilted against the sunlight, young women sit studying art and language books. Now and then they raise their eyes and watch a lone kayaker paddling by. When the wind blows, they gracefully brush a stray strand of hair behind an ear and go back to reading their books.

In the Boboli Gardens, I see young women dotting the landscape like flowers. On the bridges, on the buses, on the terraces, on the piazzas, at the *stazione,* in every pizzeria and trattoria, beautiful women abound. Many of them are students who come to study the *David* of Michelangelo, the beauties of Botticelli, the doors of Ghiberti, the madonnas of Cimabue, the dome of Brunelleschi. Like the young beauties Maria and Patty, who live in the downstairs apartment, these young women come to Italy to enlarge their lives, to soak in culture, to have adventures, and, if possible, to fall in love.

But the ones I observe reading along the river, or sunning near the copy of the *David* on the Piazzale Michelangelo, or leaning over the wall of the Ponte alle Grazie to throw crumbs to the ducks are not the native beauties of Florence. Mostly, they are from France, America, Yugoslavia, Germany, Sweden, Spain, Brazil. Often they are daughters of affluent families, education-minded parents who are happy to lend a

hand with tuition, room, and board while their daughters "go abroad" to soak up the glories of the Medici civilization.

The Florentine-born beauties are in another dimension. I see them working as waitresses in the trattorias, as agents in the government offices. They ride to work on their motor scooters, dressed in suits and high heels and with their leather purses on the floorboards. Many of them, with tendrils of hair curling about their faces in the wind, could have stepped straight from *The Birth of Venus* or *La Primavera*. They are not in such a hurry to fall in love as the visiting girls are. A young American male student told me, "American men have it the worst. The Italian girls want nothing to do with us, and the foreign girls, including the American girls in my classes, love Italian men. So that leaves us nowhere!"

"Why do you think Italian women aren't interested in you?" I asked him.

"They're stuck up," he said. "They want to marry money; they want a nice house and good furniture. They don't want a poor guy in torn jeans from California."

Patty, the girl downstairs, the corn-fed, blue-eyed redhead from Kansas, is in love. Maria, the dark-haired Brazilian girl, is in love. One of the girls in Joe's class is in love with an Italian who stopped her in the street and said, "I love you," in three languages, till he found the right one.

"How can you love me? You don't even know me," she said.

"But I do. You will see. I love you with all my soul."

Marta, the singer, is in love with an Italian. "He doesn't talk much," she told me, "but there's something about him. Those brooding eyes."

When I receive an invitation from Sara, who was one of the guests I met at the Jewish New Year's dinner, I agree to go with her to a meeting of a group called Network. Its members are all English-speaking (mostly American) women who came here as students, fell in love, and married Italian men. Now they have children, speak fluent Italian, and tangle with the government bureaucracy about matters they took for granted in the United States. (Sara tells me that foreign-born married women in Italy have to sign a yearly affidavit that their husbands support them and that under no circumstances will they become wards of the state.) She says the women formed Network in order to meet once a month for support, sympathy, and encouragement.

"Encouragement?" I ask.

"Mainly for dealing with their husbands' parents," she says. "Italian grandparents are very pushy. They know exactly how they want their grandchildren raised, and they're not bashful about saying so."

The meeting is at Piazza Savonarola, in the building owned by Syracuse University, one of many American universities that maintain campuses in Florence. The sound of women chattering in English feels like home to me. Inside, about thirty women are gathered around a buffet table, holding paper plates on which they have piled snacks of a highly recognizable sort—crackers and cheese, carrot and celery sticks, salted peanuts, potato chips. (Notably lacking are Italian appetizers such as *crostoni* and *prosciutto e melone.*)

Sara introduces me to a few people who at once ask where am I from, what am I doing here, am I going to live here? Do I need some advice?

They are very eager to give advice—those who have been in Italy a long time have important news for the newcomers. They know the best hospital in which to have babies, the best doctors (especially those who are familiar with the American style of practicing medicine), the best place to buy bagels, the best way to deflect the unwelcome advice of the in-laws.

Do I need anything to read? They have a private lending library and pass around precious paperback books from the United States, some sent by relatives, others brought by friends. They exchange names of baby-sitters and recommend good places to get cheap clothes. (The American Church has a thrift shop in its basement.)

Knowing I am a writer, Sara introduces me to a group of women, all of whom are aspiring novelists. One of them tells me her husband is a construction worker. "Marco couldn't care less that I have my master's degree, and I couldn't care less that he hacks away at the insides of old buildings. Our real life is wonderful—we drive to the beach or the mountains or go skiing, and we cook magnificent food, and we make love. We even visit his parents every weekend; it's not so bad. In the United States, I would have had to marry an academic and join the PTA. Here, I make risotto and write mystery novels set in Pisa or in Siena."

"I'd like to write about Italy," I tell her.

"Be our guest," she says. "There's nothing better to write about than Italy!"

25

Sciopero! (*Strike!*)

The weather has turned suddenly bitter—rain, wind, lowering skies—and Joe and I have both caught the germ that the students have been sharing among themselves by offering one another licks of their gelato cones and sips from their four-dollar cans of Coke and by their constant hugging, kissing and grooming of one another. This physical need they have for touch and for sitting in one another's laps (at least the girls do this) must be a function of their being far away from home. The girls spend hours, often in public places, braiding and arranging one another's hair, and three of the boys have hired Rosanna to dye their hair brilliant red, orange, or purple. They think it a lark to call one another "Pomodoro," "Arancia," and "Porpora."

In the apartment today there is no heat and no running water. I call downstairs to see whether Maria or Patty or their landlady, Paola, knows the reason for the trouble, but no one is home. Joe is getting ready to take the bus to *il centro* to teach his class. He bundles up in sweater, raincoat, and hat. I—rather than stay in the apartment and freeze—decide to go to the *tabaccaio* and buy *francobolli*—stamps for the postcards I want to send to friends.

We part at the bus stop; Joe rarely has to wait more than five minutes for a #14 bus, though—if I'm with him and one passes by just as we approach the corner—I always cry out, "Oh, no, oh, wait, wait!" as if this bus were the last one on earth. As I walk the two blocks to the *tabaccaio* (a capital "T" is posted outside the store as an indication that bus tickets and stamps may be bought within), I look in the window of the *pasticceria,* where the most luscious fruit pies are displayed, along with cream puffs and lemon cakes. I pass the *libreria* (the book store), and the *macelleria* (where beef and chicken parts hang on hooks in the window.) Much further down Via Aretina is David Due, a trattoria and pizzeria that has a statue of David (wearing a green loincloth) in the entryway. (Their pizzas, like most pizzas in Italy, are baked in a wood-fired oven, and come out deliciously thin and crisp, with every possible adornment, including *tonno, speck, funghi, prosciutto, cipolla, melanzane,* and all varieties of cheese. It's always eaten with a fork and knife, never by hand.)

The rain is coming down hard now—I think of getting back to the apartment, lighting the oven, and sitting in the kitchen to keep warm. My problem is that I manage to get the oven lit only half the time. Most of my efforts conclude with the match burning down to my fingertips so that I have to drop it and then mash out the flame with my foot. That, or the gas simply does not ignite. When the smell of gas becomes too strong, I give up, in fear of an explosion, and open the windows to air out the kitchen.

The last time I visited Santa Croce, however, I sinned in the desire to get my oven lit. Although I put 200 lire in the offertory under the table where votive candles are lit, I didn't light a candle. Instead, I put one in my backpack and took it home in order to light the oven with a long taper instead of a one-inch match.

Today, in the *tabacccaio,* the young woman who greets me has sold me stamps before. She knows my routine—I tell her that I want *"dieci francobolli per cartolina USA,"* and she does the rest of the figuring out. Each stamp to the United States costs 1,250 lire; they come in denominations of 1,000 and 250. There is no way I am able to say in Italian, within a reasonable frame of time, the numbers represented by the necessity of buying ten 1,250-lire stamps. She knows my dilemma; she even puts the stamps in a little cellophane bag for me. She takes my money, she gives me change.

I indicate *"freddo"*—it's cold out. I further indicate—by a pantomime and a serious mangling of her language—that there's no heat in my apartment. I also indicate somehow that the *fiamiferri*—the matches—are too short for lighting the stove.

She smiles and offers me solutions. First she presents me with an *accendigas*—a flint lighter for the stove. This device, by a simple squeeze of the handle, produces a spark that lights the gas without a flame. I'll buy it!

She then produces the next item to help me through the winter: a hot water bag! It's made of bright green rubber, with a red stopper. She indicates that I can fill it with hot water and take it to bed with me. (Yes, if they ever turn the water on in the building, and, yes, if I can light the stove to heat the water . . . and if I can fill the hot water bag without burning myself. . . .)

I leave in high spirits, having spent a good deal of money, but with the prospect ahead of warmth and comfort.

It's pouring when I get home, and it promises to be a long, dark day. My little Walkman radio plays comforting tunes of America—Cher, Elvis, the BeeGees. I do manage to light the gas burners easily with my new *accendigas,* and I sit reading in the kitchen till suddenly the key turns in the lock, and Joe appears in the doorway, completely bedraggled and soaking wet.

"What happened?"

"No bus came," he says. "I waited and waited."

"All this time?"

"Yes, till a man on a motor scooter passed me by and said didn't I know there was a *sciopero*? A bus strike?"

"You waited all this time? In the pouring rain?"

"He said in Italy there's a strike every few days—trains, mail delivery, banks."

"Well, don't worry about missing class. Most of your students who take buses won't be there either," I remind him.

I help him peel off his wet clothes. On the stove (lit with success by the *accendigas*), I heat the water that's still in the teapot and fill the hot water bag with it.

We get under the covers with the rubber bag between us. The sheets begin to warm at once. I offer Joe one of the Walkman's two ear pieces and fiddle with the tuning dial until I find music: Puccini's *La Bohème*.

Perfect. We snuggle together, listening to the tragic tale of love, in a freezing garret while thunder rocks the countryside and lightning illuminates the sky.

26

The Five-Hundred-Year-Old Farmhouse

A friend of my friend from California calls and invites me to her five-hundred-year-old farmhouse on Mount Morello, high up in the hills northwest of Firenze. Cornelia, an Englishwoman who met her Italian husband at Oxford, has lived for thirty years in Florence, where her husband is a professor at the University. She herself is a writer and art critic. She promises that one day she will take me for coffee in her favorite bar on Borgo San Jacopo and that from there we will go to the reading room of the British Institute Library on Lungarno Guicciardini, where I can sit in the reading room and watch the Arno flow past. She tells me that she and her husband have lived in the historic house I am about to visit for only six years, but all the years before they dreamed of buying such a place.

She picks me up in her little car in front of the Grande Mondo Ristorante Cinese on Via Aretina. She warns me to buckle up. Driving in Italy seems to be a contest, much like the bumper-car ride I passed one day in the park near the Bellariva swimming pool. There is much honking, cutting off of other cars, edging-in-front-of, short stops, and a general sense of frantic busy-ness: drivers are constantly shifting gears, slamming on brakes, and swerving suddenly.

Cornelia asks whether I would like her to take the country route.

When I agree, she guides her little car through the rapids of Florentine traffic till she turns off on a narrow, cavernous street that becomes a steep mountain road. Within minutes, we are at the crest of a great downward slide: a green vista lies before us, a country scene of olive trees and yellow flowers and stone walls that hug the edge of the road. Cornelia apologizes for having to honk her horn constantly, but it is a safety necessity, honking wherever the road curves, wherever a narrow road exits from an olive grove, wherever the pebbled driveway of a house intersects the main roadway. The air is dotted with the staccato beeps of cars. The drivers all honk, but no one slows down. As Cornelia takes a sharp curve, we are suddenly confronted with a car coming our way—on a roadway wide enough for only one to pass. Cornelia brakes, begins a long backing-up, manages to clear the stone wall by half an inch as she pulls as close to the side as possible while the other car squeaks by.

As she continues on, she points out to me the shops in Piazza Niccolò da Tolentino. The baker delivers fresh bread up the mountain every morning; the grocer drops off cartons of bottled water. The butcher will bring a roast, a chicken, a ham, and wonderful sausages.

After climbing the road ten minutes longer, she slows and parks on a dirt area—I hear the tires scrape and feel them bounce over small rocks.

"Here we are," she says, with pride and pleasure in her voice.

I look about for her villa, her palazzo, her country mansion, and what I see is a tiny little house, the kind a child would draw: two windows up, two windows down, a door, a little step, and a chimney.

Her youngest of three boys, Marlowe, is at home, a six-foot-tall teenager who talks with perfect British pronunciation. Cornelia tells me they speak only English in their home, whereas, out in the public world, they speak only Italian. "We live in two worlds here," she confesses.

The whole of the downstairs of the house is visible from where I stand in the entry: in front of me is a worn stone staircase, to my left is a small room, to my right is the main room of the house, living and dining rooms in one. Cornelia points out the original stone hearth, where food was cooked five hundred years ago and up to the present until they broke through a wall to what is now the kitchen. The room, no wider than four feet, used to be a dog kennel. Cornelia explains: "It is illegal to carve this opening in the wall, there are strict rules about any changes being made in these historical buildings. You can't so much as put up a shed without a permit, and even then the structure must be able to be disassembled with the removal of a few screws. A storage area must not have sides or rise higher than the edge of the wall around the property. Of course, the government knows people make some changes in order to live—and so, from time to time, they offer a *condono*—a pardon, if you file papers about the changes and pay a fee. Then your home is legal in case you want to sell it, and they make a profit."

The dining table is set for five; Cornelia says it's possible that her other sons may appear for lunch—though she can never be sure. "They don't live in the house—there's no room," she tells me. "We actually rent a flat for them in the building just adjacent—so the two older boys live there! You can see this house is not very spacious."

She leads me up the narrow flight of steps to the second floor. The stones are so polished and slanted that I must hold on to rope banisters on either side of the wall to keep my balance.

We enter her bedroom, big enough only for a double bed and one armoire. The walls are painted white; the stucco is uneven, as if layers of plaster have been added over the centuries. But then Cornelia throws open the shutters, and I understand her passion for this house. This is a view as if from heaven itself—a vista before us of sky and cloud and mountain and meadow.

"We often see the weather moving in over the plains," she says, and that simple sentence evokes a sense of centuries of sunrise and sunset, winter storms and spring breezes. "It's the quiet I love here; I need this peace to nourish myself."

At that instant, as if by signal, a roar overhead is audible; a jet plane swoops skyward and flies directly over the house. Cornelia laughs. "Ah, well," she says, "it is still the twentieth century, and the Peretola Airport is just over there. They do sometimes fly very low."

Lunch is risotto with peppers and onions, a meat roll with roasted potatoes and oregano, sweet corn (canned), hot fresh Italian bread, wine, ripe peaches. For dessert, Cornelia serves *panforte,* a delicacy from Siena, a kind of gummy, sweet fruitcake.

After lunch, she tells Marlowe we are going out to tour "the property," and we walk out the door into a vista of olive trees and grapevines. "Over there is our own little spring, and here, this is our well." My feet sink inches into the damp soil.

"Oh, dear, we have had so much rain. You'll ruin your shoes." But I am looking at the mythical fruits of Italy, grapes and olives, all taut in their shining skins, bright in afternoon light.

"We have picked most of the grapes, but the olive picking will take place in a week or two. Perhaps you would like to be here to see it?"

"I would love that."

We walk and walk, beyond her property and along the road, backing ourselves against the stone wall whenever we hear the honking of an approaching car.

"In that villa," she says, "lives Flavia Colacicchi, the widow of the famous painter Giovanni Colacicchi. His paintings hang in the Galleria di Arte Moderna in Palazzo Pitti and his self-portrait in the Corridoio Vasariano of the Uffizi. Her paintings are really wonderful, I think. The Palazzo Pitti recently bought one. Flavia is a very old woman now, one of my close friends. I think she'd like you; perhaps when you come again you would like to meet her."

"Oh, yes, I would!"

I feel already as if my future time in Italy has been enriched by promises of delights to come. I am grateful to Cornelia, and to my friend at home who put me in touch with her.

Back in the magical house, we have tangerines and tea and talk about writers and writing. We discover that we both love the work of Arturo Vivante, an Italian writer who moved to America and published many stories in the *New Yorker.* What's more, it turns out that Flavia Colacicchi knew him as a boy in Siena.

As the afternoon begins to darken, Cornelia suggests we drive to the piazza where I can catch the #14 bus that will take me right back home. I can feel a chill settling on the house, the cold rising up from the terra cotta tiles. The small radiator in the living room has come on but warms only a small area around it.

I have wondered all afternoon whether I could live here, live this way, without my space, without my comforts, in a primitive house like this. The answer comes to me as we walk outside into the sunset. I take into myself the beauty of the land, this quality of light. I feel myself falling dreamily under the spell of the perfect ovals of grapes and olives.

27

Losing My Way,
Discovering Treasures

My technique for shopping now includes taking our suitcase-on-wheels to the supermarket. Admittedly, I may look a little strange to the locals as I hoist my suitcase into my wagon and wander the aisles buying buffalo milk mozzarella (soft white balls of cheese packed in water), and *biscotti alla mandorla*.

On the day that I want to buy bread crumbs but don't know where to find them, I ask the clerk where there might be *panne macinato*. (I have seen the word *macinata* on the packages of ground beef; I therefore assume ground bread might be what I want.) He leads me right to the spot; I feel triumphant. (The word on the package is *pangrattato*—grated bread, close enough.) But my small creative victory allows me to feel closer to conquering my sense of helplessness. I also want to bake some corn bread but have no idea how to find baking powder, baking soda, and vanilla. I have no approximations to offer the clerk, but I lead him to the packaged cake section and try to indicate that I want a product that makes a cake rise up. To do this, I lift a cake over my head. This is becoming a little like a game show. He cocks his head as if trying to think of an answer. Then: the light bulb smile. Does he have the answer? He motions for me to follow him along the row of flour, sugar, and farina bags till he stops at a little pile of blue and white envelopes.

He offers me one. The package reads *Ottimi Dolci con il Lievito Va-nihliato.* This must be it, something that levitates my cake! Something with vanilla in it. In the small print it says *"Bicarbonato di sodio, Piro-fosfato acido di sodio."* I'll take it. Another triumph of intelligence, the clerk's and mine.

I travel along, piling my wagon high—a large chicken (headless), pounds of potatoes, a bag of onions, a kilogram of mushrooms (bright, white with their roots still attached to clumps of dirt from which they were pulled), shining purple eggplants, four liters of natural mineral water, boxes of pineapple, pear, and orange juice. For good measure, I buy ice cream, as well.

When I check out, I hoist my suitcase onto the counter and fill it up as the checker rolls my purchases along. I pack carefully, the heaviest items on the bottom, the most fragile toward the top. The customers and the checkout girl watch me with some degree of wonder. Most of the local women shoppers carry their bags home in their two hands, except perhaps on Saturdays, when they come with their husbands and load up the cars with bottled water and wine.

After I pay my bill, whose numbers are stratospheric, I maneuver my suitcase out the automatic door with one hand, pull the wagon along with my other (to retrieve my 500-lire coin when I return the wagon to the locked position behind the others), and wave to the young black man who daily spreads his wares on a blanket in front of the supermarket. (Like so many other young black men I see walking the streets with huge packs on their backs, he sells cheap socks, umbrellas, children's toys, wallets, key chains, and pencils.)

I pull my suitcase over the stones, up and down curbs, past the *tabacchi,* the *pasticceria,* past the gas station, feeling quite confident and proud; I can negotiate this universe.

When I get home, I enter the front gate with my key, go straight ahead to the glass door (which is open), and up in the elevator to my floor. The problem is, my key will not open my apartment door. I try it every which way. I shake the doorknob, I kick the bottom of the door-frame, I poke and turn and twist and pull. I can't get in. My ice cream is melting, my buffalo cheese will go bad. What shall I do?

I try to think of what might be wrong. Who can I call? Will I have to drag my purchases back to the market? Find a phone and call the school and tell Joe to come home? My landlady's phone number is locked in the apartment. I am completely baffled and perspiring profusely.

But just then I look at the door I've been trying to open and notice some initials carved in the wood. I don't remember seeing them before. A warning bell goes off in my head. Could this be the wrong door? Could this be the wrong *building*? Our apartment building is one of three identical structures—could it be I have simply gone into the wrong one?

I take the elevator down and see that instead of going to the far right, to our apartment building, I entered the middle building! What if the tenant had been home? What if she had flung back her door and confronted me?

I pull my suitcase outside and down the steps, drag it along to my rightful building, go up in my rightful elevator, enter my rightful door, and collapse in my kitchen in profound embarrassment and confusion. So much for my feeling a new sense of ease about getting along in Italy. So much for thinking how competently I'd learned to maneuver in this new country.

After unpacking my groceries (and what was I thinking to even imagine I could possibly fit that much food in my tiny refrigerator?), I am still thrumming with adrenaline. I can't rest or sit still. Joe won't be home for hours; I must go out again.

This time I leave my suitcase behind and take only my mesh carry-bag to the open market. Vendors of all sorts have set up their wares in the parking lot opposite the Chinese restaurant on Via Aretina. Outside, under awnings rigged up on wires like sails, there are a thousand things to buy: fruits and vegetables, fish and octopus, shoes and linens, clothing and housewares.

I bypass the produce, avoiding also the fish seller whose display includes great open tins filled with tuna packed in oil (upon which flies are landing in large numbers). In the next stall, I see an enormous roasted pig: its head, with open mouth, is partially severed from its body and tilted back so its dead eyes are looking skyward. Just behind the head, the pig's skin has been peeled back. With a huge knife, the butcher is cutting slices of roast pork. Animated by bargaining and dealing, waving his knife in the air, he cheerfully cuts and wraps the meat, while his wife weighs and takes money for it from the line of waiting women.

At the housewares booth, I see what I want: an espresso coffee maker, shining and new, standing atop its box. *"Quanto costa?"* I say, and it's done. I don't bargain, I happily hand over 15,000 lire and take my prize. I also buy two dozen brightly colored plastic clothespins, as well as an oil and vinegar dispenser made of plastic. Finally, I choose three nested, covered, plastic containers—objects I have been missing desperately, something in which to store leftover pasta sauce.

The clothing stalls are next. Though I know Florence is famous for designer clothes, for elegant leather and shoe stores, for the finest in high fashion, I am drawn to a huge pile of clothes tossed on a table. Every size, color, and style are jumbled together. I watch what the natives do. The woman I take as my guide is choosing articles of clothing, one by one, holding skirts to her waist, examining shirts and dresses for holes, feeling fabric with the fingertips of an expert. Once she decides, she tosses her choice over her arm and moves on to the next article. After a time, she hands the whole pile to the owner, he counts, he thinks, he gives her a figure. She gives him one back. They argue briefly. She counts out her bills, and he places her purchases in a plastic bag.

I choose for myself a brushed cotton flannel overblouse, scoop necked, wild with colorful flowers, and a warm ankle-length paisley skirt. For Joe I pick out a pair of men's pajamas, gray, with a sailing ship embroidered over the pocket. I hand them over to the man, he praises my good taste, he gives me a figure (less than the espresso maker!), and I half-heartedly say *"Posso de sconto?"* (which I know is only half the sentence Joe told me I must say to ask for a discount). But he knows exactly what I mean. He can't possibly, he says (he guesses I am from "Oosa," he even asks me where and tells me his brother lives in California, near Hollywood), but still I come away flushed and happy. I have turned the day around. Now I own an Italian wardrobe!

I make one last stop at the button and jewelry stand, where a great jumble of earrings is for sale for 3,000 lire ($2.00) a pair. What takes my fancy is a pair of clip-on loops with large gold plastic polar bears swinging from them. They are both ludicrous and magnificent at the same time—I must have them. I buy a second pair as well, for my friend Jenijoy at home. She and I are probably the last holdouts in California; neither of us has pierced ears. Why would we want to do something as barbaric as making holes in our ears, we ask each other. Now I have to refrain from asking myself why on earth we would want to wear large gold polar bears in our ears, either.

On the way home, when I stop to extract my purchases from the bag, I discover that the clothes turn out to have labels from China and Hong Kong. Never mind; I bought them in Italy and Italian they are.

As if I have not had enough adventures for one day, I discover, as I walk homeward, a tiny store I hadn't seen before, on the corner of Via Aretina and Via Filippo Turati. There is no sign over the door, yet a steady stream of people go in and out, some arriving with full plastic bags and going out emptyhanded. I take a chance and open the door. To my utter delight, I find myself in a thrift shop.

A flyer on the wall reads *"Mercatino degli Abiti Usati (Giacche, Camicie, Pantaloni . . .),"* which I understand means "used clothing." There seems to be some political literature for sale, books about Gandhi, poems by Kahlil Gibran. Products like tea and coffee, made elsewhere. There is a pile of reprints of a newspaper article about (as far as I can understand) exploitation in third-world countries. Whatever cause or charity the owners espouse, it seems a good one. I won't mind spending money here.

Up on the shelves are little baskets with signs reading *"donna intimo"* (ladies' underwear) and *"sciarpe e cappelli per donna"* (ladies' scarves and hats).

As if I haven't bought enough today (how will I ever fit these items in our luggage when we go home?), I get busy shopping. I shop with a sense of mission, unearthing treasures I consider to be of exceptional beauty and value (and these, when I check, have labels that read "Made in Italy." Nothing from China here!)

I caress a particularly lovely scarf, printed with pink and yellow roses—"100 percent *lana*," all wool. I have seen these at the vendor stands near the San Lorenzo open market for 15,000 lire and up—and when I hold up the scarf and ask the kind-looking woman sitting at a flimsy wooden table, "*Quanto costa?*" she says, "*Duemila*": 2,000 lire, equivalent to $1.30!

Oh, wonderful. I search and I discover: a leather purse (a designer purse?), several of the lovely undershirts that Italian women wear (I saw them for sale in the open market, hanging on hangers above the crowd, marked 30,000 lire). These are made of a wool blend with a lovely, lacy V-neck, designed to peek out of one's blouse. I find an item that at home I might see in a fancy lingerie store like Victoria's Secret: a pink satin nightgown with peek-a-boo hearts throughout. All of these I lay on the table, and the smiling woman adds them up. They are all "*duemila*"—and the purse is "*quatromila*"—about $2.50.

I pay, we smile, I recite my endless refrain: "*Sono americana, non parlo italiano.*"

"Aah, aah," she says. She lets me know that she, too, has a relative in California. She takes my hand as if I am her relative. I want to hug her. I tell her, "*Mio marito è un professore a scuola Dante Alighieri.*"

"Aah, *si*," she says. "*Molto bene.*"

"*Per tre mesi*," I add. "*Solo.*" I am getting into deep water here.

She looks sad that I will be leaving so soon. Next time I come in (and I have just decided I will come here every day), I will definitely tell her I am a *scrittrice*, a writer, and perhaps someday I will put her and her *mercatino* in a book.

She seems to want us to exchange further confidences. There is something in her gaze that seems motherly, protective. I have for such a long time been unmothered by my sick and aged mother, unprotected by her, that I long for someone to care about me in this way. Perhaps I can adopt this sweet soul for my mother, and she can adopt me.

Reaching for her purse on a shelf, she pulls out a postcard that shows a church surrounded by a group of low buildings. Pointing at one of them, she indicates that she lives there, in a convent, alone, and that she has no children.

"Come si chiama?" I ask her.

"Mi chiamo Paola." She tips her head toward me, wanting to know my name.

"Mi chiamo Merrill."

"Aah!" She holds out her arms to hug me. I come into them and we embrace, strangers in needy communion. I decide I love her and always will. When I finally leave the store, I feel tears in my eyes.

28

Cinderella in Drag: A Night at the Ballet

After dinner—hamburgers on *pane bianco* with ketchup (Del Monte) and *maionese*, accompanied by the cola I bought (not very good) and plumcakes for dessert (why are these dry tasteless packaged objects called plumcakes?)—we get ready for our night at the ballet. The class has tickets to see *La Cenerentola* by Prokofiev at the Teatro Comunale.

I wear some of my new finery from the open market, the long skirt, the polar bear earrings, a blouse I bought at a return trip to the *mercatino usato*—and my mountain-climber's shoes. Every outing I take in the city requires the heaviest shoes I own, with the thickest soles; otherwise I cannot negotiate the streets of Florence, the curbs, the flagstones, the staircases polished by five hundred years of wear. I've made my peace with fashion. Thick socks and warrior shoes—like it or not, these are my trademark.

Joe looks distinguished in his suit and tie; we check each other out, and we approve. A dab of perfume for me and we're ready for our night on the town. I'd prefer to have a limousine picking us up, but it's the #14 bus as usual.

The students are resplendent tonight. The girls whom I've seen wearing nothing but jeans and sweatshirts are glimmering in crushed red velvet evening gowns, black satin pantsuits, silvery shawls, and wonderfully high heels. A few have had their hair bleached or cropped or dyed by Rosanna. This group appears to be an entirely different species from the kids who wander into Joe's class and fall asleep over their notebooks. The boys look as if cardboard is holding them up in their stiff shirts, polished dress shoes, and dressy jackets.

Phil and Sara, our students who are now quite clearly in love with each other, are asking their friends to take dozens of photographs of them, in various glamorous poses. A brief pang of envy shivers through me.

Our Chinese student, Mai Jing, has come with her landlady, with whom she has formed a deep bond of friendship. Nicoletta's sister has arrived from Rome, and the two beautiful women (*two* Sophia Lorens!) are talking at high speed in Italian.

The class disperses to find their reserved seats scattered through the balcony. I feel more than ready to be entertained. It's been so long since I've seen a movie or even watched a television program! I'm looking forward to my eyes being pleasured with scenes of classical ballet and my ears being soothed by the universal language of music. For once, my lack of Italian should not impede my understanding. We are about to witness the comforting tale of goodness rewarded. Cinderella, who cannot go to the Prince's ball will, in time, win out over the cruel stepsisters and the villainous stepmother and capture the handsome prince as her own true love. I settle back and wait for the curtain to rise, for the conductor's baton to signal the orchestra to begin.

The first problem seems to be that there *is* no orchestra. A rather thin, whirry sound track comes from the rafters via speakers. We are being treated, in the great Teatro Comunale, to canned music. Next, the curtains part, and Cinderella, dressed like Charlie Chaplin, revolves on the hands of a clock under a huge tilted mirror. Now the other characters enter: the cruel mother has a head bare as a billiard ball, and the two ugly sisters have calves like football players. I take out my opera glasses. Indeed, these women are men!

Cinderella, however, dressed in pants and suspenders like a man, is clearly a gorgeous young woman. When the Godmother arrives with her dainty helpers, she also brings along Elvis Presley, who appears on-stage with his fake guitar, his sideburns, and his thrusting hips.

In time, the ugly sisters, in their scratchy tulle gowns (and stomping about in their flat-footed gaits), leave for the ball. But suddenly (and this is what I have been waiting for), Cinderella appears, in glittering white . . . dressed as Marilyn Monroe. She is wearing the white halter dress that Marilyn made famous. She sports a blonde wig, and she dances her longing and sadness in a few dainty modern-dance steps.

My attention wanders during the ball scene, but I'm roused by the clock striking midnight. Cinderella, of course, runs away. In no time, the Prince is on the prowl for his dream girl, the one who will fit the glass slipper. The messengers fan out into the city, carrying the slipper, to find Cinderella. Only, as it happens, the messengers are pizza delivery boys wearing roller skates.

At this juncture, I become aware of breathing down the back of my neck. I turn around and see a heavy-set man leaning forward, his elbows on the back of my chair, his chin nearly on my shoulder. I frown at him. He merely leans further forward, the better to see the stage, I assume. Joe also turns to see the man thrusting his head between us; we are both inhaling the scent of onions on his breath.

"*Scusi,*" I whisper, indicating we are most unhappy with this intimacy. The man does not budge. His eyes are fastened on the stage below, where, gyrating to the scratchy sound track, the hero and heroine are enacting the finale.

The Prince, having discovered his Princess, is dancing with Cinderella, but the two are spinning about the stage separately as if they have been to too many discotheques and have forgotten how to be romantic.

The man behind us snorts and sneezes. Joe and I both stare fiercely at him, but he stares at the stage with dumb blankness. We are *trying* to pay attention to the final love scene. Joe finally surrenders his seat and stands in the aisle, attempting to watch the end of the ballet.

The man behind us takes this as an invitation, and moves forward into Joe's seat! Is this an Italian custom? The man and I are nearly cheek to cheek. Custom or not, I can't bear it. I jump up to join my husband in the aisle. Blocking the view of others behind us, we're confounded. Where shall we go?

We sit down on the steps of the aisle, but then we can't see the stage.

But just then the ballet comes to its conclusion. We've missed the end of the story, but we don't much care. We are merely relieved it *has* ended.

Out in the night air, we stand among the milling crowd, wondering how to get home. It is nearly midnight. When the clock strikes twelve, do all the orange buses of Florence turn back into pumpkins? (Or eggplants?) Most of our students have departed; many live within walking distance of the theater. Many are not even going home but, dressed in their best, are going to a disco to round out the evening.

Just then Mai Jing comes rushing up to us, her cheeks flushed. "Mr. Joe," she says (which is what some of the students call my husband—a title between a more formal last name and a too-informal first name), "would you like my friend Massimo to give you a ride home?"

"Indeed, we would," I reply before Joe can demur. "Thank you."

Massimo turns out to be a wild and handsome Italian; he has parked his car right in the center of the intersection in front of the theater, blocking traffic in four directions. He wears a three-day beard (which seems to be the fashion of choice among young Italian men), and he cheerfully squeezes us in the back of his tiny car with Mai Jing's landlady. The five of us shoot off into the night at an incredible rate of speed. I don't have time to get my bearings—we are on a roller coaster ride!

"Massimo doesn't speak much English," Mai Jing turns to tell us.

"That's all right," I reply. "I don't speak much Italian."

"He is happy to help you," Mai Jing says.

I hold on for dear life as we careen around the city. Joe tries to explain to him where we live— "*Abito vicino a via Aretina*"—but Massimo is not too interested in directions. I fear that he might just let us off in the middle of some street and wish us luck getting home. Mai

Jing's Italian landlady is clutching my arm—she's too astonished to speak.

Miraculously (how does he know where it is?), Massimo pulls up at our gate. We have been riding perhaps five minutes on a trip that takes us twenty-five minutes by bus.

He says something to Joe, who translates for me. "One day Massimo says he would like us to come to dinner at his apartment."

"Oh . . . that's nice."

"He says he will be happy to pick us up."

"I'm delighted," I say, hanging breathless onto our gate. "Any time."

"Very soon," Mai Jing adds. She is happy to be of help to her professor.

It occurs to me that all the students on this trip with us in Florence are having amazing, glorious, romantic adventures with new people.

Joe and I will just have to be satisfied with each other. Grateful to be alive, we clasp hands and make our way upstairs and to bed.

29

"Rita, You Are the Girl
I Have Loved . . ."

Looking for the post office one day, Joe and I take a street north near the open market, pass under the railroad tracks, and find ourselves almost in the foothills that, when we see them from our roof terrace, seem a great distance away. We walk past rows of ordinary apartment houses, cross some fields where new construction is taking place, and beyond that find ourselves in pure country: unpaved roads, overgrown grassy fields, and the smell of the sun hot on vines and vegetable gardens. Behind a fence, some chickens scurry about, clucking and scratching for feed. A rusted sign says *"Privato,"* but we continue on, crunching over the stones and dried clumps of dirt.

On our right is a large villa, but bigger and more official seeming than a villa, more like an institution. A plaque on the side of the building says *"Sordomuti,"* which Joe tells me means deaf-mute. We look for signs of movement or people but see nothing. Are the deaf and mute inside? Is it a school? Living quarters for the students?

So much of life in a foreign country has to be guessed at, surmised, imagined. How they do things here, what they think about the smallest matters, is an issue of constant discussion between us.

For example, each morning at 8 A.M., as we have breakfast, we hear a great commotion from outside: the bleep-bleep of emergency horns growing in volume till the walls shake, the beeping of car horns, the roar of motorcycles, the shriek of an ambulance. Each morning we rush to the window and see an impressive entourage coming into the city from the *autostrada:* motorcycles, police cars, a military truck with armed soldiers, automatic weapons at the ready and pointed from the windows. Overhead there is a helicopter hovering, and, following all this, escorted by the weaponry and the doomsday warnings, is a big black bus with blackened windows. Whoever is inside is hidden, apparently someone either of great importance or extremely dangerous.

Once the bus is gone, followed by its tail of noisy protectors, we forget it and go about our day's work. However, at six in the evening, the same cacophony alerts us to look out the window, from which we see the return trip of the parade: police, ambulance, armed soldiers, big black bus. While ordinary traffic comes to a halt, the caravan races along at high speeds and zooms onto the *autostrada.* We always watch till the line of vehicles disappears in the distance.

In the days following we ask people we know: could it be the President of Italy? Could it be royalty? When I ask Cornelia, she says it might be the defendants involved in a big Mafia trial (taking place in a hidden venue). She is certain the cortege travels fast so that no one can assassinate the criminals or the *pentiti* (the ones who have spilled the beans to save themselves) before justice is done.

But, still, we never learn what it's all about. The procession takes place every weekday, and at breakfast and at dinner we wonder about it. Joe jokes that our terrace is the perfect place for an assassin to situate himself. He would have ample warning of the approach of the black bus and could take clear aim. But of what or whom we will never know.

Now, after we pass the deaf-mute building, we continue along the country road, discussing the apartments we have seen under construction. We've heard stories about the shortage of housing for young people in Italy. A young man named Riccardo who has begun coming to our apartment once a week to practice English/Italian with Joe has told us that he and his fiancée, Angela, have been waiting for ten years for their house. The two of them, now in their thirties, each still live with their parents, and each year the red tape surrounding their hoped-for apartment gets more dense. In spite of the fact that years ago they put a large down payment on a yet-to-be-built apartment, there now seems to be doubt as to whether it will be completed. There is also a lottery involved—for who gets the apartments as they are built, who gets the ones on the upper floors with views, or who gets any at all.

The Mystery of Italy. We are infants here, barely comprehending what goes on about us.

At the end of the long *"privata"* road, a nailed-together wood and tin shack lies hidden in an overgrown grove of trees and vines. As we approach it, a German shepherd rushes out at us, teeth bared, growling. I can almost feel his teeth sinking into my leg.

"We should have paid attention to the sign!" I accuse Joe. We have lived our entire lives by the rules. I want to ask him how come we decided to stop just now.

Joe just says to the dog, "Shh, shh," as if he is calming a restless baby. The dog halts in his tracks, looks at us, and begins to wag his tail. From somewhere in the forest of green growth, a woman emerges, wearing an apron over her dress and calf-high rubber boots. She is holding a shovel. Her hair, long and blonde, is tied back with a barrette. And she greets us with a smile.

Joe says, *"Permesso, Signora . . ."* and then begins to speak to her in Italian that seems impressively smooth and confident to me. She answers in a gracious tone, apparently not angry that we have trespassed upon this private property. In fact, she seems quite appreciative of company and conversation. With half an ear I listen to them speak, Joe asking questions and the hearty-looking woman answering in long, musical sentences. The Italian language comes from her lips like a song.

I walk a little way from them and kneel down to make friends with the dog. There is a hush upon the woods, a sun-lit quiet that weighs down the foliage and makes space even for the buzz of small insects. Though we are not so far from the streets full of motor scooters (or even the *autostrada* with its black bus and police cars), we are in an-

other world here, insulated, fragrant with the tart smell of ripe tomatoes on the vine and rustling with the movement of the wind.

I imagine what it might be like to live here, to live in that little cabin
(not a villa, not an apartment, but almost a tent), to step outside into
this ocean of stillness and lie in the grass with my face to the sun. For
that moment, I almost cannot bring to mind a picture of my home in
California, its many rooms furnished with years of accumulations, the
closets full of old photographs, the file cabinets full of writings and tax
forms, the kitchen cupboards bursting with old and new pots, salad
bowls, blenders, and coffeemakers and the pantry holding a hundred
cans of beans, juice, soda, soups, vegetables, and fruits bought in another world, in another time. I experience the amazing certainty that,
should I—at this moment—be given the news that my entire house in
America had vaporized into thin air and vanished, I would greet the information serenely, go on with my walk in the country, my arm linked
in my husband's, and never grieve the loss.

I am here and nowhere else. This is life, now, on this little country
road. We are on the face of the earth and alive. Only this matters.

Who knows how long we stand there with the farm woman? As we
walk back along the road, Joe tells me what he learned from her: that
this whole private country road and the property on either side have
been sold to a contracting company that will build apartment houses
here. That if we followed the road we were on further up into the
mountain, we would eventually arrive at Fiesole. (But a warning—
there are dangerous German shepherd dogs that guard the passage.)
That the *contadini* (the peasants) who live in the shack have permission
to stay there and farm until the ground is broken for construction.

Joe says, "She spoke in that beautiful Florentine way, did you
notice?"

"I noticed she was beautiful," I tell him.

We are walking not back toward the post office but further east, paral-
lel to the railroad tracks, hoping to find a crossing that will bring us
back to the main street—and from there we will reckon how to get

Message of love on the wall

home. The road is narrow; each time a car passes, we flatten ourselves against the high stone wall. From time to time, we pass an iron gate and look between its rungs to see endless rows of olive trees and, in the distance, a villa with its tile roof and green shutters.

I am beginning to be thirsty; we have been walking for hours, but where are we? I begin to wonder if we could be lost, if we will be here after nightfall, if the dangerous dogs will find us. . . .

Joe knows there will be a crossing soon. "All these cars, they have to have a way to get across the tracks."

We walk on, hand in hand. I love this little adventure; even my small fear that we could be lost is exhilarating. When did I last experience this sense of discovery, the knowledge that every step ahead of us will bring sights we have never seen in our lives?

We cross a running stream (on its bank, nearly in the water, is the chassis of an old motor scooter), we pass what seems to be an old age home (in the open courtyard there are a dozen old men, at tables, playing cards or talking), and, just when I feel I can walk no longer, we come to a crossroad that leads under the railroad tracks to the other side. This passageway is blocked to cars by steel pipes implanted in cement, but bikers and pedestrians may cross.

A beautiful young woman, long black hair streaming behind her like a comet's tail, flies past us on her bicycle. As Joe and I enter the overpass, I see, written on the wall, high up, in blue paint, a thrilling bit of graffiti:

RITA SEI LA RAGAZZA CHE HO AMATO DI PIÙ IN TUTTA LA VITA
BY
SAMU

Though I know what it must say, I ask Joe to translate for me.
"Rita, you are the girl I have loved most in all my life."
If this poetry is graffiti, then let the world be covered with it.
"Will you write my name somewhere in Italy before we leave?" I ask my husband.
In reply, he takes a ballpoint pen from his shirt pocket, draws a little heart on the wall of the overpass, and inserts our initials in its center. I take the pen from him and add an arrow to pierce the heart.

30

The Incorrupt Body

Too many of the hallowed dead in Italian churches are not hidden below in the crypts and catacombs or laid to rest just under the marble floor or even in the raised biers with saints posed in effigy above them. Instead, in many cases, the sainted dead, in whole or in part, are there in person, above ground and under glass, like *The Sleeping Beauty.* Those with limitations in the number of their remaining parts reside in small silver reliquaries or in tabernacles with windows for viewing. Even those with no remaining parts are not kept from being celebrated—witness the Shroud of Turin and Saint Peter's Chains (minus Saint Peter) in Rome.

A finger is a strange souvenir (Galileo's finger bone stands upright along with two of his telescopes in a glass case at the Museum of the History of Science). An enshrined lock of hair of a departed human is enough to give one pause. But what of a head? An entire body?

On a cold, rainy day when I am on my way to the University of Florence to visit a professor of literature to whom I have an introduction, I stop for shelter from the wind and take a moment to sit down in the church of San Marco. At this early morning hour, there are not yet any tour buses pulling into the piazza. The interior of the church is dark, peaceful, and empty except for a monk moving about in the dimness.

When I have caught my breath (and because I am a little early for my appointment), I look up to admire the artwork of the ceiling, the elegance of the altar, the embellishments and decorations that are present in every detail. Though there is not time today, I will return another day to visit the monks' cells in the Convent of San Marco, which contain the frescoes of the life of Christ painted by Fra Angelico.

Rested a little, and grateful for the absence of wind and for the small warmth afforded by the enclosure of marble and stone (though on warm days these same stones keep the churches blessedly cool), I get up to walk around the church. In a chapel to my left, I see one of those long glass cases that must be yet another coffin of a saint.

Since I began visiting churches in Florence, I have much preferred the lit displays of effigies of Christ or the Madonna to the embalmed bodies of saints. Often the Madonna is encrusted with jewels, her wrists wrapped in gold bracelets, a single teardrop pearl adorning her pure brow, her neck ringed with gold chains and precious stones. (Joe says this is a subliminal reminder to support the church generously.) Christ, when displayed, is waxen faced, supported upright on the cross, nailed and forsaken, a crown of thorns upon his head, or supine, in utter, defeated weakness, an embroidered cloth over his limbs (one cloth was vivid with red roses), his head languishing to the side, his ragged breast wound pouring out his life's blood.

The power of these displays always brings a gasp to my throat. How can I not experience this mother's loss, this son's death of unimaginable pain? How can any writer, even if not previously stopped in her tracks by the powers of Shakespeare or Virginia Woolf, dare to put pen to paper after experiencing the sweep of *this* story?

Though the body of the saint is protected behind golden bars, I am able to approach—with some trepidation—quite close to the glass coffin, whose lid and base are made of engraved gold. When I look at the dead man, I see my mother's face. Taking a rapid step back, I have to lean for support against a pillar. Despite the bishop's pointed hat, his curled elfin gold-cloth shoes, despite his priestly robes, this man wears my mother's face. His pointed nose and chin, each curving toward the

Jesus under glass

other, are not so much the generic stamp of old age as they are my mother's actual features. Though his skin is brown and leathery, whereas my mother (if today, this very minute, she is still alive) has the pinkish color of life in her cheeks, he is in every way her twin.

Am I having a visitation? Could this vision be a message in no un-certain terms that I should never have left my mother at her great age and so close to death? Is it a warning to me because for all the weeks I've been away I have been celebrating each day that I wake and think, with relief, "No visit to the nursing home today"?

When I have recovered my ability to see and breathe, I write down the information from the plaque: "The Incorrupt Body of San Antonino Pierozzi, 1389 to 1459, Founder of Saint Mark's Monastery, reformer of the Dominican order, archbishop and protector of Florence for thir-teen years, celebrated for his spiritual direction. He gave all to the poor and died impoverished. The thanks of those who turn to him cannot be counted."

I wonder what the kind man would think of himself being on display this way. He surely looks a little overdressed, and, though he must have lived a life of humility, now his casket is a place for tourists to stop and take photos. Maybe this good man should have been allowed the dignity of burial and the dark peace of eternity.

Though the time has come for me to continue on to my destination, I find it hard to make the transition from five hundred years ago, when the saint lived, to the present moment, when I must unfold my map and travel on. I am in the strange space between thoughts of the afterlife and the concerns of today's journey. How can I pull myself away from one and enter the other?

Just then, a strange and secular sound comes to my ears, leading the way back to reality. What I hear are sounds like that of a jackpot being struck in Las Vegas, a distinctly worldly melody of coins falling into tin. I look around in the dimness, seeking out the source of this cascade of money. When I locate it, I recognize—at the point of its origin—the monk I had seen roaming about earlier. He is bent forward, holding in one hand a tin bucket beneath the offertory where the votive candles are lit. With his other hand, he is sweeping a waterfall of coins into the container. The sparkle of falling coins seems to go on forever. The music they make is like voices echoing in a celestial concert. The shrill tones made by this hallowed money ride up to the dome of the church, modulate, and come gently down—in a shower of tinkling stars—upon the heads of saints and sinners alike.

31

The Altar of the Virgin of Siena

To take a day trip to Siena, we first must learn to read the *orario* posted at the SITA bus station (which is tucked away behind the Santa Maria Novella *stazione*). The options are many; we may take a one-hour bus trip via the *autostrada*, a two-hour bus trip via a succession of small towns along the way, or a combination trip, half *autostrada*, half hill towns.

We choose the longer route since we have no reason to edit our experience; everything we behold will be new to us, everything a surprise. We board the bus with sandwiches and drinks, and my usual burden of camera, water bottle, jacket, and fanny pack. We take just enough lire for the day's contingencies but leave our travelers' checks and passports hidden in the apartment in a box of Krisiriski rice cereal.

The SITA buses are luxurious compared to the city buses—reclining upholstered seats, foot rests, mesh bags on the seats in front to hold water bottles, curtains across the great touring windows to shield one's eyes from sun. Our round tickets for this trip cost less than ten dollars each.

Almost as soon as we leave the city and pass the Carthusian monastery just outside Galluzzo (whose cells resemble condominiums modules climbing the steep incline), we can see hills rising up on either side of the road. In no time we are in another country, far less populated than Florence, bright with open sky, feathery clouds, and the sheen of sun on cypress trees and the roofs of country houses.

There are so few times in my adult life that I've had this sense of absolute expectation, of openness to what's coming—without an accompanying awareness of personal problems, duties, obligations to consider. Today there is just a feeling of well-being, and of living in the here-and-now.

The bus lets us off near the great Gothic church of San Domenico, which is listed in the guidebook as a "Don't Miss" since it houses the head of Catherine, the patron saint of Siena. Joe and I agree we won't begin our visit here. We'll leave the head for last.

The city is a maze of steep narrow alleys that slant and arch and angle at every turn. Each new street is an opportunity for a beautifully framed photograph. My breath comes out in a series of gasps as one extraordinary view gives way to the next, with only a few steps taken in between.

Outside a *fruttivendolo,* a display of mushrooms is advertised: PORCINI NOSTRALI (home grown), 35,000 kg, GIALLARELLA (yellow), 19,500 kg, and TRUMBETTO DI MORTO (little trumpet of death!) —with no price listed. If (I calculate) the *Porcini Nostrali* cost about $24 a kilogram, I suppose it's best not to ask what the Trumpet of Death costs. Or what it does to you. These fungi are already eerie, in their weird, asymmetrical shapes, their bloodshot colors, their ominous names. In English a sign above them says, "Don't touch."

"I definitely don't want a *funghi* pizza for lunch," I tell Joe. But he is already at the next shop, examining a poster that looks like a shelf of real books, presenting the illusion of one leaning upon the other, some open, some with pages falling out.

"Stand still right there," I tell him and snap his picture.

"Would you like me to buy you a poster like that?" I ask him, but now he's moved on to stand in front of the *latteria* which advertises "PANINI (sandwiches), BIBITE (soft drinks), DOLCI TIPICI (typical sweets)," and I snap another photo. Then I hand the camera to him and

"Mushrooms of death"

hurry to pose myself under the mounted head of a boar wearing a red ribbon pinned above his brow. Joe positions himself like a tripod, squatting on one knee, squinting his eyes, gritting his teeth . . . and takes my picture.

Photography, to him, is just an interruption in the flow of images. To me, photos are the safe deposit box of my journey. On any trip, information flies by so fast, so many things are glanced at and forgotten, scenes are admired but fade like a dream. The camera is my magic eye: it remembers the details for me. Later, at home, in quiet attention, I am able to recreate my trip and discover things in a photograph that I never saw in the scene when I snapped the shutter.

As we enter the Piazza del Campo, I feel that recognizable (Florentine) sense of coming out of dark canyon into a heavenly flood of light—and there below is the great shell-shaped piazza. Off to the left is a large fountain, rectangular in shape and decorated with statues. As we descend the wide, shallow flight of steps into the piazza, I see a flutter of pigeons landing on one of the fountain's sculptures—a kind of wolf-dog with sinister, sharp teeth. A stream of water spurts from his open mouth. The pigeons land on his paws and head to drink, while his eyes, wary and conniving, focus directly on the one bird balanced upon his snout—as if he will in just one instant snap his jaws shut upon it.

We walk on till we come in view of the zebra-striped Duomo of Siena, a brilliant combination of alternating black and white stone with a bell-tower and dome amazing to behold. In the courtyard I pause to marvel at the facade, that strict geometry of black and white. A winged angel is poised at the very top of the church, and just below is a painting, glittery with gold leaf, of Jesus, with his golden halo, crowning the Madonna, while at their feet lies a semicircle of haloed worshippers.

Inside the dim church, we gaze up at the starry ceiling (each stone of the cupola has a golden star set in its center), staring into the light till the sunshine flooding into the church nearly blinds us.

Then, somehow, Joe and I become separated. I don't go looking for him because we each like to wander about at our own pace, pausing to examine what catches our attention. We both know we'll find each other soon enough.

In front of me now is the Chapel of the Virgin of the Vow, where a framed painting of the Virgin is the centerpiece. Golden bronze cherubs dance about her head, statues flank her handsomely on the right and left, great pillars of green marble decorate the altar, and the Virgin herself, bearing a weighty, bejeweled gold crown on her head, holds in her arms the Christ child wearing an identical but smaller bejeweled crown. They wear matching necklaces made of ten strands of silver beads, one strand of each necklace bearing a heavy cross. On the breast of the Virgin is pinned what looks like a large heart with a flaming tree growing out of it. The heart has inscribed in it the word "PACE," followed by some numbers I cannot read.

On a little wooden table to the side of the chapel, a visitor's card displaying a photo of the painting—with a prayer to the Virgin on the back—is offered for sale on the honor system. The prayer is authored by "Gaetano Bonicelli, Archbishop of Siena, March 25, 1995." It reads:

Before You, Holy Mary of the Vow, past generations bowed with humility. Now no enemy army is staying at the gates of our homes any more, but snares are threatening our minds and hearts every day. . . . On the threshold of the Twenty-first century do teach us the way to faith serenely and discovering the secret of Your fidelity to Almighty's project. Oh Virgin Mother of God and Our Mother! We want to commit our young people to You so that the future will not be hopeless. . . . Oh beloved and sweet Mary of the Vow, don't allow troubles of our material life to close the horizon of our eternal destiny, where one day we'll be beholding You together with the Father, the Son Jesus in the unity with the Holy Spirit for ever and ever. Amen.

After I pay my 200-lire coin for the prayer and add another coin to reimburse the church for the small flat candle in a plastic cup that I'm supposed to light—but don't, I want it for a souvenir—I find my way to the ladies' rest room and, with due respect to the material life, pay to use the facilities.

Coming out the door of the ladies' room, I bump into my husband coming out the door of the men's room. I throw my arms around him as if I have not seen him for centuries, overcome by the amazing coincidence of this meeting. I feel as though the Virgin of the Vow has had something to do with this coincidence. I feel blessed.

I embrace my husband so passionately that he asks me whether I found a flask of sacramental wine in some corner. Then together we go into the gift shop, where we see other signs of the material life—postcards for sale, little statues of the Virgin, plastic trays embossed with images of the bell tower, of the *Fonte Gaia* (the wolf-dog fountain), guidebooks of the city, maps and directories of the churches. There's more: pens and pencils, ashtrays, key chains, scarves, rosaries, reliquaries. Which reminds me—we have yet to see Catherine's head.

We decide Catherine's head will be the last stop. Having eaten our lunch sandwiches impulsively on the SITA bus toward the end of the two-hour bus ride, we are hungry now for dinner. We walk back along the slanting streets toward the Campo till we find, among all the many trattorias and *gelaterias,* a pizzeria.

We each order a pizza. Mine will be topped with *prosciutto cotto* (ham), and Joe's will be *quattro staggioni* (four seasons), with artichoke hearts, black olives, and champignon mushrooms. We order red wine (Cokes are three to five dollars each in restaurants in Italy, and wine is cheaper and better) and settle back to rest in the hard wooden chairs.

After a time, our waiter brings our pizzas steaming to the table. Each pizza, taking up a whole plate, has a paper-thin crust, brown at the edges, olive oil lying in rivulets on the melted cheese, bits of tomato flung upon the surface, and—still steaming from the wood-fired oven—generous portions of the decorations of our choice: paper-thin *prosciutto cotto* for me, and lovely vegetables for Joe.

We are getting better at eating pizza like the natives, with fork and knife, delicately, in no great rush—and we do so admirably here, I think. This pizza is so delicious, I feel something like religious ecstasy. I suspect this may be the closest I will ever come to it.

Joe and I toast one another, pour again, and toast again. We eat and drink. Then, rested and replenished, we begin the walk back to San Domenico and Catherine's head.

I tell myself I am ready to face up to so small a thing as a head if I have already beheld the entire incorrupt body of San Antonino Pierozzi in San Marco, but I feel squeamish nevertheless. I have seen shrunken heads in museums, heads on poles with long locks of stringy hair hanging from the scalps (and still growing?); I have seen heads (and feet) packed with my chicken from the *macelleria*. But a woman's head? And if it is a woman's head, who cut her head from her body? If Catherine was so revered, who had the audacity to bring out a saw? And why— as we have read in the book—did the lower part of her body go to Rome and the head stay here? And how does one maintain a head—is it dusted? Perfumed? Has it been embalmed?

Better not to know. Joe, in his history professor's voice, often explains bizarre customs, both to me and to his classes, by saying, "That's what they did in those days." To him it makes perfect sense. What they did in those days was what they did. It's our job to figure out why.

I don't look at Catherine's head too long. Her separated head is in a box with a glass viewing window. She is wearing some kind of head covering. Her face is brown and leathery, her eyes sunken. She is not pretty. She is not adorned with glittering jewels or gold crowns or heart pins with burning trees. She wears no necklaces (she has no neck to speak of).

I feel sad to read that she took the veil at the age of eight, that she received the stigmata, that she died in Rome and was canonized in 1461. I feel sorry that during her life she wasn't living in some gorgeous Italian hill town, her window looking out upon the mountains glowing with cypress trees. I wish for her, retroactively, a life of love and beauty, a cherishing husband, and the precious joy of holding a sweet tiny baby in her arms. I wish for her, it seems, an unsainted life.

32

La Bocca della Verità
(The Mouth of Truth)

In the bowels of the Santa Maria Novella *stazione* is a veritable carnival of shops, vendors, food stalls, and beggars. Blankets line the tunnels, and on them are little jumping and dancing plastic toys from Hong Kong and Taiwan, many of them wind-up toys that play the same music but at different times, resulting in a crazed-sounding din. The sellers are situated only inches from one another—each one beckoning and calling to passing travelers to stop at his blanket and buy his wares.

Joe and I have four hours to kill. We have already—early this morning—taken the #14 bus to the *stazione* and then the SITA bus to the Peretola airport on the outskirts of Florence (the same airport from which jets take off and pass over Cornelia's five-hundred-year-old house). We arrived at the airport intending to meet our oldest daughter, Becky, flying from California to stay with us for a week—only to learn that she had missed her connection in Brussels and would be delayed for four hours. We decided we could have lunch at the airport—but the cafeteria was *chiusa,* and the bar was smoky and crowded. There was nothing for us to do but take the bus back to the city, have a meal, and spend time till it was necessary to go back and meet Becky's flight.

Thus we find ourselves in the underground corridor of the train station, examining the wares. There's a certain kind of jacket for sale all over Florence this time of year, costing in the range of 15,000 lire, made of a washable nylon pile, hip-length, with elastic wristbands and a zipper up the front. They seem inviting to me, warm and soft, and I decide this is a good time to buy one. The patterns on the cloth are often of geometric, American Indian designs, and the colors are shades of blue, or brown, or mixed pastels—all very pretty and soothing to the eye.

As soon as I tentatively touch a plastic-wrapped jacket displayed on a table to look for the size label, the salesman has it out of the bag and is holding it open for me to try on. In no time he is praising my beauty in it, my absolute breath-taking gorgeousness. I hear a string of *bellas* enough to turn my head. Joe can't help smiling. It's settled, then. I buy the jacket, then I buy another one for my sister. I consider buying others, for my friends, aunt, daughters, but Joe reminds me of our suitcases, how they were already straining at their zippers when we arrived in Italy.

He gets me free somehow, and we wander along the tunnel. Little gypsy girls run at us with their hands cupped for money. The gelato stand calls to us with its great tottering column of stacked sugar cones dipped in chocolate. Everyone wants us, courts us, makes us feel important, desirable. Up ahead we see a kind of waterfall, an underground, train-station waterfall. Nothing is surprising in Italy. You see everything here; you expect not to be surprised.

In a little alcove we see a photo booth. Beside it, mounted on the wall, there is a large carved stone displaying a moon-faced creature. The sign proclaims *"Bocca della Verità"* (The Mouth of Truth). The visage, with its wild beard and hair, has intense staring eyes and a fiercely open mouth. It seems to have been transported directly from some ruin to this wall. (The original was an ancient sewer cover, at the Church of Santa Maria, in Rome.) If you put your fingers in its mouth, it promises to read your hand and tell your fortune . . . for only 1,000 lire.

"Oh, I must . . ." I tell Joe, and he finds coins in his pocket for me to use. I drop the money in a slot, lay my fingers between the creature's

Merrill's fortune from the Bocca della Verità

teeth, and rest them on the flat chilly stone inside. I hear a motorized whir and fear for a moment the teeth will bite down. But my fortune emerges on a thin sheet of paper, computer generated. Joe translates for me from the Italian:

THE MOUTH OF TRUTH TELLS YOU THAT
YOU ENJOY A ROBUST CONSTITUTION AND WORK HARD
YOU WILL BE DISAPPOINTED AND UPSET BY TAKING GAMBLES
YOU ARE NOT SUSPICIOUS OR EXCESSIVELY CAUTIOUS
IN ORDER TO REALIZE YOUR AMBITIONS DO NOT LOOK ANYONE IN THE FACE
YOU WILL HAVE FINANCIAL DIFFICULTIES THAT YOU WILL EVENTUALLY SUC-
CEED IN CONTROLLING

"But only," Joe adds, "if you don't buy any more jackets or put money in any more machines."

"Wait, there's more." On the bottom of my fortune is a scale that shows my level of *Vita, Amore, Fortuna, Salute,* and *Sesso.* I seem to be well above average in Life, Love, Fortune, and Health—but *Sesso* goes off the chart. What could that be?

"Sex," Joe says.

"Well, lucky you," I tell him.

For our next entertainment (we still have three hours left before we can meet our daughter), we decide to have a long, luxurious lunch at Trattoria Alfredo near the Palazzo Vecchio. We have seen the sign for a *menu turistico* posted outside, promising a flat 25,000-lire price for "*primi piatti* [soup or pasta or risotto], *secondi* [meat or fish], *contorni* [salad or vegetable], and *dolce* [dessert]"—the entire works.

Like all the trattorias we have visited, this one is cozy (crowded would be the word in the States), furnished with simple wooden tables and chairs, and owned and run by family members. Here there are two brothers, both wearing red aprons, who welcome and seat us. An additional menu is offered for *bistecca alla fiorentina,* a specialty steak of Florence, famous for being seared and salted on the outside and dripping with blood inside. This delicacy generally costs 45,000 per kilogram for the meat alone, more than our budget will comfortably allow. We settle for the *menu turistico* and make our choices with difficulty, considering the many possibilities. We decide we will share everything.

My *primo* is lasagna, Joe's is *pappa al pomodoro,* a tomato and bread soup, flavored with garlic and basil. The soup has the consistency of oatmeal but tastes delicious and could be a full meal. Next we have *osso buco* and *fegato alla veneziana,* with side dishes of peas and ham, and *insalata mista* with the ever-present dressing of fresh pressed olive oil (greenish in color), poured from a glass pitcher with a spout, and the accompanying vinegar. A platter of bread is set before us, thickly sliced, rough textured, with the flat taste of unsalted bread that Italians favor.

Still, our feast is sumptuous. We eat leisurely, having time to observe and comment upon the other customers. None of the guests at this hour seem to be tourists—we hear rapid Italian being spoken at every table and conjecture about the relationships of the parties in each group. Are those two beautiful women mother and daughter? Then who is the man? Is he the daughter's lover or the mother's? Or their brother? Father? Husband? And what of that sullen young couple in the corner, she pouting and he drinking glass after glass of wine? There's a father and his young son, the boy perhaps twelve or thirteen; they seem to love one another seriously, they talk in a gentle way, as if cooperating, confiding important messages. If only we knew what these people's lives were like. We can wonder, but can only guess. We will never know how they rate in the areas of *Vita, Amore, Fortuna, Salute,* and *Sesso.*

Dessert is tiramisú for me, macedonia for Joe; again we share. The tiramisú is a scrumptious confection of cream, espresso coffee, sponge cake, shaved bitter chocolate, and liqueur; the macedonia is made of fresh, hand-cut squares of fruit: plums, oranges, apples, pears. And then coffee is served in small white cups, dark, rich, foamy with its own bubbly sheen. The bill never comes till Joe asks for the *conto*—it's considered rude in Italy to rush patrons on their way till they make it clear they're ready to leave. We notice we have whiled away the better part of two hours, and now it's time to take the bus back to the airport in the hope that our child has arrived.

In front of the Peretola airport is a huge, chunky, ungraceful statue of a big brown bird.

"What is *that* doing here," I ask Joe, "in this country of great art?"

"I think it must be Michelangelo's first sculpture," Joe says.

The arrival area (which we are prevented from entering) is glassed in; however, the top three-quarters of the glass is painted black. In order for me to see whether our daughter is coming in from the landing field, I am required to lay myself down on the floor and look at the shoes of the incoming passengers through the clear lower part of the glass partition.

Furthermore, having the intention of taking her picture ("Becky's First Moment in Italy"—to go in the albums with "First Smile," "First Steps," "First Day of School," "First Prom"), I have to aim my camera blindly toward wherever it is that I think the passengers' feet will first appear.

This prohibition—the blackened glass—seems typically Italian to me. Italians are masterful in thwarting the wishes of the public. Like their closing the cafeteria exactly at the moment when we reasonably expected to wait there and have a meal, they now do all they can to prevent me from seeing my beloved daughter arrive in Florence.

But I won't be thwarted. I have no shame. I station myself on the floor, lying on my side, having a fairly good view of the shoes coming in. Joe pretends not to know me. He's waiting to the side with a luggage cart, wishing (I'm sure) that I were able to exercise more self-control. But there are times I have little regard for propriety.

I want to get this photo, and I consider the barrier an interesting challenge. I can't be certain I will recognize my daughter's shoes, since I probably haven't accompanied her to buy shoes for twenty years or more (probably not since she was fourteen), so watching for her shoes is a matter more of intuition than of knowledge.

As passengers begin to arrive, I know which shoes are not hers at once: the cowboy boots coming in the doorway from the tarmac are not hers, the shiny Italian leather loafers are not hers, the backless clogs are not hers, the high-heeled pumps are not hers, the basketball sneakers are not hers. But, wait, there's a pair of tennis shoes coming in the doorway now, worn down at the outside edges in just a certain way, the walk familiar enough to make my heart flutter.

"She's here!" I cry to Joe and begin snapping photos blindly, holding my camera at floor level. "Yes, yes, I'm sure it's her."

Joe says, "Maybe there's a reason the windows are blacked out. Maybe they don't want you taking pictures of everyone's feet. Maybe it's a security measure, so that no one gets assassinated when they arrive. Maybe you'd better get up off the floor."

The tennis shoes, connected to our daughter, come around the corner and out into the waiting area, where we are overjoyed to see her. The first hug is the best, full of reunion, delight, the sense of solid flesh in my arms. My daughter says, "I knew you were here, Mom, I saw your camera there on the floor, aimed at everyone's shoes. Who else could it be taking pictures like that?"

We ask about the flight, about her delay in Brussels. She tells us that, because of the unexpected layover, she was given a coupon good for "a free snack"—which she greatly appreciated since she had no local money with her. We discuss the merits of the various airlines, and I decide that flying from Los Angeles to Brussels and then directly into the Florence airport is a far better arrangement than the flight we took from Los Angeles to New York to Rome (after which we still had a long, tiring journey to take to Florence.)

We ask Becky about matters at home; she assures us her husband will manage perfectly well for the week. She has been to visit my mother, who is holding her own, been to greet my cat, who has taken up a firm friendship with the boy who is feeding him. My sister is well, my plants are thriving. No crooks have ransacked the house, no earthquake has brought it to ruin.

We make our way outside and see a city bus waiting at the bus stop.

This, we learn from the posted sign, goes from the airport directly to the Santa Maria Novella station, for the usual city fare of 1,200 lire. We elect to take this bus, rather than the fancier SITA bus, which—in this case—costs five times that price and follows exactly the same route.

Just as Joe punches our tickets in the box on the bus, an older German tourist couple arrives at the bus. They drag their heavy suitcases aboard. The husband removes his wallet and takes out some bills, offering them to the driver. The driver shakes his head. Via pantomime and the pointing of his finger, he explains more or less that he doesn't sell tickets. He directs the couple back toward the airport terminal, where they will have to buy tickets from a machine, bring them back to the bus, and have them punched. Of course, by then, the bus will have left for the city, and they will have another hour's wait.

I want to leap up and explain to them that *this once* they can ride without a ticket. That dozens of Italians play this game every day—they ride the buses and hope no ticket controllers (I think of them as the bus police!) will leap on and confront them, asking to see a punched ticket. I want to beg them to take the chance, that soon they will be spending many dollars honestly on buses (and everything else). That foreigners are not likely to be fined if they plead ignorance (which they obviously have in good measure). That this unfair welcome is just an accidental oversight of the local authorities. They don't mean to be this inhospitable. (Do they?)

The tired German couple is already confused and sweating; I somehow want their first moments in Italy not to be ones of exhaustion and frustration (as mine were). I wish the driver would invite them to ride this little trip into the city without forcing them to drag their luggage back to the airport terminal, without requiring them to find the ticket machine and read the directions on it (impossible to understand), without having them realize they don't have the proper change for the ticket dispensing machine (which I'm sure they will not, since the man seems to have only some bills with him that he now is offering the bus driver, beseechingly, as if to say, "Please, take *all* my bills, just let us stay on this bus.")

But, no, to be in Italy is to have this pure Italian experience. Defeated already, the man drags his luggage off the bus, helps his wife down, begins to trudge back to the terminal. The bus driver checks his watch, starts up his motor, and, with only my husband, our daughter, and me aboard, departs without apology for the city center of Florence.

33

The British Institute Library, Jane Eyre, *il Porcellino*

With the arrival of our daughter, I suddenly become a specialist in Italian culture, a connoisseur of Italian life and customs. On the first rainy day of her visit, when she sees women across the courtyard hanging out clothes covered with plastic sheeting, I explain that the clothes dry faster outdoors under these "raincoats" than they do inside (whereas mine, hanging over cold radiators all around the apartment, tend to develop a moldy-dishrag odor).

When we stop at the *rosticceria* on our way home one afternoon, I interpret the traditional take-out foods for her: the balls of spinach, the fried polenta, the *patate rosta* and *patate fritte,* the *crostone pomodoro e aglio,* the steaming pot of *ministra di fagioli,* and the shop's main attraction, the *pollo* (or *mezzo pollo*)— chickens turned over a blazing fire till their skins are crisp and delicious and their meat is rich with the flavor of fresh rosemary. We buy a little of everything to sample tonight for our dinner and carry the greasy plastic bags home, feeling the heat from them warm our legs as we walk. Overnight, it seems, I have gone from being a beginner in matters Italian to being an expert.

We pass the little church on the corner (where there is a small plaque to the Jewish war dead), and beside it are the offices of the *Misericordia*—the mercy team (or the modern paramedics), which started out in the Middle Ages as a confraternity of lay church members who (wearing hoods to keep their acts of mercy secret) removed the dead during the plague years. There is a line of white ambulances outside the church, and a group of young Italian men and women, wearing shirts of a uniform color and style, stand talking amiably with one another, apparently waiting for emergency calls.

I tell Becky what Cornelia told me when I asked her how we could get our flu shots in Italy. First we must go to the *farmacia* and buy the vaccine; then we must carry it to one of the paramedic stations and try to find someone who will be willing to inject us. We have not done this yet, not certain who provides the needles, not sure, exactly, how to ask someone to inject us—and not sure we want to.

When we get to our building, Signora Carezza, the old woman who lives in the first-floor apartment, is out on her terrace and greets us. She wears her hair in a long gray-blonde braid down her back. Much of the day, when the weather is fine, she sits on her terrace and pets her orange cat, who lies in the sun and accepts the attention with haughty tolerance. Signora Carezza walks each morning, leaning on her cane, to the little church down the street, where she attends mass. When I announce that Becky is *mia figlia,* the old woman reaches across the low terrace wall to touch my face, then touches Becky's. She studies us, then begins to talk very fast. In the crush of words she sends forth that I don't understand, I do understand she is saying we look alike, like sisters, *tutte e due, giovani, belle, belle.* She smiles and nods. She holds up her hand to signal us: wait a moment. On her terrace is a small pomegranate tree in a pot; she plucks a fruit and offers it to my daughter. Becky accepts it with pleasure and says her first *grazie.*

When we get upstairs into our apartment, I tell Becky the sad story that my landlady, Rina Masotti, told me about this neighbor: years ago, her only child, her son, committed suicide. She keeps his room as a shrine and tells everyone that he works in Milan, managing a bank, and that he speaks seven languages.

The next morning, Becky and I ride into the city, planning to visit the British Institute Library (of special interest to Becky, since she is a librarian). We take the number #14 bus, which is already crowded when it stops for us. Even as I am explaining to her the uncertainties of the Italian bus system, our bus grinds to a sudden halt, throwing us against each other. On Via dell'Agnolo, one of the narrowest streets on the route, road construction is taking place. The bus driver is peering out his front window. On one side of the bus, where construction work is going on, is a deep hole surrounded by chicken wire; on the other side is a car—a BMW—parked illegally. The bus cannot pass.

The driver opens the doors, gets out of the bus, examines the difficulty, gets back in, and inches the bus forward by a fraction. He then turns off the ignition, gets out, and once again assesses the situation. He climbs back in. He starts the motor but doesn't move—we all know by now he can't get by without scraping the car or causing the bus to tip into the hole. He makes a call on his radio and has a loud conference with someone for a long time. Soon he is shouting and gesticulating to the person on the other end, as if to convince him of the impossibility of further travel. It's hot on the bus, people are getting restless. Half the riders get out and contemplate the problem. Everyone seems to have his own solution. A few people disembark and begin to walk to wherever they were going in the first place. The others, mostly older women with shopping bags, wait patiently on the stalled bus, beginning to talk to one another.

Becky and I get out with the others and stand around in the street. The BMW looks cocky, black and shiny, parked indifferently, wherever was easiest for the driver to leave it. (This is nothing new in Italy. I have been blocked by two Italians who stand talking on a narrow sidewalk and never even consider stepping to the side to let me pass.)

Suddenly, four young men who were sitting in the back of the bus come jumping out the front door, bypassing the driver, who is sitting in his seat with his head in his hands. The young men saunter over to the BMW, position themselves at its four corners, shout a signal, and, with one grunt, in unison, lift the car and move it over to the sidewalk as far as it will go. They let go of it so fast it bounces. They brush off their hands, smile at everyone, and climb back on the bus to a round of applause. The driver, shaking his head, lights up a cigarette, takes a few drags, and throws it out the window. Then he starts the motor, and we are on our way again.

The British Institute Library, where Cornelia showed me around the week before, is situated on Lungarno Guicciardini, on the south side of the Arno, overlooking the river between the Ponte Santa Trinita and the Ponte alla Carraia. Street numbers in Italy are often not sequential—they hop about all over the street and you can easily find a "45" next to a "125," a result of a system in which residences are numbered in black and shops in red. We finally find #9, which has no nameplate over the door, but, once inside the library, we find the flyer announcing:

> The Harold Acton Library of the British Institute of Florence
> Palazzo Lanfredini—Lungarno Guicciardini 9

As soon as Becky and I pass through the imposing heavy wooden doors, nod to the Italian watchman at his desk, cross the dark and echoing entry room, climb the stairs, go through an outside corridor to the floor where the library is situated, we enter a different world.

"Good morning," says the woman at the desk, in a crisp British accent. The words are music to my ears, as comforting as a mother's lullaby. I am back in a land of my own language and full of gratitude. The reading room is furnished like an English drawing room, complete with overstuffed chairs and tall brass reading lamps, each exuding a dim light. Tables are spread with issues of the *Spectator* and the *Times Literary Supplement*. An old gentleman has fallen asleep in one of the chairs with a copy of the daily *Guardian* in his lap.

Seeing the librarian to whom Cornelia introduced me, I introduce Becky to him. He's a tall, gracious man with a ring of curly hair around the bald crown of his head. I tell him that my daughter is also a librarian. He bows to her in a courtly manner and says, "Then may I get you anything to read?" In view of the towering shelves of books all around us, we can't help smiling. He begins by showing us the ancient card catalog, a shelf of miniature leather-bound loose-leaf books about six inches high by eight inches wide, with each page noting the name of a book, followed by typed information about it. There does not seem to be a single computer in the building.

I leave Becky to explore the library holdings on her own while I sit down in a soft green chair beside a bookshelf. My hand idly pulls a volume from the shelf, and I open it to the first page:

There was no possibility of taking a walk that day.

Jane Eyre! Just those words—and the story jumps into my consciousness in all its complexities. How astonishing that this forgotten tale still lives in me like my own heart. I lean back and close my eyes, thinking of all the books that reside in me that I can enter at will, thinking of all the journeys I have taken between the covers of books.

When Becky finds me there much later, I am almost asleep, half-dreaming of the book I will write one day about Italy.

Our next stop is the Mercato Centrale, the great food market across the river, not far from the train station. Becky has an unerring sense of direction. She can unfold the map of Florence, balance it on her palm till some aspect of it faces the way she is facing, and then go directly (on many indirect streets) to her destination. I let her lead me to the giant indoor market.

In the area surrounding it are dozens of discarded shipping crates and cartons into which pigeons swoop and scatter, looking for bits of fruit and vegetables. Once we get inside, I have a sense of being in a warehouse, an armory, a factory—a bit intimidating, perhaps inhospitable.

But, no—I'm wrong about hospitality. No sooner are we within than we are greeted by the man selling meat—his counter is filled with hanging carcasses, chickens, turkeys, rabbits, ducks—not to mention pigs, entire pigs with their heads and feet still on them. He beckons us closer, to examine them. I see that some vendors are more circumspect—they are selling huge cured hams, *prosciutti,* already wrapped and hanging in amorphous reddish lumps as if they have nothing at all to do with any creature with a head, eyes, four legs, and a heart.

Becky is intent on the cheese wheels at another counter; she wants to buy Parmesan-Reggiano for her husband, in a size suitable for transport home in a small suitcase. While she contemplates cheese, I spin on my heel, dizzied by all the competing food counters, dozens upon dozens of vendors selling delicacies, specialties of Firenze, more cheeses than one could imagine, some of them fragrant with a kind of ripe, almost moldy odor, both alluring and repellent at the same time.

The market is vast, two stories high. There is an escalator, but we can't use it. A rope is tied across it, and a sign announces: "*NON FUNZIONA*." We walk up an iron staircase and gaze at the displays of vegetables (huge, yellow squash, monumental zucchinis, tomatoes big as suns). A vendor beckons to us, invites us to examine his wares, tries to guess whether we are French, German, American. Becky and I are impressed. All the consumables human beings have devised to eat are here.

But who could ever imagine that this much perishable food could be sold before it's spoiled or rotten? Who could possibly buy this much? Eat this much? But Italy is a hungry country; Italians love to eat. At every counter there are women (most of the shoppers I see are women, except for a few tourist couples), demanding, bargaining, cajoling—"that piece there," "put in one more slice," "give me the thick piece in the middle."

How I'd love to be invited to the homes of these women for dinner. How I'd love to have them teach me to cook!

We are losing steam, Becky and I, but this is our day on the town. She wants to buy a bottle of Italian wine for her friend, Maria, leather belts for her husband, Gary, and woolen scarves for her sisters, Joanna and Susanna. We make one last stop at the Straw Market in Piazza della Repubblica, where booths fill the square and leather merchants offer us their shiny leather coats, wallets, and purses, where hanging tapestries move in the wind, where silk ties beckon from decorative wooden posts. Trinkets and statues, earrings and bracelets, scarves and hats, aprons and umbrellas—they all cry out for our attention.

After we have walked two blocks to the south, we come upon the famous boar in the Loggia del Porcellino. He's situated above a little grate (is it a fountain?), his body is the dark brown color of bronze, but his snout is gleaming yellow, like gold, thanks to the superstition that anyone who rubs his nose will return to Florence.

We can't pass it by. Becky and I each give his golden nose a rub. We each add our 200 lire to the coins lying below the grate. We want what everyone who touches *il Porcellino* wants: the chance to come back to Florence one day.

34

The Uffizi, the Spanish Chapel, and *Madame Butterfly*

The week has flown by, and there is only today for Becky to see the rest of Florence—impossible to accomplish, but we try. The three of us, to get an early start in the line for entrance to the Uffizi Gallery, arrive at the door at 8 A.M., only to learn that the museum is *chiusa* for a meeting. We and a hundred others are turned away, some having only this one day in Florence, some who will never come back here and will forever miss seeing *The Birth of Venus* and *The Primavera*, who will miss not only Sandro Botticelli but also Raphael, Leonardo, Michelangelo, Filippo Lippi, Giotto, Rembrandt, Rubens, il Bronzino, Rosso Fiorentino, Piero della Francesca, Paolo Uccello, Masaccio, Caravaggio, and El Greco—and heaven knows how many others. (I have been reading Joe's guide to the Uffizi, so I know what's to be missed.)

We cross the Ponte Vecchio, go past the enormous span of the Pitti Palace and down the street to where Elizabeth and Robert Browning once lived. Their little house is open to the public . . . but only on Wednesdays and Fridays after 3 P.M., which this is not. We consider heading back toward the Boboli Gardens, but Joe checks his museum list and is certain the Spanish Chapel at Santa Maria Novella is open; in fact, he happens to have the Spanish Chapel guidebook in his backpack. He opens it to recommend to Becky the "Allegory of the Sacred

Sciences and the Liberal Arts"—the giant mural that, as the book says, describes "the activity of human intelligence under the influence of the holy spirit."

We trudge along in the direction of the *stazione* till we reach the church that, miracle of miracles, is indeed open. We pay our money, walk through the cloisters in a biting wind, and enter the Spanish Chapel, which at this hour of the morning has no one in it but us and a lone museum guard in a blue uniform. He is sitting in the freezing room on a metal chair next to what seems to be a portable radiator. A little red electric light glows beside the switch, indicating the heat is on, but the room is truly tomb-like, the stone walls exhale waves of cold.

Joe and Becky stand still in their tracks and gaze upon the walls (wall after wall after wall, in fact)—at a monumental miracle of art, wisdom, and sheer patience. If I am restless after being here for three minutes, how did the artist (I check the guidebook for his name), Andrea Buonaiuti, manage to work here for years?

I read to myself the description in the guide book under the heading "*Cappellone degli Spagnoli* (Spanish Chapel)":

A beautiful stone portal, on whose architrave are sculpted the Martyrdom of St. Peter of Verona and the Guidalotti Coat of Arms, the walls inlaid with black and white marble, and the two magnificent mullioned windows with the twisted marble columns, announce the old chapter hall of the convent. It became known as the Cappellone Degli Spagnoli in 1566 when it was granted to Eleonora of Toledo, wife of the Grand Duke of Cosimo I, to be used by the Spanish colony in Florence as a place of worship.

This is exactly the kind of commentary I cannot read standing up, while at the same time looking up, in a freezing cold room when I am also beginning to get hungry. This is one of the many moments when I know I am not suited to tourism. However, I do not wish to let my daughter know how juvenile my attitudes are, so I read further. "Upon entering we render homage to the patron. His body still rests under the old monumental slab, in front of the altar."

I look around, wondering where exactly underfoot this corpse might be. But then I do look up, I *really* look up, and there above me is

Christ bearing the great burden of his heavy cross on his thin shoulders, and then Christ crucified (in agony), and then Christ's descent to limbo (horned devils and evil winged monsters with cloven hoofs are threatening him), followed by (of course) his resurrection, in which he floats aloft in a hallowed circle of sun, whose fiery sunspots glow while beneath him winged angels praise his glory. (And all this is executed only on two walls of the chapel.)

We haven't yet begun to study the allegorical figures, the historical figures, the evangelical symbols on the other walls. There are fourteen women painted in individual stalls, each one doing some symbolic act (reading, looking in a mirror, holding a scorpion, or a sword or a scroll or a fig or a harp), and beneath the women sit the men, who, the book reports, are Justinian, Clement V, Aristotle, St. Jerome, St. John of Damascus, Dionysius the Areopagite, St. Augustine, Pythagoras, Euclid, Ptolemy, Tubal-Cain, Pietrus, Cicero, and Donatus or Priscian (they don't know for sure?). Somewhere in all this glory of faces and objects and painted detail are represented Fear of God, Knowledge, Counsel, Wisdom, Intellect, Pity, Strength, and the various Heavens of the Gods, in addition to the areas of Civil Law, Canon Law, Philosophy, Sacred Writing, Theology, Contemplation, Preaching, Arithmetic, Geometry, Astronomy, Music, Logic, Rhetoric, and Grammar.

I am humbled by my ignorance, which I suppose is a good beginning. I am also still hungry, more than ever, and I'm really cold. I go and stand beside the museum guard, sharing the faint warmth of his little radiator. He smiles at me, and I wonder—is he honored to be guarding these old ruins, or is he just phenomenally bored? All of Florence is really one enormous old ruin—ancient and extraordinary in every block of stone.

In California, I suspect, buildings this old might be torn down to build condominiums. But here, in this cold dusty chapel, standing under the awesome weight of all art, all religion, and all knowledge, I feel the power of age and history. Perhaps I even feel a fraction of the grace the artist must have felt as he labored for years of his life to paint this mural that encompasses almost all that was known about all things in his time.

For lunch we go to Teddy's, a fast-food hamburger place on the south side of the Arno just to the east of the Ponte Vecchio. The singular attraction of this place is that we can sit at a table overlooking the river. The food is ghastly, a floppy patty of gray meat on a soggy bun—and there's an extra, outrageous charge for ketchup. I order a Coke and get a small paper cup full of lukewarm brown liquid that bears no resemblance to the drink I thought I had ordered. What's more, as I carry my tray to the table, I trip on a small step, and my Coke goes flying. Joe brings my empty cup back to the counter, asks for a rag to clean up the mess, and orders another Coke. For which he's charged an additional three dollars.

"Don't get upset," he cautions me when he hands me the new Coke, knowing me too well. "It's just the price of travel. *Non importante.*"

Becky and I discover that the glass plate overlooking the river is actually a sliding window that we push to the side so we can peer out directly into the water beneath us.

There, below, we see a rat-like animal larger than any we ever imagined could exist. It's as big as a beaver, in fact. Bigger. We watch it paddle in the dirty water, diving for bits of hamburger that people at the next table are tossing from their open window. Because I have never seen an animal like this, because I am in a fabled place, because I have just come from a chapel where Christ was crucified and reborn, because all the allegories of life have just passed before my eyes, I sacrifice my entire meal to this fantastic creature and, for good measure, sanctify his environment by blessing the water with my entire cup of brown liquid.

Our last stop of the afternoon is Piazzale Michelangelo. High in the hills of Florence, we have a view from this wide open piazza of the entire city. The Duomo and the green dome of the synagogue are clear in the distance. Souvenir stalls are spread across the piazza, and a copy of the famous *David* towers above us. (Joe tells us a question he is going to ask on the next quiz he gives his class: "What is Michelangelo's *David* wearing?" The answer? "A sling.")

Becky and Joe decide to climb the hill to the church of San Miniato al Monte, but I'm too tired to budge. (Besides, the day isn't half over. Tonight we have tickets to see *Madame Butterfly* at the Teatro Comunale, and tomorrow, the last day of October, Becky must leave for California. She'll be home in time to welcome trick or treaters for Halloween.)

She and Joe deposit me at a little cafe called the Parlour of Florence, situated on Viale Galilei, where I order a glass of wine (having not had my Coke or any lunch to speak of at the burger place) and wave them off to see San Miniato. I sit on the terrace at a small table with a checked cloth, sip my wine, and breathe in the fall air. A wind is shimmering the leaves of the trees above me, and, with each strong gust, a shower of button-shaped leaves comes streaming down upon the tables, upon the terrace, and upon my hair.

I sit there for perhaps an hour. I am alone on the terrace except for two lovers who are sharing one of the delights listed on the menu under *Specialità Gelati di nostra produzione*. Perhaps it is *Ananas Surprise,* which contains "*Banana—Datteri—Cioccolato—Maraschino—Panna liquida.*" Whatever it is, it looks tall and cold and sweetly made with the most delicious confections. I am absolutely happy at this moment. I am bathed in beauty, limp with contentment, and hungry for everything that Italy offers: food, love, and life.

When Joe and Becky come back, they are famished, too—and we order a meal we trust will be better than our burgers: *Pizza con mozzarella pomodoro e funghi.* And vino, of course. They tell me the wondrous scene they came upon in the churchyard of San Miniato. Because All Saints' Day is approaching, hundreds of people were there, in the graveyard, placing flowers on the graves of their loved ones.

In this never-ending day, we get off the bus on Via Aretina, and, though Joe goes on ahead to our apartment, I urge Becky to come with me, for just a minute, into the *mercatino usato*. This is the third time in a week I have visited the used-clothing shop with my daughter, and each time I have looked longingly at a certain coat: a pink coat, a pink silk coat, pink on one side, purple on the other. A reversible coat. A coat embossed with many Chinese acrobats, on both sides. Each time we have stopped in, today included, I have tried on this coat. Each time (not counting today), I have sensibly put it back on the shelf.

Paola, my friend, the kind woman who runs the shop, admires me in this coat. *"Bella"* is what she says, and I know it's true. This coat is *me*.

I know I don't need a coat, I have no room for a coat, I already have two coats with me in Italy, one happens to be purple already, and one is my down coat. But to look at these amazing Chinese acrobats, the smooth cool silky padded jacket. . . .

Becky says to me, "Mom, you've tried on that coat three different times. I think you must really need it. I think you should buy it!"

"You do?" I say in surprise.

We already know the price, a mere 15,000 lire, a minuscule ten dollars.

"You definitely need it, Mom."

"I do," I agree. "To make this day even more perfect."

Then, walking toward home, I decide we should cross over to the river and avoid the fumes of the cars and motor scooters on the street. We walk in the direction of the bridge where the *autostrada* begins; we walk arm in arm, my daughter and I, knowing we will have to say good-bye to each other tomorrow. I am wearing my new pink and purple silk coat, and Becky is carrying my old purple nylon coat. We walk on the path beside the river. We pass the Orto del Cigno trattoria and pizzeria on the river's edge. Becky says, "Look at that interesting piece of sculpture."

I look and note an object deposited on the wall, just above the restaurant's menu. It is a sculpture indeed: a piece of erotic art-graffiti, you might call it, a carefully formed set of male genitalia, in papier-mâché, painted in various tones of pink. The papier-mâché, when I lift it off the wall, to Becky's embarrassment, is still damp.

"Mom, put it back." (She knows my habit of picking things up from the street.)

"Someone will just throw it away. You know it was left here as a joke. I want it—an original piece of art from Florence—for a souvenir."

"You can't take that home on the plane! What if they pull it out of your suitcase at customs? Daddy would be mortified."

"What's the difference between this and the naked *David*?" I ask her.

To her credit, she doesn't dignify that question with an answer.

I am so tired at the opera I can hardly keep my eyes open. At least, this time, there is a full orchestra (not like the tape played at *La Cenerentola*). Nicoletta is there, and most of the students. I know this is a great opera, but I am exhausted. My mind is full of today's adventures. I am grateful that we have had our daughter with us for this week. I am sad she is leaving.

I find it hard to concentrate on the operatic plot, the baby born out of wedlock, Lieutenant Pinkerton coming back to claim him, with his new wife, Kate. The distraught mother, Cio-cio San, thinking he is coming to see her, Suzuki, her maid, always at her side, Madame Butterfly beside herself with grief when she learns the true meaning of his visit (oh, I do this story grave injustice)—but even as I sit, half asleep, in my seat, a woman comes down from the balcony and sits herself on the carpet between my legs just where the glass partition overlooks the stage. She sits between my legs!

"*Scusi?*" I say, leaning forward. And she says to me, in Italian, but simple enough for me to understand, that she is tired, she had to go home from work and get dressed and rush back, and now she can't see the stage from her seat, and would I mind?

Between my legs? And as she watches, she leans her head on my thigh! And falls asleep!

Madame Butterfly is dead by her own hand with the ceremonial dagger; the last sad notes of the opera have died away. I politely tap the sleeping woman and push her slightly forward while I lift my leg over her head. "*Ciao,*" I tell her as she wakens. She smiles groggily and lifts a hand to me so that I can help her up from the floor. As soon as she is properly balanced, Joe and I make our way to the exit.

There's no time to linger now, breathe the night air, take time for a gelato. We must rush back to the station to catch the last bus home. As we wait in the wind, wait for the (now beloved) sight of the orange bus that will carry us home, we see yet one more sight that will last forever in our minds.

On the corner across the street from the station, two young men are having a fight. This isn't a for-fun, I'll-show-you-who's boss-fight, it's something sinister, a brutal, to-the-death fight.

We watch from just across the street in horror as the two of them punch at each other, beat each other about the face, use all their strength to bring down the other. And one of them does knock the other to the cement and proceeds to bang his head, his skull, into the sidewalk. All those on the street and at the bus stop are paralyzed, as we are. No one moves, no one intervenes. No one breathes. How can we permit this? Yet what can anyone do?

And when it seems it will never end, two men in blue uniforms come rushing out of the station—(bus drivers, perhaps? Train conductors? Not policemen). Together they use brute force to try to pull the man off the man on the ground. And they do, after a time, succeed.

We watch to see whether one man has killed the other. But, no, the one on the ground slowly gets up, staggers to a post where he had placed his motor scooter helmet, picks it up, and walks away, blood dripping from his face. The other man, with fury still raging in him, punches at the wall of a building.

There are no arias in this opera, no songs to justify this violence, no finale sung by a chorus. It is raw hatred we have just witnessed, without benefit of art, with no redeeming meaning. We have seen all we can take in for one day. We must, we must, go home to recover.

35

Halloween in Tuscany

Joe's students invite us to a Halloween party. No sooner have we seen Becky off at Peretola Airport than we begin to discuss possible costumes we might wear. As a teacher, Joe is not strictly required to appear in full dress, but he wants to wear something to show he's a good sport. We are supposed to invent our costumes, but we don't have enough clothes with us in Italy to be creative. Though we know Italians celebrate All Saints Day, we doubt that we will find a store on every corner selling monster, vampire, and ghost costumes.

Just as we step off the bus that takes us from the airport to the station, I see at my very feet a crumpled cap in the road: it's a workman's hat, and on it is printed:

Pucci Corsi & Capecchi, SNC
Materiali Edili
Via G. D'Annunzio, 84
FIRENZE

"What does *Materiali Edili* mean?"

"Materials of the building trade. It's a construction worker's hat."

"Then this can be your costume! You can wear it with your navy thermal undershirt that I splashed bleach on, and your gray pajama bottoms."

"And you?" Joe says.

"I'll wear my gold polar bear earrings and my pink Chinese acrobat coat. That should take care of both of us."

The apartment in Borgo San Lorenzo, in which six of the female students live together, is a fourth-story walkup in one of the ancient buildings in *il centro*. We ring the bell, are buzzed in, and labor slowly up the slippery stone stairs, polished by hundreds of years of wear. The staircase is so narrow that I am able to support myself by pressing my palms against the walls on either side. There's a special smell in these ancient buildings, difficult to describe—an aroma of stone dust, with an overtone of boiled cabbage or cauliflower.

We have arrived promptly at nine, a serious error. We are always mindful of the deadline of the last bus leaving the Duomo at midnight. If we are to party, we must begin early in the evening. However, this is far too early—as we quickly understand.

From upstairs, we hear girls shrieking, "Where is my mascara?" "The Scotch tape! Where is the tape for the spider?" "Who forgot the wine? Who forgot the *wine?*"

We stop on one of the landings in order for me to catch my breath. The door opens, and a sour-faced woman looks out, tilts her head upward toward the noise, and scowls. Joe and I nod a greeting to her. She retreats and slams the door, hard.

I am seriously out of breath; my knees are taking these steps hard.

One more flight and we're there. The door to the girls' apartment is open—there's pandemonium inside. The rooms glow with a dim red light. Weird and deformed creatures shriek and dash across our path. The atmosphere is smoky with cigarette smoke and incense.

"We're not ready, we're not ready," one of the wraiths cries to us and disappears into the dark corridor. Joe and I hang our coats on the rack in the hall and stand there, uncertain about what to do.

On the wall, in the eerie glow of light, I can see a typed sign:

RULES OF THE HOUSE
1. NEVER DATE AN ISRAELIAN
2. DON'T PUT CONDOMS IN THE TOILET
3. DON'T STICK YOUR FOOT THROUGH THE WINDOW
4. THROW UP NEATLY

I reach for Joe's hand and lead him to where there may be a place we can sit down. The flitting figures of semidressed and undressed young women appear and disappear in various doorways, silhouetted by light from their bedrooms. One has her hair wound in wires, Medusa-like; her face is painted half-black, half-white. Another is in medieval dress, or possibly she's dressed as Snow White.

We make our way to a couch and sit down. An enormous orange balloon with a hairy black spider planted on it is suspended from the ceiling. (Where did they find these items?) Someone dressed as a cat, with whiskers pasted to her face and a long sinuous tail flicking behind her, offers us each a glass of wine.

We're relieved to hear the bell ringing and loud voices in the hall as a few newly arriving guests are buzzed in and come shouting up the stairs. Nicoletta has not yet arrived, nor has Mrs. Pedrini. They may have been wiser than we, realizing this party might be better left to the kids.

No one has remarked on Joe's outfit of bleached-out shirt and builder's hat (he really just looks sloppily dressed), and I have no real semblance of a costume, either. It's already almost ten, and nothing resembling a party is under way. Some phone calls are being made

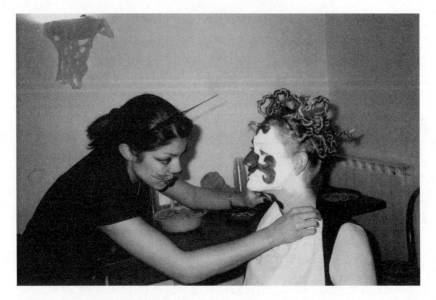

Getting ready for the Halloween party

regarding whoever is bringing the music; people rush back and forth across the room. Occasionally one of Joe's students remembers we're sitting here and offers us some chips.

The most recent arrivals are dressed as a pirate with eye-patch and a serial killer (a girl who has pasted cereal all over her face). Another student is wearing a gas mask.

A scream from the hall brings us all to attention—two of our students have just clattered up the stairs, two men: one in clogs (he's dressed as Madame Butterfly) and one in high heels (he's dressed as a hooker). Someone turns up the light so that we can all get a good look at them. Madame Butterfly is in full geisha costume, with flowers wound through her hair, a silk kimono wrapped around her body, an American flag draped over her shoulder. She flutters her fan before her eyes and flutters her eyelashes, as well. The hooker outfit can't quite disguise Phil, wearing a tight satin blouse (over an extremely well-padded bra), a short leather skirt, black tights, earrings—and for the occasion he (or Rosanna with her beautician's tools) has dyed his hair platinum blond. It's an amazing transformation—with perfectly applied makeup

"Madame Butterfly" at Halloween

Merrill and Phil

he looks like a practiced transvestite, this tall, good-looking American boy who is usually in torn jeans and an old army jacket. The pair express relief they weren't arrested on the way over. Everyone wants to pose with the hooker and Madame Butterfly. The girls take turns sitting on their laps while their friends snap a dozen pictures. "Get my camera now! Here, now take me."

Phil, who is genial and well mannered, offers *me* a chance to pose with him; how can I refuse? He hangs his arm over my shoulder and purses his lips. The camera clicks.

His girlfriend, dressed as an Arabian princess, gets to take the most pictures with Phil (or "Lulu," as he says he wants to be called); their romance is clearly well advanced, though they also, whenever I see them together, seem to have many arguments, periods of pouting, separations, and reconciliations.

Now—finally—many of the other students are arriving, all carrying bottles of wine and beer. Natalie arrives with her Italian boyfriend, Cesare; he looks older than the rest of the students, a little shy, dressed quite formally in dress pants and shiny leather shoes, but in no time at all, as soon as the music gets going, he and Natalie begin doing some wild and sexy dancing. It's not at all the kind of dance that is subtle, it suggests nothing—it's just totally explicit and hot. And, shortly thereafter, many of the other students (those shy girls I imagine would hardly do the fox trot) are dancing that way, and without embarrassment, in front of their teacher! The racket is tremendous. The plaster of the ceiling vibrates, the ancient stones of Florence rattle in the walls.

Joe and I don't know quite where to put ourselves. We've been known to dance at weddings and once at my high school reunion to "Love Is a Many-Splendored Thing"—but this? We stand near the table and consume many potato chips, trying to be cool about the spectacle, but we're of another generation. We did this sort of communing in the backseats of cars or in dark movie theaters. We were *discreet*.

But the agony is not long-lasting. In no time the police have been called by the old lady downstairs. Joe is summoned to the door by the girl dressed as a cat to explain to the *carabiniere* that these are American students (as if no one can guess this by now), they are celebrating an American holiday, he is sorry if they were making a disturbance. My husband's Italian fails him in view of the hopelessness of justifying the reasons for this racket. The warning is serious—when the police leave, Joe suggests to everyone that they could end up in Italian jails with the Mafia as cellmates. The first thing he does is to turn down the volume of the music.

I decide I need another drink. I refill my wine glass, leaving Joe, who is now reassuring Noreen and Clarita, dressed as belly dancers, that they're not really likely to land in jail. I wander down the hall to one of the empty bedrooms whose window is open over Borgo San Lorenzo. I push the shutters forward as far as they will go and lean out over the street. Below are people strolling by, enacting their business of the night (none of it seems to concern Halloween). Vendors are selling prints of the most famous paintings, *The Birth of Venus, The Primavera,* the same two little angels that appear everywhere (on calendars, aprons, and stationery), originally from Raphael's *Sistine Madonna* (which we have yet to see; perhaps we will on our trip to Rome, which is coming up soon).

Lovers walk hand in hand in the street with a certain confidence, leaning together, owning one another, full of entitlement. I see the lights of a bakery, a pizzeria, a cafe; all the shops below are busy. Florence does not sleep at night.

And then I glance up: there, close enough to touch, it seems, is the lantern of the Duomo, illuminated, keeping watch over the city. It's as enormous as the eye of God and inspires in me a sense of awe that is not familiar. I remember that from almost every narrow street in *il centro* I've seen the Duomo looming, a presence to make me gasp. Whoever sleeps in the bed in this room can see the lantern from her pillow. What dreams it must inspire I can only guess.

Sometime after eleven a few more students arrive, dressed as Martians or monsters or Madonnas (they must have spent their entire Italian budget creating these costumes). The noise (though less than before), the smoke, the heat from their dancing bodies, the disco atmosphere they aspire to spin around them, creates a kind of inferno, perhaps not so different from the one in which Dante wandered.

Joe and I have sunk, forgotten, on the couch. Drink has dulled the awareness of the party-makers; they don't know we're present. One girl collapses from too much drink and has to be carried to one of the bedrooms. Another runs—sick—to the bathroom.

"I think we should leave," I whisper to Joe. "We have to catch the last bus, you know."

He nods, takes my hand, leads me through the labyrinth of gyrating bodies. We say goodnight to no one. As we pass the door of the room from which I looked upon the lantern of the Duomo, I see two figures sitting on the far edge of the narrow bed: the princess and Lulu, or Sara and Phil, or Beatrice and Dante, it hardly matters which. These two are clasping hands, looking deep into one another's eyes. They are young, they are in Italy, and, clearly, for this moment, they are wildly in love. What more can one ask for life to offer?

36

Gypsies (*Zingari*)

We see gypsy women everywhere. In the entryway of every church an old gypsy woman sits nodding or sleeping on the floor, her head covered with a kerchief, her little dish of coins held in her hand or on the floor beside her. Young gypsy women accost us in the piazzas, at the train station, in front of monuments and fountains, on street corners. They come at us in groups, in their thin flowered dresses and shawls, their dark ragged hair flying about their faces. Surrounding us, chattering, they hold out their hands cupped as if to catch rain. It's a strange song and dance they do—a chorus of distraction, pleading, and threatening all at the same time.

On the day Joe and I visit the Brancacci Chapel at the Carmine church, a flock of gypsies swoops upon us like angry birds, circling and chanting. Two are holding babies in their arms. One of the women holds up in front of Joe a piece of torn cardboard as if it communicates an urgent message, as if he must read it and learn an important lesson. Puzzled but polite, he leans forward to see what it says. Suddenly the woman throws the cardboard at Joe's face, at the same time grasping his arm in her claw-like fingers and moving so close to him that her face almost touches his.

Startled, Joe uses his fists to punch the air about him, showing he will be quite willing to punch the woman if she persists. I see her face turn dark and ugly, she snarls at him— then hisses what must be a curse—and in a flash of skirts the gypsy thieves are gone, dispersed to the four corners of the earth. Joe checks his wallet and finds it still in his pocket. A strange expression stays on his face for a long while afterward; not so much anger as disappointment, not so much fury as sadness.

A few days later, when I arrange to meet Cornelia for lunch in front of the Grande Mondo Ristorante Cinese, I arrive early and stand outside the restaurant, watching a pretty gypsy girl of about ten as she walks out in heavy traffic on the corner of Via Aretina and Via del Gignoro. When the traffic comes to a halt at the red light, she moves about between the cars, knocking on the drivers' windows and proffering her red plastic dish for money. She has a sweet, almost ethereal smile; not many refuse her. Women, particularly, open their purses and toss a few coins in her dish. When she's rejected, she smiles just as sweetly and shrugs—then moves on to the next car.

I wonder, is her mother nearby watching? Or is the child set down here to do her day's work, left alone in the middle of a busy thoroughfare? When the light changes and the traffic moves on, the little girl comes to stand near me in front of the restaurant. Together we watch the fish in the aquarium displayed in the window. In the tank are two long gray eels and a number of goldfish.

The little girl reaches up and touches the fringed edge of my pink scarf, the one given to me by my friend Paola in the *mercatino usato*.

"*Bella,*" she says. "*Molto bella.*" The gold threads of the scarf glitter in the sun.

"*Un regalo,*" I say, hoping this may explain to her why, because it was a gift to me, I can't give it to her. Perhaps I *should* give it to her. It would surely please her. But then her mother (she could even be the same woman who threw the cardboard in Joe's face) would take it from her and sell it or keep it herself. I move cautiously away from the child, worrying about where her fingers will go next. Her eyes stay upon my face. She says something to me, holding out her dish, and I make my usual apology.

"*Sono americana. Non parlo italiano.*"

She smiles all the more fetchingly.

"*Non in scuola?*" I say. However wrong my construction may be, she understands, smiles and shakes her head.

Encouraged by the possibility of conversation, I continue: "*La macchina—non pericolosa?*" meaning to say isn't it dangerous for her to be out among the cars?

She nods and shrugs—as if to indicate the danger goes with the territory. She reaches up to finger my scarf again. Just then Cornelia appears around the corner and shakes her head at me in warning.

"I've been talking to my new little friend," I say. Cornelia turns to her and says a few words in Italian. They converse. The child tells her name: Antonella. Cornelia opens her purse and places a 500-lire coin in her dish. They talk a little more—something about school, something about don't you want to go to school? The child nods—she wants to. But she can't. In fact, there is a red light now, and the cars are stopped. She hurries back to work.

In the restaurant, the waiter seats us just beside the fish tank at the window that looks onto the street. We watch the fish, and, beyond, we watch the little girl begging with her little dish held out in traffic. After we order our meal, Cornelia tells me how the gypsies know how to steal from almost anyone, true acts of magic and mystery. How even a man whose wallet is buttoned into his pants under his long coat will find it missing after an encounter with gypsies. "They have lessons for this," Cornelia says, "they are trained in the ancient art of thievery." She explains that a gypsy woman who appears to be carrying a baby in her arms may actually have a false arm, a wooden shelf, supporting the child, while her free arm can slip under your coat and steal your wallet. "The gypsies are a great problem in Italy," she says. "They have no written language, they refuse to let their children go to school. They live in caravans at the edge of the city. They live by scavenging and stealing."

We look through the water of the fish tank and watch the child standing in the stream of cars and motor scooters, a small vulnerable soul in a red jacket. When she acquires several donations, she quickly takes the coins from the dish and deposits them in her jacket pocket.

Cornelia suddenly taps the glass—at first I think she is calling to the child, but it's not that—the goldfish in front of our eyes is eating, bite by bite, the flesh of one of the eels in the tank. The fish attacks the eel with his mouth, and a small wound, like an ulcer, appears on the skin of the eel. With each attack, the hole grows larger.

"Oh, how awful," Cornelia says. "Scavengers and thieves on such a pretty day."

When our appetizers are served, Dragon chips and *primavera* egg rolls, Cornelia and I eat and talk, no longer thinking about the gypsy child till we hear a tapping on the glass. Outside, the little girl is standing at the window, now holding a large baby in her arms and smiling at us. The baby has a great round head and huge black eyes.

Antonella stares hungrily at the food on our table. Her eyes take in the white tablecloth, the stemmed crystal glasses filled with ruby-colored plum wine, the golden crisp steaming egg rolls. The Chinese waiter arrives with more food—our first course of sweet and sour pork, and *pasta al pomodoro alla cinese,* fragrant with bits of ham, shrimp, and chicken in it.

There is so much poverty and pain in the world, so much grief. Cornelia and I agree we would like to fix it, for everyone.

When we look up again, the child has disappeared, but the goldfish, pecking and digging at its prey, continues without mercy to make its meal of the eel.

37

"A Pistol That Shoots a Big Nail in Front of the Animal"

Our landlady, the Countess Rina Masotti, calls long-distance from her *fattoria* in Colle Val d'Elsa to invite us to visit her farm. She wonders whether we would like to come next weekend or wait for the day in December when the pigs are slaughtered. I tell her, as politely as I can, that I'm not sure I'm ready for that experience. What happens on such a day?

"Oh, it's a long and complicated story," she says (she means too long to explain by long distance, as the phone *scatti* click by). "But you have e-mail, yes?"

"Yes," I say.

"I'll write to you about it. Tell me your e-mail address. Then you can decide, and we can set a date for you to come."

The next morning when I log on to check my e-mail, there is a letter from the countess.

> *Subject:* PIGS
> *To My Dear American Friends,*
> *If you would like to come on the day the three pigs are transformed into "salami" etc., etc., you will see the "special-*

ist" whose" profession" name is "NORCINO". *The day before
the pigs will be killed with a kind of pistol that shoots a big
nail in front of the animal and it dies immediately. The blood
is collected to be used for a special kind of "salame" made
with blood, fat and salt and spices. Each pig is cut into several
pieces, after having taken away the hair with very hot water.
This day there are at least three men helping the "killer" who
is not the "norcino": he will come only the day after to transform the pieces of pigs' meat into salami, finocchiona (salami
with seeds of wild fennel), ham (the typical Tuscan one which
is rather salted, that matches very well with our unsalted
bread), sausages (excellent with beans and tomato sauce!!!)*

*With the head of the pig we make a very good tasting food
named "soprassata" also with salt and spices and, in addition,
garlic and some lemon. Here they say that of the pig you eat
everything, and it is true. The remaining fat is cooked and it
will be used, instead of the oil, to fry potatoes (delicious!)*

*I could continue for hours to list food made out of pig
meat or fat. The day of the processing is an exciting and important day for the farm: the farmers join us to help the "norcino" (who acts like a surgeon) and all are busy around. Outside there are two fires burning: one has a huge cauldron
where the heads of the pigs are cooking and the other is used
to cook the fat that will become "strutto." Inside, in the large
kitchen a lunch for the "staff" will be prepared, using also
some fresh meat of the pigs. Believe me, it is a rustic, old-
fashioned and very interesting happening! I do not like to see
animals be killed—but I must accept the way of living in a
farm.*

*If this will be too difficult for you to see, I understand of
course, and we will be pleased to have you come another day,
and perhaps share a small light lunch with us.*

On the day we travel to Col Val d'Elsa, the next weekend (I have told
Rina—with some relief—that we must forgo the December slaughter

invitation since we have reservations to fly home on December 5), a freezing fog hangs over Firenze, and the same route we took on the SITA bus toward Siena is today buried in a gray, dull haze. Without the sunlit fields, the high blue sky, the mountainous clouds, the trip is tedious and seems endless. Furthermore, there are five travelers more than there are seats, and the four men and one young woman who stand in the aisle beside us, though patient and uncomplaining, manage to make me extremely uneasy. I know Joe is likewise discomforted; he may be wondering whether he should give the seat to the young woman, who is at least thirty years his junior, whereas many hale young men on the bus seem to feel no obligation to do so. This is not a route on which people get on and off the bus at every stop—once boarded, one is pretty likely to be going all the way to Siena, or Poggibonsi, or to a city at least an hour out of Florence.

I begin to redesign the laws of Italy in my mind: there will be no more tickets sold than seats on SITA bus routes, for one thing. Bus drivers will be permitted to sell tickets *on* the bus to confused tourists who have no idea when they first arrive how the bus system works. Banks and museums will never close their doors upon a whim. Strikes will be limited to two a year and announced in advance. Better heating will be provided in the cold museum rooms where guards have to sit all day. The postal system will not charge an additional tax when delivering a letter or parcel from someone who has already paid a high postal fee in her country. Flu shots will be made available in a logical manner so that a person does not have to buy the vaccine and go in search of a needle. Sidewalks shall be designed larger than ten inches wide. Pooper-scooper laws will be instituted and enforced. Airport waiting rooms will have clear glass windows that permit one to see arriving visitors. Mufflers will be required on motor scooters. Water will be served without charge in restaurants. And, finally and of great importance, no-smoking laws will be enforced in all restaurants, bars, trattorias, and cafes.

There, I have already improved the quality of life in Italy a thousandfold.

When I look out the window again, I see that the sun is glowing behind the fog. Its heat is drying the water droplets, lifting them bodily from the hills, the treetops, the orange tile roofs, the spires of the churches, the skins of the olives. The curtain of fog rises slowly as we speed along the curving road, revealing a scene that cannot—by any law—be improved upon. The Italians around me are sleeping, or talking to their companions, but not one is looking out the window. I tap Joe's hand and point. The landscape is as soothing as a balm to the eyes, green and gold, curved, slanted, shadowed, and magnificent.

Joe considers the view. He says, finally, "That's exactly what they saw, the great painters. They saw it, and put it in their paintings."

My camera is a sorry substitute for art, but I raise it, aim it out the window, and capture what I can of this dream-like vision.

Rina has directed us to inform the driver to let us off at *fermata Hotel Belvedere* just past the main city stop of Colle Val d'Elsa. Though Joe told the driver this when we boarded, it is now two hours later, and I urge him to remind the man again. He resists, I insist. (I see ourselves going all the way to Naples before we get off the bus.) But the same instinct that keeps men from asking directions must keep my husband from questioning the driver before there's absolute reason to. I bite my tongue, trying to figure out how we will get back to wherever we should have got off the bus in the first place. We are now at least a mile or two past Colle Val d'Elsa. But Joe is vindicated when the bus stops at what seems the middle of nowhere, and the driver looks back toward us and nods.

"*Grazie, grazie!*" I call down the aisle. I am grateful and embarrassed to have doubted the man's abilities. I wish I could make it up to him somehow. I do wave to him as he drives away. As for apologizing to Joe, I hold to my belief that I always prefer to be safe rather than sorry.

The Hotel Belvedere stands facing the highway in palatial splendor. It looks like a five-star hotel (though I've never stayed in one), but we don't stop to visit it, since Rina advised me to walk "right past the hotel, up the dirt road beside it to the *fattoria,* where I will meet you. I will know the time the bus should be here."

And she does meet us, there she is, my beautiful landlady, right on time, wearing rubber work boots, pants, and a jacket, smiling warmly as she walks forward to greet us. The grass is soaked by the morning fog, and already my shoes are completely wet.

"Forgive me, that I did not meet the bus on the road, but I have been busy with Roberto feeding the horses just now, and I must hurry back. Will you mind walking around yourselves for a while? In that direction you will see the turkeys and rabbits, and beyond is the garden and the small pool (the larger pool is at the hotel), and here just behind us are the pigs."

The pigs! The doomed-to-salami pigs! My heart goes out to them even before I see them: three, enormous pink creatures with curly tails and intelligent eyes. They have just come out of a rather fine stone hut, with a red-shingled roof, surrounded by a fenced yard. They look at us inquisitively, trustingly. They don't know what we know about the pistol that shoots a big nail into the animal. They don't know about salami seasoned with seeds of wild fennel or that their heads are destined to be transformed, with lemon and garlic, into *soprassata.* They certainly don't know, on this fine fall day, that their skins will be removed from their persons and dumped into a boiling cauldron. I wish I didn't know it myself.

"Which way are the gardens?" I ask, and Rina directs us, telling us she'll meet us in just a little while in the main dining hall, where we will all have lunch.

The formal garden is simple and elegant, a few pieces of statuary, some small lemon trees in large terra cotta pots, a line of cypress trees on either side of the path. Further away, the small circular pool is covered by a tarpaulin, and close by it is a caged area in which several large turkeys and a few hens are clucking and foraging for seed. The turkeys have brilliant red necks and heads, black feathers, and a ring of ridged white tail feathers. They, too, are no doubt destined for the dinner table. This is a farm, I remind myself, and this is what farms are about.

I prefer not to contemplate the ends of these animals' days but rather to walk in the vineyards and olive groves. I take Joe's hand and urge him to follow me toward the fields, far from the animals. When we come full circle around the garden, Rina is waiting for us outside the dining hall. She tells us that they have prepared a very simple lunch—please to come in and sit down.

The count himself is setting the long dining table with lovely painted dinner plates; he puts out wine glasses and a bottle of his very own vineyard's Chianti Classico wine. Rina says, "And please meet Roberto, my husband." We both shake hands with him. Roberto tells us has heard from Rina that Joe is a professor; he, too, is a teacher, of math and of geology. The farm is a family responsibility they have taken on in order not to lose the land that has been in his family for seven hundred years. Did we notice the dovecote? That is their next project—to make it into additional apartments to rent to summer visitors. This whole business, this *agriturismo* has become very popular, especially with German tourists, who want to come to Tuscany, but not so much to the busy city centers as to the countryside.

"Let us eat, we can talk as we eat," Rina says to us. "Would you like to wash up?"

Even the bathroom is rustic, farmlike, the shine of years is on the floor and walls, the towels, dried outside on the line, are rough to the touch, perfumed with the scent of fresh air.

The most ordinary matters of Italian life seem to me, at times, the most desirable, the most perfect forms of existence. To think that Italians take these daily moments for granted, to know that such scenes and scents and tastes are their due, is an astonishment to me. Is heaven only heaven when you may not have it?

When I return to the table, Rina announces. "And look, in your honor, finally, the sun has come out with all her smiles."

The brightening light gleams through the glass double doors onto the red-and-green checked tablecloth, illuminating a large basket lined with dried fall leaves and filled to the brim with oranges, pears, and apples. Roberto has poured wine that has been transformed to rubies in the shining goblets. Rina begins to slice a crusty loaf of coarse bread

Farm fruit and wine

on the cutting board. Crumbs fall onto the tablecloth and lie there like tiny jewels.

I take out my camera to capture this moment for later, our friends' good will, this gift of still life, the glowing shape and shadow of fruit, wine bottle, sunlight, and bread.

38

A Farm Feast, Colle Val d'Elsa, Bongo Drums for the Bishop

Hot spaghetti, swimming in olive oil, garlic, red pepper, and parsley, is dished high by Rina upon my flower-encrusted dinnerware till I cry *"Basta!"*

"I hope you don't mind garlic," she says. This does not seem a problem for me, since, once I begin to eat, the wine dilutes most pleasantly any shock to the tongue, whether induced by too much garlic or too much *peperoncini*.

While we swirl the strands of spaghetti around our forks, the Count and Countess tell us of their busy lives, lived half the year in Florence and the rest at the farm. Their *Fattoria Belvedere* is one of a group of seventeen farms in the area between Florence and Siena that offer rustic accommodations at a much lower price than a hotel vacation would cost. (An apartment for two in *Fattoria Belvedere* costs this year about $300 a week.)

All those who run the farms cook home-made food (or sell their farm products to the visitors who may want to cook in their own apartments) and offer activities such as cooking classes, horseback riding, folk dancing, country hikes, fishing, and various activities for the children.

In addition, Roberto tells us, here at the *fattoria* they make their

189

own wine, and if, after lunch, we'd like to see his small wine-making apparatus, he'd be pleased to show it to us. The wine, he tells us, is made from their own grapes: Sangiovese, black Canaiolo, Tuscan Trebbiano, and Chianti Malvasia. (Rina says it is all written in their little booklet, if we'd like to have a copy to take home with us.)

When I have eaten all I can of the pasta and imbibed all I can handle of the delicious wine, I push my chair back, expecting we will shortly leave to see the wine cellar, but Rina goes to the kitchen and comes back with an enormous bowl of green, ragged-edged escarole. She disappears, to return again with a pottery casserole filled to the brim with beans and sausages. To all of this she adds additional slices of the coarse Tuscan bread.

"You said a simple lunch! A light lunch!"

"Oh, but this is. This is what we eat every day at lunch. We work so hard, we are very hungry at lunch time."

"If this is simple, then what is a fancy meal?"

"If you could come next Friday night, you would see. That's when we make the farewell dinner at the end of the season for all our guests. On that night, we serve all our special recipes. After that we shut down the farm for the winter and do all the repairs and work on the apartments."

The beans are delicious, plump, and tender in tomato sauce, but when I cut into the thick, round sausage, oozing with juices and fat, I see the curly tails and the bright eyes of the pigs in their pen. I do the best I can with it, not wanting to offend our hosts, but in the end most of the sausage remains on the plate.

"Don't worry," Rina says, clearing my plate away. "We know Americans these days don't eat so much meat as we do."

This time I don't make a move to leave the table. I wait for the last course, which is dessert, a cake made from chestnut flour and pine nuts, dark, delicious, and sweet. Rina serves it with espresso coffee, strong and pungent. I sigh with contentment as we sit, relaxed, and talk about our lives and children. Again I have the sense of how Italians live in the moment, take their reward after working hard, and relish the gifts of food and rest well earned.

Roberto leads us to the small stone building that houses the wine cellar, while Rina stays behind to tend to the kitchen. We follow him carefully down the stone steps to a chilly room, where he shows us four tanks for storing red wine and only one for white wine. (This last has an engraving on it of grapes and grape leaves painted in pastel colors, an image that lends a warmth and softness to the chill of the cell-like room.)

I open the brochure Rina has given me and read:

Fattoria Belvedere wine is characterized by a lively ruby-red color; the bouquet is intensely vinous with hints of violets; the taste is dry, harmonious, sapid, slightly tannic, lively, and full-bodied. The alcoholic strength is around 12 percent. It is a wine for the entire meal, best with pasta dressed with meat sauces, boiled and stewed meats, but also excellent with roast white meats and sheep's milk cheese of average ripeness.

This is the same wine we had for lunch, with pork sausage and beans. I am certain that no matter what food it accompanies, it must bring a thrill to the veins, a limpness to the limbs, and a dreamy glow to the mind . . . as it has to mine.

When we return to the dining hall, Rina suggests we might like to see Colle Alta, the ancient medieval city high above the farm fields and pastures, famous for its crystal glass works and for having been the city where Arnolfo di Cambio was born, the same man who built the Palazzo Vecchio in Florence. She suggests that Roberto and she drive us up to the top of the mountain and leave us there to explore the city. Then, if we would like to join them for dinner, Roberto will pick us up at an appointed time and place.

There is a problem with this plan—the last bus to Florence leaves Colle Val d'Elsa's main square at 8 P.M.. Rina agrees that dinner would barely be on the table by that hour. So we decide that we'll say goodbye in Colle Alta. We'll find our way down the mountain ourselves (at least it will all be downhill!) and catch the bus to Florence at the scheduled hour.

We climb into Roberto's Jeep-like vehicle, Rina in the front and we in the back—and he pulls out onto the dirt road. Our teeth shake as the wheels take the ruts; the metal frame rattles and clanks as we begin the climb to the medieval hill town.

He lets us off at the Palazzo Campana, a handsome, four-hundred-year-old villa built on a viaduct that now serves as the arched gateway to Colle Alta. Roberto and Rina bid us a warm farewell, making us promise to visit at the farm again sometime. Then they are gone, leaving us in another world, mountainous, picturesque, alarmingly fortified, as if each family living here still feared invasion and attack.

The city wall along a precipitous cliff is dotted with narrow peepholes from which Joe says, centuries ago, watchmen stood guard. The streets are arranged, maze-like, angling suddenly into unknown territory, a torturous and twisted set of pathways and alleys between buildings. We set out to see it all, this embattled, threatened world. Yet children are playing in the street, a gelato cup stands on a stone stair, dogs and cats are basking in the sun. Clearly it is a city under siege no longer.

Passing the shops famous for crystal, we study the shimmering inventions in the window. My gift-seeking sense is always on the alert, but as soon as I imagine packing glass in my stuffed suitcases I relinquish the impulse. (Though I did buy my daughters tiny blown-glass cats in Venice, they will occupy not two square inches in my suitcase when I go home.) These crystal objects are large, imposing, heavy, elegant. If I must spend money here, a gelato will do.

We walk all afternoon, from the city's gateway at Palazzo Campana to the very far end of the hill town where, at the tip of the world, a great open piazza looks out over all of creation. Such a view seems to inspire young lovers, for at every lamppost there stands a melded form, two closely entwined figures wrapped together and contemplating an eternity of love.

By dusk, we realize we may have a very long walk down the mountain to the city center below, where the SITA bus arrives at 8 to take us back to Florence. We begin our leisurely downward trek. Coming back through the city, we notice a great crowd forming in front of the town's duomo—all the townspeople apparently turning out for some event. The men are in suits, the women in fine dresses, and the children in Sunday best.

I take Joe's hand and lead him in the open door of the church, where, apparently, some kind of ceremony is being prepared for. A silken cloth has just been laid at the altar. A gleaming silver chalice is set out, and golden candlesticks. Is this going to be *un matrimonio religioso*? If so, I badly want to stay for the wedding ceremony! I must stay! "Please," I tell Joe, "let's just take a seat and wait."

But how long can we wait? What about the 8 P.M. bus? That's still an hour from now. But how long will it take us to walk down the mountain? What if we miss the bus? We can always go back to the *fattoria* (if we can find it!) and ask for lodging at the farm. There might even be a hotel in the town. Or we could stay at the Hotel Belvedere, why not? (We have our credit cards with us!)

Just then two young men wearing especially shiny black shoes arrive in the church, each carrying a set of bongo drums! And two other men follow with speakers, wires, a microphone, electric amplifiers. Is this to be a rock concert?

I notice a pile of flyers in a little box on a table near the entrance. I take one and ask Joe to decipher it. He studies the page. "It says something about a dedication by the bishop. Or to the bishop. I can't tell."

"Could this be it happening right now?"

Joe doesn't have a clue.

"Should I ask someone?" But there is no one to ask without seeming intrusive. We know we don't belong here.

The guests who have been standing outside are filing in and taking seats. Some of the women wear large hats with flowers upon them. Perhaps whatever is bound to happen will actually take place now. But, no, our impatience is not rewarded. The musicians plug in the machinery, test it, and unplug it. Joe assures me that whatever is supposed to happen will take hours to begin and hours more to take place. If it's a dedication, there will be long speeches; if it's a religious service, there will be lengthy prayers. It doesn't seem to be a wedding; no bride is in evidence. I try to reconcile myself to the fact that is not our fate to be at this ceremony in Colle Alta. It's our fate to take the bus home.

We do have to hurry. The downhill walk is extremely steep; in certain places the narrow road slants down in an almost vertical drop. As cars pass us by, we must flatten ourselves against the wall of rocks bordering the road. My knees are aching from the strain. I have the sense I could tumble forward and somersault all the way down the hill. But the descent is surely a longer distance than we thought it would be, and the hour is later than we thought. We rush along, thinking of home, of Florence, and how it seems absolutely essential to get back tonight, to our safe apartment, to our comfortable, most desirable basket of a bed.

When we come in view of the city center, our bus is already in the square, parked and waiting to leave. The driver is inside; the doors are still locked. I immediately take my place at the front door, first in line. (Others seem to be waiting for the bus on the edge of the square, talking with one another. But I am so tired! I must get a seat for the two-hour trip home. If I had to stand in the aisle, I'm sure I would collapse.)

We wait. We wait even longer. It is well past 8 P.M. Finally, the driver opens the front door. I step up into the bus (Joe is behind me, tickets in hand.) But the driver holds me back. Shakes his head. Points toward the rear door of the bus, which he has now opened. People are pouring in. Many people. Maybe more than there are seats on the bus.

"But, but . . ." I sputter, meaning: I was here, I was waiting patiently in line, I did the right thing. But apparently it's the wrong thing. The driver says something gruffly about *controllo*—I'm in the wrong place for the wrong reason. The ticket machine is at the back of the bus; that's where I must get on. I look at the line waiting to get in the back door, and now we will be at the end of it.

Oh! *Keep your Italy!* I think. *Keep your dumb rules, your bishops and your bongo drums, and all the mysteries I can't in the least penetrate. Keep your palazzi and your magnificent views and your lovers. Just let me on the bus. Just let me get a seat home.*

39

Picasso in the Dustbin, Windmills on the Wall

On Saturday morning Joe calls me to the window. I have been writing e-mail letters home to my children and sister and have just called the Compuserve phone number in Rome. I am counting the *scatti* as they click by in rapid fire while I am waiting for the "connected" signal to appear on my computer screen.

"Come right now," says Joe, and I jump up, thinking the Mafia bus must be passing at this unlikely hour or that a monster has risen straight out of the Arno.

As I approach the living room window, Joe says, "A woman just dropped a painting in the dumpster out there, a big framed painting, and then she jumped in her car and drove away."

"And?"

"Well, I know you don't like the decorations in this apartment very much. . . . "

"*And?*"

"I thought you might want to go down and look."

"You want me to go hunting in the *garbage?* I thought you don't approve of me doing that sort of thing."

"Well, I thought you might want to see what she put in there."

"What if someone sees me?"

I don't even want my husband watching. I still remember, all too clearly, the magazines-in-the-trash episode and how Joe responded to it. I prefer to be alone when I pick up discards. Still, I get my key and tell him I'll be right back. The tiny elevator carries me down. On the first floor landing I smell the aroma of vegetable soup coming from Signora Carezza's apartment.

The garbage dumpster is just across the road from our outer gate; at least I should have remembered to take down our own kitchen trash. Even when I tie it up in a plastic bag and leave it directly in front of the door, I tend to forget to take it down when I go out.

The dumpster (what Cornelia calls a "dustbin") is a large blue metal container on wheels; it has the distinct advantage of being able to be opened by a foot pedal. I put my weight on the pedal, and the lid flies up. I peer over the edge. Sure enough, there's a large framed painting inside, sitting on top of the bags of trash. I haul it out. It's heavy, I have to use two hands (and still keep my foot on the pedal). For a moment I fear my keys will slip out of my right hand and fall to the bottom of the garbage heap.

But I manage to hang onto my keys and keep my grip on the painting, too. It's a Picasso, of course. If you're going to find a painting in the trash, it might as well be a Picasso. This one is a charcoal drawing of Don Quixote (with his sword and shield) and Sancho Panza, both slumped on their nags, on their way down the hill to where the windmills sit. It's a portrait of two adventuresome souls, like Joe and me these days. And, like us, they go on, exploring the world, looking a little dopey, a little bedraggled. Providence must have sent me this picture.

I hoist the painting in my arms and glance up toward our apartment. Joe is out on our kitchen terrace watching me. Why doesn't he come down and carry this!

Now I begin to worry about why it was left here. Why would anyone throw away a beautifully framed-behind-glass print? Unless, maybe it isn't a print. Maybe it's a stolen original. Maybe this is a drop-off point for hot merchandise and in one minute the pickup guy will be coming along to get it. He'll find me here with it, stealing it, and he'll mow me down with a machine gun! No wonder Joe sent me down and

Picasso in the dustbin

stayed safely upstairs. No wonder he's watching from up there, in case he has to wave his final good-bye to me.

I had better make my getaway while I can. If I'm murdered, Joe will never find our plane tickets in the cereal box and will never get home to our daughters. He won't have any money left, either, since whatever traveler's checks remain require my signature.

Does he think it's so easy for me to carry this thing first through the gate, then through the door, and then try to fit it into the elevator? I can't get over the fact that I'm holding three famous men in my arms, Don Quixote, Sancho Panza, *and* Picasso.

When I get upstairs, I set the Picasso on the couch. It seems to be in perfect condition; the paper backing is untorn, unmarked. The frame is metallic silver, modern and elegant. I worry a little that Joe will make me go down and put it back for some reason, but he's already checking out the window for further suspicious activity—and sure enough! He calls me over to see—a white van has just pulled up behind the dumpster, a man gets out, looks around, then lights a cigarette and stands leaning against the side of his vehicle.

We confer about the meaning of this, considering the timing. Is the man waiting for the drop-off of stolen goods? Why doesn't he look in the dumpster if that was the prearranged plan? After twenty minutes of standing there, I get tired of watching. The van looks like some kind of repair truck. The driver just seems to be taking a break.

I try to think of another reason a woman would throw out a Picasso. She was tired of it? She hates it because it was a gift from Picasso, her lover?

"Was she an *old* woman?" I ask Joe.

He says he couldn't really see.

Maybe she found out from certain recent biographies of the artist that he was unfaithful to her (an easy guess), so she wants it out of her house; she never wants to look at it again. If that's the case, then it's an original and is worth *millions*! Should I even share this windfall with my husband, who did none of the work of retrieving the treasure? On the other hand, it was he who gave me the hot tip.

The man downstairs finishes his last smoke, gets in his truck, and drives away, leaving us, as usual, without an answer.

I hang the artwork on the wall opposite our bed and spend a good deal of time studying the two travelers. In the white space of blank paper, with just a few evocative strokes of his charcoal pencil, Picasso has captured the entire story of travel: excitement, anticipation, challenge, weariness, confusion, exhaustion. Even thus challenged, his duo of travelers go forth undaunted, persevering, tilting at windmills. It's a lesson for Joe and for me as—daily—we apply ourselves as best we can to unraveling the mysteries of Italy.

40

"Tabu"

Professor Mario Materassi, who teaches American Literature at the University of Florence, invites me to speak to his class. It seems extremely lucky for me that he is an expert in Jewish American women writers, since I happen to be one. I'm especially flattered to be invited to talk about "Tabu," a story of mine that he has photocopied from one of my books and distributed to his class. But he cautions me that his students are not like the Italians in my story.

Italians in my story? I have no recollection of this. Since I have with me in Italy the collection of my stories, *Chattering Man,* in which "Tabu" appears, I look it up and leaf through it until I find what must be the relevant paragraph. To my dismay I read:

Five Italian boys I recognized from the lunchroom at school were there in Ruthie's living room, slouched on the couch and slumped in the two armchairs. They looked as if they didn't belong on furniture, but should instead be on leashes or in cages.

So much for tact and my effort toward good Italian-American relations. I will have to make my apologies to the students and explain something about the context of my insults.

Professor Materassi has a university office on Via San Gallo that must once have been a room in a great *palazzo*. The elaborate ceiling, high above a gilded border of engravings, is three dimensional; various creatures (cherubs and satyrs) peer down from above. The paintings on the walls, separated by great arches, depict dramatic events: two shepherds, one holding a great wooden club, look upon a felled enemy who lies bleeding on the ground, while in the background two sheep and a black-faced lamb lie nearby watching. If these are depictions of allegorical tales whose stories I should know, I don't. Yet I am quite willing and able to marvel at their grandeur, their awesome size—and to think: all this in a "mere" university office.

The professor tells me he has prepared my class for two days for this discussion of my story (and mentions, offhand, that, from the beginning of the academic year, the class has been discussing Faulkner's *The Sound and the Fury*). Of course I am pleased by his serious attention to my work.

When he leads me to his class, I do my best to speak in slow and precise English that the students seem to understand quite well. They are attentive and respectful and look much as students do in an American university: blue jeans, book bags, and radiant young faces (especially here! So many beautiful young Italian men and women). I try to communicate how this story of mine came to be, based as it was on a party I was forced to attend as a thirteen-year-old. The villainess was a sexy beauty who lived across the street. Her mother insisted that she invite me, a neighborhood kid, to her birthday party.

I'm tempted to apologize to the professor's class for how the Italian boys are viewed in the story (also to explain how Italian boys, in our neighborhood, were reputed to be the most handsome, sexy, and dangerous!). The students have already read the other passage in the story about Italians, which I hope they will take in the spirit intended:

We were in the first year of high school that winter. Ruthie had begun traveling with a different crowd. Dark, handsome Italian boys, who wore the top three buttons of their shirts undone and sported large crucifixes that gleamed aggressively from the swirls of their black chest hair, circled about her in the lunchroom. As if witnessing a miracle, they hopped about and genuflected as she delicately dipped potato chips into a swirl of mustard that she had dabbed onto the center of the cellophane bag.

"I hope you understand," I tell them, "that when I was thirteen years old I desperately wanted an Italian of my own." They are kind to me and laugh.

When class ends, the professor introduces me to one of his students, Emanuela de Carlo, who has asked him whether she may translate several of my stories into Italian for her graduation thesis. She is a dark-eyed, dark-haired beauty who speaks English carefully and profoundly. I am touched that she would want to spend months bringing my words into the music of the Italian language. When we talk for a while after class, I realize she has already read all the stories in my book that Professor Materassi has loaned to her. She knows them better than I do, she can quote phrases to me. "I will send to you my thesis when I have finished it," she tells me.

When we part, I can't stop myself from hugging her. I have been away so long from my daughters! This young woman is so sweet and warm-hearted that I love her already. In all the ways that Italy has become part of me in these weeks I have spent here, I'm thrilled to think that, with Emanuela's help, I will—in some small way—become part of Italy.

When the students have departed, Professor Materassi takes me to a small cafe on Via San Gallo, where we are joined by his wife, Millicent, who asks what I would like to eat. I defer happily to her to choose my food. She orders us each a small *panino* of salty ham and cheese, followed by an eclair filled with custard and iced with chocolate. "The salty first," she says, "and then the sweet." And always the cup of espresso to add richness to the tongue and energy to the body.

(This is not lunch, she reminds me, but a mere midmorning snack. I am invited later to their apartment for an Italian *pranzo*—to share pasta and other delights.)

Professor Materassi must return to his teaching duties, and Mrs.

Materassi offers to take me with her on various errands and to show me more of the city. Near the hospital of Santa Maria Nuova, on Via della Pergola, she points out the ticket windows of *Amici delli Musica,* which is in the Teatro della Pergola—a grand old eighteenth-century music hall where concerts are performed. We must not miss seeing one; she will arrange for tickets for us at the earliest opportunity.

We take a bus across the river to the Red Cross shop, where Mrs. Materassi leaves off a bag of donations and I buy a wonderful pink sweater (to go with my Chinese acrobat coat); the sweater has a floral design on one half of each sleeve and a geometric design on the other. "Very Florentine," Mrs. Materassi assures me—and, for only 5,000 lire, a bargain. Another good place for bargains is the thrift shop, open on Wednesday morning, at the American Church on Via Rucellai, not far from the station.

I almost cannot keep up with her—she maneuvers the streets with speed and expert knowledge. ("Better to walk on the other side on this street, the sidewalk isn't as narrow," and "This is the finest gelato place in Florence; the owner has lemons shipped in from Sicily because their taste is the best.") Mrs. Materassi, who invites me to call her Millie, is extremely accomplished, knowledgable about all things in Florence that I yearn to know, expert in literature, film, and art, in food, and in all necessary practical matters. The daughter of a Korean ambassador, she speaks Italian with perfect fluency (as does Cornelia), while I can't imagine myself ever getting beyond *"Buon giorno. Sono stanca."* There is something about my mind (stubborn? lazy?) that cannot seem to retain verb forms, although Joe says that isn't true, that I just haven't tried hard enough or practiced long enough.

"When we come back to Italy to live here in our retirement," I tell him, "I'll learn how to speak Italian."

But not now. For now I will happily trail after Millie Materassi, listen to all her tips, recommendations, and bits of advice, and follow her back to her house to share lunch with the professor, their beautiful daughter, Luisa, and their impressive cat, Figaro.

41

Daughters of Florence

The girls downstairs, Maria and Patty, have love problems endemic to young women living the artistic life in Firenze. They are in love with art, with youth, with their own beauty, and with the illusions engendered by living under the eye of the surreal Tuscan sun. Patty's boyfriend thinks he is following in the steps of Michelangelo; he has left her to work with a sculptor in the country and has apparently lost his sex drive, a consequence of using all his creative energies (he tells Patty) for his art. She, on the other hand, wonders whether there is a real-life female model working out in the country with the two men.

Maria, in her quest to enlarge her horizons and to learn the English and Italian languages, traveled from her homeland in São Paulo, Brazil, to study first in England, then in Italy. While in London, two months ago, she fell in love with an Englishman named Morris. He has lately been writing that he wants to marry her. Last weekend she flew to Paris (with tickets he sent her) to meet him again and to allow him to plead his case. "Two days in which to fight, to love, to plan," Maria told me. "How can we know if this is for a lifetime? In my own country I would understand so much about a man, how he is with his family and with mine, what kind of character he has. This is too fast."

Now that her studies are over in Florence, she is leaving to return to Brazil this very afternoon, to go back to her family and her job, and to reflect on the strength of her emotions at a distance from the romantic haze that shimmers in the atmosphere here.

When I find a notice mistakenly put in my mailbox announcing that a package is waiting for Maria at the post office, I knock on her door to give it to her. (I have also received a notice that a package is waiting for me.) Since I don't know exactly where the post office is, I'm planning to ask Maria whether I may accompany her if she plans to claim her parcel before she leaves this afternoon.

She flings opens the door of her apartment wearing only panties and a bra; the smell of floral shampoo wafts to me from her wet hair.

"You should *never* open the door dressed that way!" I say.

"Oh, I saw you through the peephole," she says, laughing. "Come in, I will get some clothes." I follow her inside to the small room she has been sharing with Patty; she jumps into a pair of slacks and pulls a snug black shirt over her head. I think of my own three daughters so far away and so removed from me; I feel a catch in my throat watching this lovely girl.

As if to verify what I am feeling, Maria comes to me suddenly and hugs me. "You are so special to me," she says. "Like my mother, almost. You understand so much."

When she sees me holding the notice from the post office, her face lights up. "Oh, I thought he was lying. He told me when I was in Paris he had sent me a present weeks ago. When it never came, I didn't trust him. How can you know if a man can be trusted when you know him only a few weeks, and then for two nights in Paris?"

I have no answer, of course.

"May I go with you to the post office?" I ask her. "There is also a package for me there."

"I'll get yours, too. I'm going to run there right now and come right back. Then I have to finish packing; my taxi is coming at two o'clock to take me to the station." And she bends to tie her shoes, hugs me again, and is off.

Her face is radiant when she knocks on my door a little while later. "Look what he sent me." She holds out a book of poetry, a silk scarf, some chocolates. Her smile is so lovely, so full of hope, so *transcendent*! She comes into my arms, and we both hug each other as if our hearts will burst, each for our own reasons. (The package she has picked up for me is a bottle of "Skin So Soft," a body lotion sent by Lesley, my good friend in the States, who swears it will repel mosquitoes. As usual, there was a 2,000-lire tax, which Maria paid for me, that mysterious surcharge on all packages received in Italy.)

Maria says she doesn't want to leave me, makes me promise to visit her in Brazil. She will send me pictures of Morris. She will invite me to her wedding. She is so young and beautiful, so hopeful, so vulnerable. I tell myself I am not envious, thinking of the struggles and experiences she will have to face, the loves and the lovers. I tell myself I am relieved to have made most of my important decisions. In a sense, my story is nearly all written, and I am forever safe from certain harms. I should congratulate myself on my sensible choices, my good husband. But somehow this knowledge does not comfort me.

Later, as the hour of 2 P.M. approaches, I watch from my window, compelled to see her departure. I think of all the times I have seen her in the weeks we have been here: Maria sunning on the terrace of our apartment, reading on a bench at the edge of the Arno, studying on the patio of the language school after her class, walking along the Ponte Vecchio (greeting me as if she had just met a long-lost friend). Her energy, her beauty, her long dark hair have become part of my life.

Now, as I see her taxi pull up, as I watch her struggle through the gate with two enormous suitcases and her backpack, I feel a knife of pain and loss go through me. I am certain I will never see her again.

I press my forehead against the cool glass and watch the driver close the trunk, open the taxi door for Maria. Just before she gets in the cab, she pauses and throws a glance toward my window. When she sees me there, she throws me vibrant, exaggerated kisses with both hands.

After the cab drives away, I feel my knees buckle. I don't understand this at all, this wash of grief that consumes me. It has been set loose by my calculations: my own past youth, my grown-up children who need me no longer, my being in Italy at a time of my life that's well past the time for certain possibilities to present themselves. How can I make sense of what has caused this tailspin? I shuffle, sobbing, to my bed, where I give myself up to the storm of passion and wait under the covers for recovery and the return of reason.

42

Massimo's Lizard-Skin Keychains, Riccardo's Castagna

Mai Jing's boyfriend, Massimo, has not forgotten his pledge to make us dinner. On a night wild with rain and thunder, he picks us up at the gate in his little red car, with Mai Jing, smiling and speechless, sitting in the front seat beside him. He tears along the lungarno and over the Ponte Verrazzano to pick up Mrs. Pedrini at her apartment. Believing that Joe knows Italian, Massimo talks at great speed, turning his head over his shoulder to address Joe, while keeping his foot on the gas and ignoring Mai Jing's cries of "Go slow, look out, be careful, you will murder us."

Faith that we will get through this evening alive is what sustains me. Faith is what got me to Italy in the first place: faith that we would have adventures (Joe promised, "I can't tell you exactly what will happen, but something will . . ."), faith that my mother would continue to live (as she has), faith that we would learn how to shop and travel and eat in Italy (we have), and faith that our adventures will ultimately be good ones.

The rain is sheeting across the windshield so heavily that Massimo must thrust his head out of the window in order to see anything at all while he drives. When he stops for Mrs. Pedrini, she runs out to get in the car, the rain plastering her hair to her face. After he takes off with a jolt, she grasps my hand and whispers to me she's lucky she's had seventy-two good years of life so far, since this may well be the end of it.

How do young men get along in Italy? Massimo's means of support is unclear. He appears to be a shining example of health, sexual energy, ambition, cleverness, good humor, and craziness. By interpreting a combination of mime, gesture, and intonation, with footnotes from Mai Jing, we learn he has been, by turns, a judo expert, a mountain climber, a student of psychology, a seller of fish, and a biker who rode 2,700 miles through the Dolomites (or *to* the Dolomites, I can't tell which); now he makes his living by "buying and selling."

What he sells, and to whom, we can only guess. There is much "buying and selling" in Florence; tourists buy, Florentines sell, everything from rosaries to rare antiques, from fake *David* statues to sets of hand-painted Italian dishes, from leather wallets to thousand-dollar Gucci handbags. (There is also the drug trade. When I walk by the river, I often see discarded needles and syringes.)

Like the young men our girls met when they first came here (the men who invited them to the clothing warehouse in the country), Massimo wheels and deals.

After another wild ride, he stops his car halfway up a curb and announces we are at his house: please, to follow him. Jumping through ankle-deep puddles, he leads us up an alleyway, around a corner, through a doorway, until we find ourselves in an ancient building smelling of concrete and cement particles, whose crumbling walls are only half-standing.

"Now just up to the fourth floor," he says, taking the steps two at a time.

Mrs. Pedrini takes my arm on one side, Joe on the other. They know my knees aren't doing that well. "Up we go," Mrs. Pedrini says. "One step at a time."

Massimo, in his two-room apartment (which he tells us he bought for the lire equivalent of $200,000!), is making fish for dinner. Not any fish, but fish fresh from the sea, brought to Florence by a "special friend" of his. He holds up two enormous silvery fish as if they are trophies. (When I shop in the market, I always forgo frozen fish, which sells for an average of about $10 for a single piece.)

We all sit at a tiny wooden table about two feet from his stove (the room is perhaps eight feet long) while he slits the fish, stuffs them with cloves of garlic and parsley, and wraps them in tinfoil. He drops them in a large frying pan over a high flame and then begins making a salad and rice while Mai Jing cooks a Chinese specialty of sausage and noodles.

I try to get my bearings. A large bicycle hangs from a hook on the ceiling. Two canaries sing in a golden cage. Large pieces of glass crystal sit on a shelf, catching the light. Goldfish skim the edges of a glass tank. This Chinese girl, this Italian man, Joe and me, Mrs. Pedrini—we can't really talk about anything meaningful to one another; we almost can't communicate at all. We mainly drink wine, stare dumbfounded, smiling a good deal, and wonder what this evening is about and how it connects to our lives.

None of us are unhappy, however—this is so very nice. We sit in pleasant communion while a wild rain drums outside, while a small fan in the kitchen window spins in the wind of the storm, while the great gray fish cook till Massimo unwraps the tin foil and shows us their dead white hard cooked eyes. I'm at home, a million miles from home, among these people who are not family members but a strange mixture of strangers. I'm oddly, sweetly peaceful, eating good food offered to me by the goodness of heart of this strange young man for whatever his reasons. I'm happy to be comfortable at his small table in his ancient apartment, drinking his wine, laughing at nothing, about nothing much, with others who are equally amiable.

There is more food than anyone could reasonably be expected to consume, and when that is done, more is set on the table. After the last sweet is passed around and the black coffee is served, Massimo untwists a hemp chair from a hook beside the bicycle hook on the ceiling and Mai Jing climbs into it, rocking gently on the rope like a weight at the end of a swinging plumb line. Time spins out, there is no hurry to accomplish anything or understand anything.

Fish dinner with wine

Just before the party ends, just before Massimo is about to drive us all home, he opens a large trunk that is filled to the top with hundreds of small red and black gift boxes. "Take one," he says. (I hope this is not, in view of the coming car trip, our last wish.) Each of us takes a box and opens it. In each box is a lizard-skin key chain stamped with the word "Firenze."

This small, solemn ritual moves us all. Where he gets these exotic key chains and what he does with them is a matter about which we are forbidden to inquire. Our mission is clear: we are on earth tonight in this small, warm Italian circle of light to accept all gifts—food, wine, and friendship—and to question nothing.

The other young man in our lives is Riccardo, who practices English with Joe while Joe practices Italian with him. Each Monday night at nine, Riccardo parks his motor scooter on the street below (I watch from the window in order to buzz him in) and comes up in the elevator, smelling of the Italian night.

Riccardo, who is a graduate student of Professor Materassi's (he

"Giuseppe" and Riccardo

has already written his thesis, on Flannery O'Connor), has a job with the university (but not as a teacher), works evenings in a recording studio with other musicians, all of whom have hopes of recording a CD, and has been engaged to Angela for fifteen years, since they met in high school. Both Angela and Riccardo—as he told us earlier—still live with their parents; they are waiting to get an apartment so that they can get married.

Riccardo and Joe have arrived at a fair arrangement: they talk for one hour in English and one hour in Italian. Sometimes I sit in the living room and listen to them. Joe tells Riccardo about matters of importance in the United States (TV shows, comic strips, movie stars, politics, traffic laws, Mexican food), and Riccardo tells Joe how things work (or, more often, don't work) in Italy. Though I usually set out cookies and soda, Riccardo accepts only mineral water, pleading that he has just come from eating his mother's huge dinner. (How lucky she is, I think, to still have him at home, this handsome, fine young man.)

When the men speak in Italian, I curl up in the leather chair and allow myself to sway in the rhythms of the language like a sea creature moving with the tides. The sounds wash over me, comforting me in their singing fluency, making me think I understand what is being said. For some reason I believe that I soon *will* understand; it's just a matter of being open, of being willing. (It can't have anything to do with reciting, over and over, *"Io sono, tu sei, lei è, noi siamo, voi siete, loro sono."*)

Sometimes I do understand half an idea and interrupt to ask Riccardo to explain something more fully in English. He is patient, extremely polite, as kind to me as he can be, but it's Joe who gets impatient; he wants to get on with the real conversation. He has paid his dues by studying hard, and I haven't. We know what he thinks of that.

Usually, then, I go to the bedroom, lie in my bed, and listen to my Walkman. With little foam earphones in my ears, I hear songs sung in English, listen to the heavy-lidded voice of Cher, the wild animation of the Beatles, the harmonious jive of the Bee Gees.

I do sometimes long to see any TV show, any soap opera, *Jeopardy,* or *Oprah,* or *Days of Our Lives,* something I am fully equipped to understand instead of always wondering what's going on here. On my laptop I have a few computer games, and sometimes I play Solitaire or Free Cell, but games never hold my interest for long. I know there's an English-language film theater in the center, but they are always playing some rough-and-tumble action film or a silly comedy of no interest to me.

From the living room I hear my husband in his new incarnation, "Guiseppe, the Italian," talking in tongues beyond my grasp. Sometimes I feel very lonely in Italy.

If I get up and look out from the back terrace, I can see into a hundred lighted apartments, and in them people are cooking, talking, watching television, raising their children, feeding their pets. This life in Italy takes me outside of my own mortal life here; this isn't real time for me, I don't get old, no decisions of consequence have to be made. I seem formless, undirected. I wish I could float across the distance between buildings and land like a feathered seed in any other body, take on someone else's life and do the impossible thing: know what it's like to live in another's soul, an Italian soul.

One of these nights, when Riccardo is about to leave after his visit with Joe, a large brown nut flies from his jacket as he swings it off the hook in the hall.

I retrieve it for him. He tells me it's a "horse chestnut," *il frutto dell'ippocastano,* a crazy chestnut with magical properties. "If you always carry one in your coat pocket, you will never get sick."

Riccardo gives me his, with his blessing. He tells me not to take it seriously; in fact, he thinks he's catching a cold: he feels a *raffreddore* coming on.

43

No Coins in the Fountain

Our schedule in Rome could kill a horse. The class will have two nights and three days in the Eternal City, during which Nicoletta, who was born there, intends for us to see every church, every monument, every statue, every fountain, not to mention the entire Vatican Museum, all of Saint Peter's, and—if possible—the Pope himself.

I bring to Rome a small, strange, indulgence: a jar of Skippy peanut butter that I find in the Conad market for an exorbitant price. I don't tell Joe that I've packed a heavy, glass object in my suitcase, along with a little loaf of *pane bianco americano* and a knife—he would think me mad. It just seems to me that I'm going to need a little comfort food to hang onto in this three-day marathon.

We are met at the train station by a large touring coach hired expressly to gather us up and deposit us at our hotel, a five-minute ride from the station. Nicoletta and Joe are using a portion of the school funds for this extravagance, convinced it's worth it for all of us to arrive (all at the same time and with our luggage) and then to be transported to the Roman Forum without mishap.

The mishap seems to be the hotel itself, from the looks of the disgruntled clerk at the desk to the smell of the large mangy dog sprawled out in the narrow reception area. The keys to the rooms, as they are distributed, appear to weigh five pounds. A leaden ball is soldered to the top of each key.

It takes forever for the clerk to find which rooms are vacant, to check all the passports of the students assigned to the rooms, and to listen to arguments about who will be rooming with whom.

When Joe and I are assigned our room (the *matrimoniale*), it turns out to be four flights up, with no *ascensore*.

"*Oh, no!*" I say, when the key is dropped into my palm. "*Not four flights up!*"

I plead my knees, which are not faring at all well lately. Nicoletta suggests we trade rooms with two of the students who are on a lower floor. I'm all for it, but the question is: who will trade with us? Joe will have to ask.

Which two students would be willing to sleep in a *letto matrimoniale,* a double bed, without having their integrity impugned? (In fact, it is already a delicate situation, my husband announcing publicly that he and I are willing [in fact, *prefer*] to forgo the delights of a double bed. Must we state our justifications? Make apologies? Must I invite everyone to listen to my knees, which make a strange crackling sound when I bend and unbend them?)

Two of the girls who are good friends volunteer to take our room. One of them is the former marine. I trust no one will draw any untoward conclusions about them. In fact, in my gratitude, I am ready to send these girls flowers and order them room service.

When we get to our room, I can tell at once by the absence of a phone that there is no room service here. I suppose we are fortunate they have furnished us with beds, by the look of things. I fall gratefully upon one of the single beds, exhausted already. The light fixture above my bed has no bulb in it; the one above Joe's does, but it doesn't go on.

The bathroom, which I can see from the bed, is an all-in-one-room affair, walls and floor made of cement and with a drain in the floor so that a shower curtain is not necessary, not even a shower stall. Oddest of all is an electric hair dryer installed on the wall in the bathroom.

With one's feet in two inches of water, once the hair dryer is turned on, the average person's survival time would likely be thirty seconds.

We have only ten minutes to rest. The bus awaits us. Joe offers me a chance before we set out on today's quest to look into one of his many guidebooks: Michelin's *Rome,* or *Rome on a Budget,* or *The Wonders of the Sistine Chapel.* I refuse. I have not even looked out the window at Rome. I seem to want—most of all—to make myself a peanut butter sandwich and take a nap.

Just as I get settled in the reclining seat of the tour bus, it takes off and turns a couple of corners, and the driver stops and opens the doors. That's it? Why can't we see the whole city from this venue of upholstered comfort? But, no, we are now required to disembark just above the Roman Forum. And what do we behold below? A wreckage! A mess of broken-down columns, cracked walls, and crumbling cement— all taking up prime real estate in the center of the world's greatest city.

All right, I should be ashamed to have such a reaction, but push a person beyond her limits and the vulgar and common aspects of her tired soul emerge. The problem is this: why should I already be beyond my limits when we have just arrived? It seems to be an emotional exhaustion, rather than physical. I seem not to want to be here. Why should that be the case? The Fear of Italy I felt when we left the States has been transformed now into Fear of Rome.

I realize that it could be that I have come to consider Florence home. I want to be in Florence! I feel patriotic about Florence. I am finally familiar with its shape, its idiosyncrasies, its flagrant noise and clutter, its transcendent beauty—and just when I have learned to embrace it, and, actually, to love it, I have been dragged away to another city, bigger, noisier, more cluttered, and totally foreign. I will get hold of myself. I am an adult, I am in control of these childish emotions. I am in Rome, the city of great art and history, where Caesar ruled and Michelangelo painted, where the mythical Romulus and Remus were discovered, where gladiators fought in the Colosseum and lions tore men to pieces, where Saint Peter was in chains and where Moses sits glowering with his terrifying horns. And where, if you don't count that the Vatican is a separate city, the Pope resides. Where I have the great good luck to be now.

I think of my friend who named her cat "Be Here Now" to remind herself to live in the moment. I will get off the bus in better humor. I will try to live in the moment. I will look around me. I will learn.

Almost at once there is an unexpected revelation from my husband. As we stand before the rather silly equestrian statue of Italy's first king, Vittorio Emanuele, Joe says to me: "That's what I want for my monument when I die."

"You want to be on a *horse?*"

"On a horse," he says.

"You on a horse? You've never even ridden a horse."

"But that's what I want."

"Who would I hire to do this sculpture? I don't know any horse artists."

"I guess you'll have to ask around, get some referrals."

"And how would I pay for this?"

"I'm sure you'll find a way."

"Yes, if we win the lottery."

"And remember—I want to be wearing a hat on my horse."

"I'll see what I can do. If it's your last wish, I would hate to deny you. . . ."

All this joking sends a chill through my bones. My life as a widow presents itself in all its emptiness, loneliness, and horror. As if my physical being hasn't been worn down enough, my psyche takes a blow below the belt. I imagine myself back in my house in California, sitting at a window on a rainy day with a cat in my lap, looking out at a statue of Joe on a horse with a cowboy hat on his head.

I suddenly lean toward him and kiss his cheek. I don't care how many students might see us, I have to seize the day. In fact, my husband is pleasantly surprised and kisses me back, too. He never inquires into these lightning changes of my moods; he sometimes even tells me he appreciates them.

I wonder: doesn't he ever want to know *why* what goes on in my mind goes on there? Apparently not. Though I'd *always* like to know what's going on in his, and ask him all the time, he rarely seems to know.

When we pass the Column of Trajan, Joe asks that I take a picture of it for him. Just as I am out of my element here, he is in his. How closely he identifies himself with the history he loves, how these great monuments move him! While he looks with awe upon the vistas of the Roman Forum, the Campidoglio, the Circus Maximus, I watch the students who—in their youth and energy—ham it up by posing in ridiculous and exaggerated postures at every famous vantage point.

At the entrance to the Colosseum, a number of the girls pose in turn with a handsome, costumed "Roman soldier" (for a tip, of course) so that their friends can snap their pictures. For the students, this trip is not about history but about themselves. In youth, all things seem to be self-referential (and self-reverential). Whereas Joe, as he gazes at these objects he has so long studied, is self-effaced; he is no more than a point of intellect feeding on these famous representations of ancient story and beauty. Nothing here is about him (except perhaps for his momentary desire to be remembered like the King of Italy, on a horse), whereas for our young students, everything here exists for them, is about them and their friends, is here for their entertainment, a prop for their antics, a backdrop for themselves as hero or heroine: ("How does my hair look?" they say, as they pose for the camera. "Wait! I want to take off my sunglasses!")

Three beautiful cats pose on the stony outcroppings of the Colosseum. As tourists toss them bits of cheese, a parade of ever more hungry cats issues forth from the crevices, their curling tails and patterned fur a design of contrast and order against the ragged stone. Joe is pointing out to his students the battlegrounds, the prime seating areas for heads of state, the boxes where the wives and women sat observing the bloody entertainments that took place below. Now only thousands of feral cats inhabit the ruins where these cruel spectacles took place. They pounce on bits of cheese and bread as the great cats must have pounced upon real men and torn them to pieces so many centuries ago.

Wild cats in the Colosseum

Following Nicoletta at the brisk pace she has set for us, we march around the periphery of the Forum and then walk to the Church of Saint Peter in Chains. There, in a gilded box with glass windows, are displayed the very chains themselves. Who exactly did these chains enchain? Were they wrapped about Saint Peter himself? In Italy, no one is permitted public doubt. No one asks for proof; it would be unseemly. A finger, a head, a chain. If they say it's real, if they display it, if they charge a price to let us see it, we are required to suspend our disbelief.

Inside we are invited to crowd around the great *Moses,* his horns ablaze, his mouth set in anger, the folds of his marble gown and his finger pressing the hairs of his beard as real as life itself. His power, his size, his strength, the burning fire of his gaze engulfs us all until the light goes out, and a visitor is required to deposit another 500 lire in the slot to turn it on.

The Pantheon, a perfectly preserved spherical temple with an open hole in its dome, is situated directly across the square from Burghy's!, a fast food restaurant much like McDonald's. The students are impatient with hearing that the diameter of the dome is equal to its height, that rain falling in the opening never reaches the floor but magically dissipates on its journey downward. They sit on benches around the sides of the structure, tapping their toes, waiting to be set free to feast on French fries and hamburgers. It's been hours since breakfast in Florence, and the aroma of fried potatoes beckons us all. But Nicoletta reminds us of our plan to eat lunch at a trattoria after we visit the Church of Saint Agnes in Agony in Piazza Navona.

The students groan. Another church?

Nicoletta reminds us that there we will see the head of Saint Agnes herself.

More groans. Another head?

"Well, do as you please," says Nicoletta, and we all run, not walk, across the square to Burghys!, where in a few moments we are devouring pretty bad hamburgers and pretty good French fries. The students and we buy packets of ketchup, caution thrown to the winds. We buy as much ketchup as we can reasonably consume, hungry for ketchup, hungry for rest, hungry for a reminder of our old safe life after the threats of Moses' glare, after looking down into the death-corridors of the Colosseum, desperate to fortify ourselves before having to look into the face of Saint Agnes's detached head.

Only after a hearty boost in our blood sugar from fries and Cokes do we set out for Piazza Navona, following in the military pace of Nicoletta's marching feet. Along the way there is so much to see, so many shop windows to examine, so many statues in the middle of nowhere to wonder at, so many pretty babies with dark hair and red cheeks to appreciate, but there will be no loitering, no lingering, no stopping to take pictures. There's a timetable to stick to, there's all of Rome to see.

I balk at the pace. I slow down, I drag my feet. But Mrs. Pedrini comes up to me and takes my arm: "Come now, darling girl, you don't want to get left behind and lost."

I surely don't. I don't even know the name of our hotel. If I get separated from the group, "lost" will be an understatement. I will be homeless in Rome; I will have to sleep under the Arch of Titus, or, worse, in the crevices of the Colosseum with the cats.

Piazza Navona is a long, open piazza with three enormous fountains spread out in great gushing majesty. One of them, Bernini's *Fountain of the Four Rivers,* boasts statues representing the four corners of the earth. How many horses' heads, dolphins' mouths, cherubs' faces can be designed to shoot forth water? More than I can count, apparently, because after a while I can't even distinguish the details of the fountains, don't know what shapes I am seeing, can't process all this information. Nor do I want to consult Joe's guidebooks to learn that "This fountain was built in ——, designed by ——, erected for the glory of the —— family, under the rule of King ——." If anything, I would like to sit at the edge of the fountain, dip my fingers into the water, watch the families strolling by, and just "be here now."

I elect to skip the head of Saint Agnes, though I do allow myself a peek into the church called Saint Agnes in Agony, feeling some sympathy toward anyone suffering agony. After several hours more of fountains, churches, more fountains, and more churches, I turn on my automatic pilot. I let myself be led wherever Joe pushes, prods, or leads me, and, when he abandons me to give a little talk to the students, I stare at the head of someone associated with our group and try to keep it in view so that, when it starts to move, I can direct my feet to follow.

At some point we all enter a trattoria for dinner, and Nicoletta orders Roman delicacies for us to try, stuffed breaded fried green olives, parmesan cheese fritters, and pickled sardines. Mrs. Pedrini orders a large flask of red wine and generously shares it with us, the grownups. I have reached a point of saturation and exhaustion, the likes of which I have never experienced in my life. I try to keep the thought in my head that soon a bed will be forthcoming; that soon I will be able to stop moving.

After dinner, we are all going to walk back to our hotel, wherever it may be. The students beg to be able to take a bus, but Nicoletta says it would be folly to imagine that all forty-one of us could get on the same bus (or even find one). "It's only a few miles," Nicoletta assures us. "And Rome is very beautiful at night. And I want to take you all to the Trevi Fountain on our way back."

I am sure Rome must be beautiful at night, but as we cross the city I have the sense only of hurrying to keep up, of trying not to be struck by cars as we race across huge, wide intersections. Somewhere, in the midst of all this, Nicoletta announces that we are now coming to the Trevi Fountain, famous in history (and in the movies), inspiration for the song "Three Coins in the Fountain." Legend has it that if you toss a coin in the fountain, you will come back to Rome someday. Our students immediately begin throwing coins (over their left shoulders) into the enormous fountain that stands, full of rearing horses and handsome half-naked men, before a magnificent building. The silver and gold coins catch the glint of the floodlights and sparkle through the air like falling stars. The shallow basin of the fountain is glittering with coins several layers deep.

"Do you want some coins?" Joe asks me, digging in his pocket and pulling up a handful of 200-lire pieces.

I shake my head.

"If you throw a coin and make a wish, you'll come back to Rome someday," he urges.

Exactly, I think. *"No, thank you."*

He knows I can't be reasoned with when I'm in this condition. He puts the coins back in his pocket, except for three, which he tosses in the fountain for himself. Fine, he'll probably come back here with his next wife.

When we restart the trek back to our hotel, apparently still miles hence, we reach, at one point, the most enormous flight of steps I have ever seen, wider and higher than the Pyramids. Mrs. Pedrini takes my arm on one side, and Joe on the other; they nearly hoist me up the stairs, one at a time, speaking to me as one speaks to a child: "Just one more, one more, one more, just one more, almost there, here we go, see, you can almost see the last step up there."

I have become a babe in arms, speechless, without volition, without reason, a ball of needs and automatic responses, bleary-eyed, shivering with cold and exhaustion, at the mercy of forces far stronger than I am.

"Almost there," Joe whispers, and then we seem actually to be there, wherever there is. There is a doorway, a large dog that smells, a heavy key handed over a desk to us. Joe leads me gently to a bed in a room, whereupon, fully clothed, wearing my heavy walking shoes and my coat, I lay my head on the pillow—and that is the last I know of my first day in Rome.

44

A Roman Ruin, I, the Sistine Chapel, and Judgment Day

Nicoletta leaves the hotel at 6 A.M. to get in line to buy tickets for all of us at the Vatican Museum. The plan is for Joe to meet her there at 7 A.M. with the students, at which time we will all be ready, at the starting gate, for entry to the hallowed halls of the museum, and, ultimately, the Sistine Chapel.

After a short ride on our hired bus, we disembark at the museum to see thousands of tourists in long lines, corralled between corridors of metal pipes, looking like cattle on the way to slaughter. Their heads are bowed forward into the blasts of cold wind. Hawkers selling rosaries, Sistine Chapel and Trevi Fountain ashtrays, statues of the *David* and replicas of the *Pietà* and *Moses,* walk up and down outside the fenced areas offering their wares. I notice that many of our students—or at least our female students—are buying rosaries.

"Do you think I can get a priest to bless this with holy water?" one of them asks the vendor. He nods vigorously: there is no doubt. If she asked him whether the Pope himself would bless it, the man would surely agree.

When the line starts to move, it doesn't inch forward but jolts into movement till suddenly we are all walking very fast, almost running between the barriers, jogging up a circular ramp, rushing so fast that it's impossible to look around and see where we are.

Nicoletta stands heroically facing us against the surging tide of people and distributes, as we run past her, the tickets she bought for our group. Seconds later they are torn from our grasp by surly-faced ticket-takers as we enter the fabled halls of art and culture and continue to rush along, the press of humanity behind us, and on either side a million marble antiquities, going by us at the speed of light.

Since I can't stop to examine even one piece of art, I begin to take photos of what flies by me, hoping that at some future time the essence that caught my eye can be considered at leisure. I photograph a marble bust of a man who has a lovely sensual mouth, even with his lips of stone. I photograph a statue of a man holding a child (when have I ever seen this combination in Italian sculpture? Surely never before). I record in rapid fire; a series of gargoyles with hideous screaming mouths decorating the edges of a crypt, a series of female heads with pensive, sweet expressions, and a series of marble men in fig leaves, whose musculature and physical beauty are thrilling, even in the half-glance I can give them at this pace.

There is the sound of the thundering hoof beats of the thousands of tourists behind me. I feel a terror overtake me; I must have air. I pull Joe out of the line and flee to an open window in the corridor. From it I can see the dome of Saint Peter's and the green peaceful gardens beneath. (I remember the movie in which Tom Conti, who plays the Pope, tired of all the pomp and circumstance of his life, wanders out the back gate of the Papal Gardens and finds his way to a small village where he befriends the simple folk and finds the true meaning of life.)

"How much of this museum is there to go?" I gasp.

Joe consults his guidebook. "This must be the Gallery of Statues. Next is the Busts Room, the Cabinet of Masks, the Octagonal Court, the Etruscan Museum, the Room of the Chariot, the Raphael Rooms, the Religious Art room, the Borgia Apartment, and, of course, the Sistine Chapel."

"Let's just go to that one and then leave," I beg him. "I think I'm having a panic attack."

Merrill and her camera in Rome

Joe says we must at least see the Raphael paintings. But how to get there? Ropes and museum guards prevent us from straying from the prescribed course. There is no wandering around at your own pace, there is no free will here at all. Various paths have been designed to bring people to the Sistine Chapel by maze-like circumnavigations. We are trapped. We must follow along the prescribed path, the only course to take.

When we do, in fact, get to the Raphael Rooms, the walls are draped in burlap. "In restauro," says the sign. Everything is in restoration in Italy. There can be no arguing with that. The entire country is falling to pieces, is itself a badly kept museum. The facades of half the churches are under burlap and behind scaffolding. Joe will surely not get to see the Raphaels today—and perhaps never.

SILENCE WILL BE OBSERVED IN THE ROOM. THERE WILL BE NO PHOTOGRAPHS TAKEN. . . . SILENCE WILL BE OBSERVED IN THE ROOM. THERE WILL BE NO PHOTOGRAPHS TAKEN.

This message is broadcast over a loudspeaker in the Sistine Chapel at brief intervals as we are funneled through a doorway and are pressed forward with the crowd from one end of the room toward the other. If silence is what they require in this holy room, I wonder whether a loud-speaker is the way to achieve it.

From one of two narrow benches along opposite walls, an Asian couple are just rising; I pull Joe with me and capture the seats in order that we might be able to sit down, lean our heads back, and look up at the famous ceiling. Above me I see God creating Adam (with Eve watching from the shelter of his arm). Those two forefingers, the finger of God and the finger of Adam, straining to touch across the vast heavens (over the vast armies of people below, over the repeated refrain of "SILENCE WILL BE OBSERVED IN THE ROOM. . . . THERE WILL BE NO PHOTOGRAPHS TAKEN") bring me to surreptitiously remove my camera from its case, hold it blindly in my lap, aim its general view-finder upward, and release the shutter. Michelangelo fell from a scaffold in this place; I will at least take this small risk to capture part of his creation so that I can take it home and look at it there. I certainly can't contemplate it here.

I wonder that Michelangelo was a mere thirty-three when he began painting this ceiling. I read somewhere that for months after, he could read mail from his father only by holding the letters above his head. A glance into the guidebook reveals to me that he wrote, when first seeing the site, "This place is wrong, and no painter I." His comment about trying to complete the task was: "I strain more than any man who ever lived . . . and with great exhaustion; and yet I have the patience to arrive at the desired goal." (Which reminds me of my single-minded desire to reach the bed in my hotel last night.)

It took him four years to do the ceiling, 5,800 square feet of surface, covered by more than 300 figures (when only twelve were originally planned). Hundreds of feet above our heads are the episodes from the Bible, the drunken Noah, the creation of Eve, the flood, the expulsion from the Garden of Eden. Those scenes across the room are upside-down to us, some depictions facing horizontally, some vertically. One would have to lie on the marble floor with binoculars for several weeks, spinning in a slow circle, to appreciate this monumental creation. Preferably without the loudspeaker, begging for silence, blasting in our ears.

Now Joe takes my hand and leads me forward to the altar, above which is Michelangelo's depiction of *The Last Judgment*. This is truly terrifying. Painted twenty-five years after the ceiling, Michelangelo seems to have had a more judgmental, less generous, view of life. In the center is the wrathful Christ with the Virgin Mother at his side, his arm raised in damnation, while all about him the sinners tumble toward hell, the damned souls harassed by wingless angels and clawed demons. Charon, with devil's horns for ears, is beating his passengers with a stick (as he ferries them across the River Styx to hell). Most hideous among the horrors is the flayed skin, the empty hanging human form (with Michelangelo's face caricatured on it, the guidebook tells me)— is this done as an expression of his sincere sentiment, or as a masochistic act, or as a cynical prank?

But the general impression of both ceiling and altar is one of roiling, writhing bodies in chaos: the whole shebang of history and religion swirling around in confusion, much like what is taking place right now on the floor of the Sistine Chapel itself as bodies pour in through the doors at one end of the chapel and are ferried along, by force, by pure bodily pressure, to take in the depictions of the horrors that lie ahead and to flee to their fates on the other side.

I see that some of our students are rebelling: they are blatantly aiming their cameras around the room, come what may, damnation and hell itself. And, like a lunatic deity, the voice from above continues: "SILENCE WILL BE OBSERVED IN THE ROOM. . . . THERE WILL BE NO PHOTO-GRAPHS TAKEN."

45

Saint Peter's Basilica and the Pope's Fishing Cap

Seven hours after entering the Vatican Museum, we are popped out an exit into fresh air again. The students collapse on benches, moaning, flinging their heads in one another's laps; even the marine takes off her steel-toed marching shoes and looks at her feet as if she expects to see snakes where her toes had been.

Mrs. Pedrini offers around a bag of pretzels, and I take one, full of gratitude for every individual grain of salt I can pick out on the surface of the baked, brown crust. Just one small grain takes on a clarity and brilliance to the eye, then a sharpness to the tongue—a single defined experience exceptionally welcome after the blurry attack of images and colors upon my senses that entered and are still knocking about in my brain.

I think I have been stricken with the disease common among visitors to Italy: the Art Overload Syndrome, or Stendahl Syndrome, named for the writer who, after visiting the tombs of the great 180 years ago in Santa Croce, wrote, "I had palpitations of the heart . . . I walked with the fear of falling. . . . I sat down on a bench." The article I read reported that an attack of this condition makes the victim want to hop on a plane and go home. I definitely have all the symptoms. I have been overcome by art.

Stillness is the medicine to cure it (or, at the very least, sitting down on a bench). The afflicted person requires a stop, some kind of rest, a pause to let the colliding molecules settle, find some pattern and coherence. But for me there is only respite, not rescue. Now Nicoletta announces we are all to follow her to a pizzeria. After lunch, we must storm the portals of the great Saint Peter's Basilica.

The Pope is nowhere to be found. However, we learn that a huge flock of his brothers in the ministry, the priests who were ordained the very same year as he, fifty years ago, have been invited this very day to Saint Peter's for an anniversary party.

As we enter Saint Peter's Square, we encounter the arriving throngs— hundreds of old men wearing long cassocks, heavy silver crosses, and white silk caps (much like the yarmulkes of the Jews), all struggling up the stone steps, all wearing plastic name tags on their priestly robes, all on their way to a grand dinner party at the Vatican.

In Saint Peter's Square, an orchestra is just now rehearsing for the celebratory concert to take place outdoors tomorrow. The entire square is roped off, barricaded, and filled with folding chairs. Around the periphery, media trucks are setting up enormous TV screens, speakers, microphones—wires are everywhere.

I look up to the high balcony draped in red velvet from which I have often seen, via the miracle of TV, the Pope give his blessings to his people, his country, and the world. Nothing is up there but a pigeon, pacing back and forth, obviously distressed by the worldly clatter and commerce taking place below.

Our class files into the church, with Nicoletta leading the way to Michelangelo's famous *Pietà* in the chapel to the right. This is the first required stop on the list of attractions not to be missed. We have all read and looked at copies of this sculpture, the limp and just-dead Christ lying in his grieving mother's lap while her one hand supports him and the other is held upward, open and relaxed, as if to accept her fate with supernatural grace. I am eager to see in person the Virgin Mother's face (looking years younger than her bearded son) while she supports his lifeless form in the shelter of her embrace. Her expression of peace is most baffling to me. Shouldn't the mother of a dead child be screaming in agony? Shouldn't she be tearing her hair?

When questioned about the beauty of this sculpture, Michelangelo wrote: "If life pleases us, death, being made by the hands of the same creator, should not displease us." It's clear to me he has never been a mother.

Perhaps I will learn some critical lesson from looking closer at this contradiction in terms. But the problem is that we can't get near the *Pietà* at all. Something in the vicinity of it or just adjacent (a wall? a pillar?) must be "in restauro." Or the rumor goes around that some-one has tried to hammer off one of Christ's toes and this barrier is for security. In any case, scaffolding has been erected all around the base of it. The Virgin's tilted head is visible only from a distance and even at a distance can be glimpsed only when a coin is put into the light meter.

I turn away in disappointment. The students groan but recover quickly. In truth, they are waiting to take on the challenge of the almost-impossible climb up to the top of the dome where one can see a magnificent view of Saint Peter's Square, Vatican City, and all of Rome. As soon as Nicoletta warns against it, reminding them we have many miles to go before we sleep, they all rush away to climb to the dome. Nothing excites youth more than a dare.

Joe and Mrs. Pedrini and Nicoletta confer: they will venture for-ward into the bowels of the church and try to discover the pulpit of Saint Peter, a great carved throne in bronze. I am certain that if they find it, it will merely be a lump under a sack of burlap. I'm not in-terested. What I want is to go outside. I'm inside, and I want to be outside—my need, for once, is that simple. I whisper to Joe that I will forgo this tour and will meet him outside, hours . . . or years . . . hence, whenever he appears.

On my way out, at the base of a great marble pillar, I find a hat— it's a fishing hat—with a wide brim and a plaid ribbon around the cir-cumference. I feel it is an omen, a message for me, perhaps from the

Pope himself. This must be his fishing cap, I'm sure of it. A consolation prize because I have not been able to touch the Virgin's marble hem or learn the secret of her serenity. I appropriate this cap and place it on my head. It is surely as good a memento as a rosary dipped in holy water.

Outside, I seat myself on one of the great staircases just against the wall and lean back to watch the continuing parade of elderly priests. I look at each of their faces, their wrinkled, mostly-kindly-looking faces, as they pass by. I wonder about the lives they've led, whether they ever regret that they did not marry and have children, whether they feel jealous that they are merely priests, while their brother in faith has climbed the ecumenical ladder to become Pope of the World.

I know my innocent and naive imaginings are the laconic thoughts of a Jewish girl from Brooklyn who understands very little of this Catholic culture. How can I really perceive the meaning and sanctity of this trinity, this crucifixion, this passion, this sacrifice upon which all Italian art is based, modeled, and executed?

That old bearded man I see down there, dressed in a brown robe tied around the waist with a rope, the man just walking past the Swiss guards—is he a monk, a penitent, a beggar, a holy man? Those geese, flying in formation overhead, directly over Saint Peter's Square, flying in a thrillingly perfect "T" (not a "V")—are they papal birds, symbolizing the miracle of faith?

The orchestra in the square is now playing music, thunderous stirring Beethoven, vibrating the very walls of the Vatican with the amplification machinery that's set up for tomorrow's event. Everything here is overdone, oversized, overpious, overcharged. I feel an impulse to cry. All my emotions and responses are bursting forth. I am sitting on the steps of the house of the man only one step removed from God. It is no wonder I am overcome.

Mai Jing and Maria come staggering up the steps toward me and fling themselves to rest on the stair below where I sit.

"Guess what? We saw the Pope!" Maria confesses.

"Yes! *We saw the Pope,*" Mai Jing repeats.

"*You saw the Pope?*" I am instantly jealous. I was right here all this time looking at birds and I missed His Holiness?

Mai Jing explains. "We got lost before lunch. We were so tired we left the Vatican Museum before the rest of you and came into Saint Peter's to sit down, and the Pope was right inside saying mass. No one even bothered us. They just let us stay and watch."

"You actually saw the Pope saying mass?"

Both girls are staring oddly at the fishing cap on my head.

"Yes, we heard him say mass. And afterward, one of the priests who was there blessed my rosary," says Maria. "My grandmother will die of joy!"

"I'm not Catholic," Mai Jing says. "I'm glad I saw him, but it really didn't mean that much to me."

"But still!" I protest. "It would have meant a lot to me, and I'm Jewish!"

"And just after that, we climbed up to the top of Saint Peter's dome. It took forever to climb up there; we were almost sick to our stomachs. The steps are slippery and slanty; you have to hold onto the walls. Some people were just hanging out the little narrow windows; they were too dizzy to go up or down. There are so many steps you finally can't breathe. But when you get to the top you see the most beautiful, most breathtaking view of all of Rome! The most amazing view in the world! Did you see it?"

"No," I say. "I missed that, too."

Apparently, I have missed everything. I have missed the Raphaels behind burlap and the *Pietà* hidden by scaffolding. I have missed the view of Rome, and I have missed the Pope himself.

While I am doing this, I begin to catalog other things I have missed in my life: the chance to be a great beauty. The chance to be rich (or famous—either would do). The chance to be a great musician (a singer with a voice like Cecilia Bartoli is what I have in mind). I long ago lost my chance to be a Rockette when, at age five, I fell off my bike and scarred my knee badly. And I lost my chance to be the first woman-something: pilot? President? Police chief?

A Mother Goose rhyme comes to my mind:

Pussycat, Pussycat, Where have you been?
I've been to London to visit the Queen.
Pussycat, Pussycat, What did you there?
I frightened a little mouse under a chair.

46

The Spanish Steps,
Desperation at the Tiber River

We have one more monument to visit—the Spanish Steps—and then (it is promised by Nicoletta), we may go back to the hotel and to bed. Tomorrow morning, she reminds us, we must be up at the crack of dawn for our trip to Ostia Antica, the ancient city that lies in ruins just outside Rome.

"Andiamo!" she says and waits for us to rise from the steps of Saint Peter's. The students who have just come down from the dome are still staggering with dizziness. *"Andiamo subito!"* We rise to the occasion, all forty of us in her thrall and at her mercy.

It must be said Nicoletta is more than generous with her city, her love of it, her knowledge of it, her pride in it. I wonder, though, is she not mortal and beginning to tire? But she can't let us leave Rome without seeing the Spanish Steps in the Piazza di Spagna, the square that English poets loved, near which Shelley and Byron lived, and the very house where Keats died.

But do I really want to see the Spanish Steps, or *any* steps? Do I want to encounter one more set of steps in this great city's arsenal of steps? Could I even walk up and down one more set of steps and live to tell the tale?

As we trudge along, more a ragtag bunch now than a marching

troop of soldiers, word comes down the line that we are going to stop at a little *salumeria* to buy food for our lunch at Ostia Antica tomorrow, which is Sunday, a day no food shops are open. When we close ranks (Joe and I are at the end of the line, both because he is supposed to bring up the rear and because I can't possibly keep up the pace set by Nicoletta), we find that all the students have crowded into a tiny delicatessen. They are swarming along the shelves and grabbing cookies, crackers, boxes of juice, tubes of mayonnaise, chips, candies, almost everything that's edible.

The couple who own the place seem astonished; this is apparently just a local neighborhood establishment, it's quite late on Saturday night, they are just about to close up, and suddenly this . . . invasion of Americans! The wife now must stand at attention to handle the cash register, and the husband hurries behind the counter where the students are yelling orders for him to slice, weigh, and wrap meat and olives and cheese: ham, salami, mortadella, prosciutto, mozzarella, gorgonzola, parmesan, ricotta, fontina—whatever is there for their proven prodigious appetites.

The counter area is six deep with our students; there's no point our adding to the crush of bodies. Joe and I remain outside and wait for the commotion to subside before we do our shopping. I realize I badly need a bathroom; this is no small challenge in Italy, where public bathrooms are never in evidence and private ones can be used only if one is a patron at the establishment. Several of our girls are experiencing this same necessity. I hear two of them talking as they eye a cafe across the street from the delicatessen.

"Just wander in as if you are looking for a table to sit at. Then run as fast as you can to the back and find the john. By the time they notice you, you're done!"

I am not in a position to mull this over for long; I take their advice. I make a dash for the cafe, am inside the shop and inside the bathroom in the blink of an eye. Deeply relieved but embarrassed, I pass by the proprietor, head down, on my speedy way out. He says, *"Signora?"* but I am out the door in a flash. Will he have me arrested? But no—several of our girls now are making the same journey I did, and the owner is generous, he understands. In fact, two of our girls stop to talk with him when they are done taking care of the necessities of nature. When they leave, I see him put two lemons in their hands as a gift, two large, beautiful lemons, each one bright as a sun.

By the time Joe and I get into the *salumeria,* the shelves are bare and the meats and cheeses are all gone! Our students have completely cleaned the store out. The last of them are checking out candy bars and almond biscuits.

We have just begun to look around when someone shouts a warning to us: "Nicoletta wants to get going."

I peer at the shelves in a kind of panic: what can we buy for tomorrow? Nothing is left but a few dry packaged coffee rolls. There isn't a bottle of mineral water or a container of juice on the shelves. The meat counter looks as if bloody carnage has taken place on it—a few scraps of skin and strings of fat are left on the cutting board.

Joe, too, is looking around for some morsel we might be able to eat in the Roman ruins tomorrow. He shows me a package of "Italian toast"—those dry crumbly things that are not, by my standards, edible. There's nothing left to drink but some expensive Chianti wines. Well, why not? We have to drink something. I choose a bottle of wine and pay for it at the cash register. Joe looks crestfallen that we haven't found food for our picnic at Ostia. Perhaps he imagines we may simply starve tomorrow— and flutter away among the stones like a pair of autumn leaves.

When we find ourselves in the street once more, we are alone. Our students have disappeared. Where have they gone? Which direction? We look to the right and left. Did Nicoletta forget us? In what quarter of the world's four directions are the Spanish Steps? Joe thinks they went that way; I point the other way. Where is the map? Our map is back at the hotel. What do we do now? The lights go off in the *salumeria* behind us; the exhausted owners are locking up and going home for the weekend.

"Should we ask someone to direct us to the Spanish Steps?" I ask my husband, knowing better. He is one of those men who doesn't ask for directions. Failure to get somewhere on his own brain power is perceived by him as a slight to his manhood. I would ask for directions at once *("Dov'è le scale Espanol?")*, but there is no one to ask at this late hour on Saturday night in this neighborhood of locked-up shops. Besides, what do I care where the Spanish Steps are? I do not want in the slightest to go there.

"Let's just go back to the hotel," I plead.

Joe is actually considering this suggestion. Could he think it might be a sane choice?

"I guess we could do that. Do you happen to remember the name of the hotel?"

"No. But I'd know it in a minute if I saw that dog."

"Do you remember the street it's on? You generally are better with names than I am."

"No, but we can always ask which hotel in Rome has guests who are electrocuted by the hairdryers in the bathrooms."

We are standing alone now in a street that is completely dark and deserted. Somewhere our students are frolicking along, swinging their bags of cheese and salami, unaware that they have abandoned us. Nicoletta probably still thinks we are bringing up the rear.

"Okay," Joe says, "let's try to find a bus that goes to the train station. Once we're there, I think we'll be able to find the hotel."

"Oh, thank heaven!" The end to this day is actually in sight; I feel my spirits rise. "Where can we get a bus?"

"Let's walk along. We'll probably find a bus stop in a minute or two."

An hour later, we come to an intersection with a bus stop sign. Joe tries to read the hieroglyphics detailing the routes and times and says, finally, "I think we can get a bus to the station here."

I lean against the wall of a building and look into the lighted globes of oncoming headlights. After I count sixty-two cars, I cry out, "I think a bus is coming."

We rush to the curb, the bus stops for a few passengers who get on, but it's not our bus. Well, the next then. Twenty minutes later, there is another. Not ours. Twenty minutes later, there is another.

"Maybe the bus that goes to the station doesn't stop here," I suggest.

"I think it does. It probably just makes few runs at night."

We go back to the wall and lean against it, each of us looking away from the other. I take inventory of my body: my heels feel as if spikes have been driven into them, my lower back is weighted by lead anvils, my stomach is convulsing with spasms of hunger, my eyes burn from car and bus exhaust, my head aches. I moan, not softly. Joe is trying to whistle a happy tune.

After six more buses pass us, Joe steps up to the sign and begins reading it again. "There's *supposed* to be a bus that goes to the terminal," he says, as if the written word could not betray us, as if the city of Rome has made a pledge to us that we must expect will be fulfilled.

"*I* am terminal," I tell him. "Please believe me. I can't stand up much longer."

He seems to be losing strength himself, staggering slightly as he transfers from one hand to another the heavy bottle of wine in the plastic bag.

"Do you want me to hold that for you?"

"That's okay."

"Why don't we open it and drink some?"

"I don't think that's the best idea. Let's wait for one more bus and then if it isn't ours think of something else."

"I did just think of something else. Remember that night we waited for a bus in Florence, on the lungarno? That night we finally figured out that the #14 bus ran one route in the day, but not at night? That we were waiting in the wrong place? See if this sign shows that the colors of the bus numbers and the background are reversed. Could that be the case now?"

Joe goes back to the Pledge of Rome and reads the bus schedule again. His head drops. "You're right," he says. "According to the sign, the bus to the terminal only runs here in the daytime."

"How come we didn't think of this two hours earlier?" What I really mean, by the tone of my voice, is "How could you be so stupid?"

When he has no adequate response I decide, in my impaired mental state, that my primary mistake in life was to marry him. I now decide to tell him this—rather loudly, in fact, adding that if I hadn't married him (with his stupid interests in history) I would not be in this horrible predicament that will probably kill me and that when I soon fall over dead it will be his fault and I am sorry I ever met him.

He listens to me patiently and calmly looks around to see whether we can get a cab on this street, which apparently we cannot. He gently takes my arm and steers me along, explaining that if we get to the road that runs along the Tiber River, we can probably get a cab there.

I walk in a catatonic haze, wherever he pushes, pulls, or guides me, up curbs, down curbs, as he drags me across streets, up steps, down steps. What makes him think he will find the Tiber River? If he does, I will surely drown myself in it. Or him. This marriage has been a mistake from the beginning.

When we find the river (what is a river doing smack in the middle of a busy city?), there are no cabs to be found. (All the cabs are at the terminal, no doubt, which is where we want to be.) As we cross the river, I stop to lean over the side of the bridge, watching the lights play on the water and wondering whether a boat might come along into which we could jump. At this point, I snatch the bag from my husband and lift out the wine bottle. I will get drunk on the bridge and be arrested; at least in jail I can sit down somewhere, and they will offer bread and water. But of course the cork requires a corkscrew, and of course my husband doesn't at this moment have his Swiss army knife with him. Now we will die because he is never prepared for all contingencies.

Perhaps I could love him again if only he would carry me in his arms, but he hasn't done that since our wedding day. (And only for thirty seconds then.)

He retrieves the wine bottle, pulls me by the hand across the bridge, and on the other side of the river calls my attention to the glorious marble buildings, floodlit, decorated by handsome sculptures and tall columns. They are full of steps, steps everywhere, Italian steps if not Spanish steps, but wonderful steps, long wide steps, steps that begin to resemble beds to my wild eyes. In fact, they are so inviting that I choose a step and lay myself down upon it. Not so bad, actually, if you don't count the sharp edge in your back.

Joe tugs at my hand.

"Leave me alone. I'm going to sleep a while."

"I think there may be a bus stop just a block or two away."

"*You think.*"

If I were my husband, I would just leave me here forever.

But with tender patience he helps me up and does actually half-carry me along. We pass some chained-off areas, we pass some statues, we turn a corner, and we find ourselves at a large bus terminal. In fact, there is some official in uniform there who can be asked a question. Joe asks the question (it must be "Will we live or die?") and seems to get a satisfactory answer.

"Bus #4 goes to the terminal," Joe turns to me and announces triumphantly. "And he says it will be here soon!"

I immediately sit down on the curb and then lie down on the grass. After an interval, Joe pulls me up and pushes me aboard a bus. We have no bus tickets, but what does that matter? Arrest has been my goal for some time now, anyway.

A group of Persian men at the back of the bus are sitting among piles of Persian rugs tied with twine. They are soft high piles of rug, perfect for sleeping on. Joe has to restrain me from climbing atop one of these piles and going to sleep. The Persian men, handsome, with big black mustaches, talk in their native language to one another. Now and then one of them catches my eye and smiles at me.

I can hardly believe we are actually on a bus, sitting among human beings, no longer lost in a maze of fountains and statues and churches. We may live after all. I may someday actually see my children and my mother again.

When we get off the bus, Joe drags me like a rag doll to the first *trattoria* we encounter, seats me in a chair, and replenishes my body with minestrone soup and the boiled flesh of chicken. He allows me mineral water (but not wine), and, when he deems us adequately restored, he lifts me from my chair and moves me forward into the night again.

We are somewhere near the train station. As we walk along the periphery of it, searching for our hotel, a trio of menacing young men steps out of the shadows to block our way. These hoods are swaggering toward us in postures that indicate definitely unwholesome intentions. I stare them down, having recently survived personally such dangers as they know not of. Let them just try something. Let them dare. I'll smash them over the head with our wine bottle.

Joe moves me forward at a rapid pace, his hand under my elbow. He would like me to lower my head and hurry on. I am totally aware of what he wants. But I'm so tired and angry, I am thinking that, if these boys mug us, I will actually murder them. Unusual circumstances bring forth superhuman strength. I'm tired enough and furious enough to take all three of them on at once.

"Is that our hotel?" my husband asks to distract me.

It could be, who knows, one fleabag place looks like another.

"I think it is," he says.

"It's too ugly to be a hotel."

He hurries me inside, away from the tough guys following a few steps behind us. And there before me I suddenly see that beloved, mangy dog sprawled on the dirty floor. I fall to my knees and embrace him. His wet tongue licks my cheek. I am in love with this gorgeous dog, and I wish I had married *him*.

Joe lifts me up and carries me bodily to our room, somehow managing to jam the key in the lock and at the same time carry me over the threshold. He staggers with me across the room to our beds, where he dumps me on one of them, loses his balance, and falls directly upon my body. *How fine and romantic,* I think one second before I conk out. *Just like newlyweds.*

47

The Mosaics and Karaoke Bars of Ostia Antica

A day in the country (and out of the congestion of Rome) is a balm, a benediction, a blessing. The bus delivers us to the seaport town of Ostia Antica, about fifteen miles outside of Rome. Once a bustling city center, Ostia now lies in ruins among trees and tall grasses brushed by fragrant, fresh winds blowing inland from the Mediterranean Sea.

The students burst from the bus singing. They remind me of zoo animals allowed outside on the first temperate spring day after being confined in their cages all winter. They whoop, they holler, they swing from the branches of the trees like monkeys, they do somersaults and headstands, they play leapfrog, they hug one another, they do wild, unrestrained dances of joy.

The moment Nicoletta buys tickets for the group and we enter the grounds (still empty because of the early hour), the students disperse to the first visible ruin, originally an amphitheater, now a rubble of bricks, broken columns, cracked stones, and high jagged walls. They arrange themselves around it as if enacting a ballet.

Some leap upon the edges of the walls, some jump upon the columns, others climb into what must have been a fountain. Two of them, Phil and Sara, the ones I am now sure are lovers, the ones who at Halloween sat talking on the bed in the light of the Duomo's glow, take each other by the hand and climb up to the highest point of the wall around the arena.

Nicoletta warns them to be careful. She has heard of students who have fallen from that height and have had to be airlifted home by ambulance. In silhouette, the lovers seem majestic and mythical to me, she tall and thin in a long black dress and he even taller, handsome as she is beautiful, a prince and a princess surveying their kingdom to come. They fling their arms toward the sky as if supplicating the gods, or thanking them that they are here, young, strong of limb, and free to court and adore each other under the sun in the Italian countryside.

Or so it seems to me, who would also like to fly to the top of that wall and look far over this ancient creation, testimony to other souls who once walked here, laughed here, and lived here. There is something undeniably sad about the vast silence and absence of movement as far as we can see. More than anywhere else I have been in Italy, I feel the immediacy of time past here, of real lives lived and deaths died.

Though Ostia is said to have been a city of poor people—laborers, sailors, fishermen, shopkeepers, and fishmongers, as well as those who transferred materials from seagoing vessels to smaller boats on their way to Rome via the Tiber River—it seems, as we begin to walk along its rocky paths, to reveal itself as a sun-drenched resort.

The community boasted a lighthouse, a tavern, wine shops, a public forum, theaters, a synagogue, and temples of worship, not to mention the elegant and elaborate bath houses, each comprising the *calidarium* (the hot baths), the *frigidarium* (the cold baths), the *laconicum* (the steam baths), and the *apodyterium* (the dressing rooms in the *thermae,* the edifice containing the baths).

Below the baths are elaborate mazes of channels and pipes, to bring water to the baths and then to drain it, as well as places for the furnaces and boilers required to heat the water.

Our students spread out in all directions, now and then passing us on a path or calling to us from over the broken walls of a *domus* (a Roman villa) to say we must not miss seeing the latrines, those amazing rows of stones with holes in them. (They wonder whether the Romans used the bathrooms as a social meeting place!) Have we discovered the huge earthen pots that once held oil? And we must be sure to see the tombs and the *columbaria* where the ashes of the dead were stored in terra-cotta containers.

Our students have suddenly become mini-anthropologists, creeping over and under mysterious structures, conjecturing about the uses of various artifacts, holes, and hiding places, musing on symbols and icons. They seem, finally, to be interested in Italian history, as if some magical wand has opened their eyes.

Everywhere underfoot we find the most exquisite mosaics, depicting gods, sea serpents, mermaids, musicians and their instruments, horses and chariots, bulls, birds, sailors, seagoing vessels, various tools and utensils.

These mosaics are there for us to walk upon, to bend down and examine, and—unlike everything in Rome that is covered, protected, and *in restauro*—these ancient works of art are unguarded and close enough to touch. I am grateful for this freedom (and for the trust it implies; after all, the mosaics are tiny stones, easily pried up and taken home for souvenirs. Their presence is testimony to the respect of visitors who have allowed the stones to stay here, almost in their original wholeness.).

In front of the theater (large enough, says the guidebook, to hold 3,500 people) are three pillars with the open-mouthed masks of drama on them. Eight of our students have laid themselves across and upon these pillars, with their friends crouching beneath or climbing atop them. They all open their mouths to imitate the ghoulish expressions on the masks while the cameras click in the hands of whichever of their friends have been designated to immortalize this moment.

Several of the girls have begun weaving garlands of flowers and vines from the greenery growing everywhere underfoot. One of them comes to me and lays a wreath upon my head.

"Why don't you kiss her?" cries Marta to my husband. To everyone's surprise, certainly mine, and, perhaps most of all, his, Joe takes me in his arms and kisses me, while the kids with cameras are quick to capture the moment.

Being together during these long adventures has humanized all of us, made us feel more like family than teacher and class. Some of the girls have come to me with their problems, and, missing my own daughters, I comfort them and advise them as if they were my children.

I wear the wreath in my hair the rest of the day, feeling like Flora in Botticelli's *Primavera*. At least as young and beautiful as she, I walk smiling in the forest, strewing flowers from my basket, accompanied by amorous zephyrs cavorting in the grass and Cupid, floating overhead, inoculating me with love. Looking up, I see Botticelli's blue skies shimmering in the heavens above me.

As the sun moves higher, the students call to one another over the stones and fountains. "Lunch time! Meet at the tombstones."

"Mrs. Pedrini says we'll all have a picnic."

"Everyone meet at the tombstones. We'll share."

Joe looks my way. He is thinking of our empty larder, I'm sure, after the slim pickings in the *salumeria* last night in Rome. He is embarrassed, perhaps, that we will have to take alms from the students. He is carrying our bottle of wine—at least we can offer something in return. I swing my backpack carelessly: little does he know what it contains.

When we get to the tombstones, long flat cement sarcophagi on which we can sit and spread our picnic lunches, Mrs. Pedrini has already distributed paper plates and cups. (She is always prepared for any contingency.) The students begin to unwrap their portions of meats and cheeses and coarse Italian bread. Nicoletta confesses that she will need donations; she admits she bought nothing in the *salumeria* last night.

When I open my pack and set out my jar of Skippy peanut butter, a gasp goes up among the students.

"Peanut butter! Where did you get *peanut butter*!"

"Oh, have I missed peanut butter," Marta cries. "Peanut butter and enchiladas. I'd give my right arm. . . ."

"Grape jelly, did you bring grape jelly?"

"Wait," I say, and now I withdraw my little loaf of *pane bianco americana* from my pack. White bread and peanut butter: we are at least a drop closer to home and heaven.

I carefully lay out upon a napkin the bread, the jar of peanut butter, and a little plastic knife; I invite everyone to share in a taste of home. Joe is astonished at the reception that greets this small contribution. Had he known I was carrying a heavy, breakable object all the way from Florence, he would surely have told me to leave it behind. But now he is proud of my resourcefulness and the response my peanut butter has elicited.

"Everyone have some," he calls out. "And we have some wine to share, too."

Now, with Mrs. Pedrini's corkscrew, we open the Chianti and pour tiny amounts into everyone's paper cups. The students generously offer us slabs of cheese, slices of prosciutto, containers of salty black olives, while they happily make themselves little hors d'oeuvres of peanut butter on white bread.

With the blue sky above, the golden bricks and stones of Ostia all around us, we spread our bounty here in the place where the quiet spirits of the dead once reposed and join our histories with theirs.

After lunch, we have an hour more before we must board the bus for the terminal in Rome and our train back to Florence. Happily fed, peaceful, and relaxed by the portion (though small) of lovely wine, we make one more exploration of the ancient city, stopping in what seems to have been a bar or outdoor tavern. We see a counter, benches, shelves for food, and even a painted fresco, faded but still clear on the stone, of bowls with fruit in them, and wine glasses with beverage painted within. On one of the narrow benches, I deposit my pack to use as a pillow and collapse in the sun, still exhausted from Rome, utterly happy to be in this place of stone and sky. Tiny mosaic tiles sparkle on the ground beneath the bench.

Marta and Mrs. Pedrini find us there, and Marta says, "I think this used to be a karaoke bar! There are lots of bars here. The Ostians must have loved to hang out, eat pizza, drink wine, make music."

She reaches down into the tall grass and brings up a bunch of weeds that she holds in her hand like a microphone. "Let's see. Let's get things moving here. What shall we sing?"

Merrill collapsed in Ostia

Mrs. Pedrini is partial to French love songs. "'La Vie en Rose'?" she suggests.

"It's not my usual," Marta says, "but you go ahead, I'll join in."

Mrs. Pedrini finds herself a microphone also, fashioned from one of the paper cups left over from lunch, and begins to sing in French.

The sound of her voice carries across the open fields. It's tremulous and quite passionate. Some tourists, now also wandering the great spaces, come closer to investigate, and soon a number of our students arrive, in twos and threes, for the concert.

Mrs. Pedrini sings slowly, expressively, sensually. She's very beautiful, a promise to us all of what growing older can mean: grace, enthusiasm, wisdom, generosity, energy. There isn't one of us who hasn't stood in her aura and benefited from it.

Marta joins in with her, and soon everyone standing around is humming and swaying, including the busload of Japanese tourists who have just arrived. I have never seen so many smiles in one place.

When Mrs. Pedrini has taken her bow, Marta sings one of her specialties, the song "Crazy," in the mode of Patsy Cline.

"I'm crazy . . . crazy for feeling so lonely. . . ."

From so small a girl, her voice is shatteringly big and resonant. In the fields of an ancient Italian ruin, we are hearing a song we all know from the records made by a woman from the American South. We have indeed mixed up the countries and centuries here, mixed up who we are with who we used to be, mixed our faces with stone masks, braided our hair with garlands of flowers—and yet not one of us, I would venture to guess, feels crazy or lonely right now. Not Joe, not me, not the students, not the Japanese visitors.

We are all residents of time and history, partaking of music and company in the presence of one another. Whoever we are and whatever our personal histories, we have put them aside for the moment to be here together, living this shared life in real time. I'm easily moved to tears in our last days in Italy; my vision blurs, clouding and softening the edges of the stones from which this lost city was built.

When the song ends, the applause echoes from the hollows of the shattered clay vessels and fades away in the gentle wind that blows over Ostia from the sea.

48

Thanksgiving *Tacchino Arrosto,* Elvis in Sequins

Nearing the three-month mark away from home, the students are notably homesick. They miss certain beloved foods more than they do their homes, families, jobs, or (according to some of the girls) boring boyfriends.

Bagels, tacos, refried beans, hot wings, and doughnuts are high on their "if I could only have . . ." list. And now that Thanksgiving is only days away, they are beginning to talk in longing tones.

Sitting on the terrace of the Scuola Dante Alighieri, waiting for Joe one day, I hear them talking:

"I've been thinking about my mother's stuffing, with pecans and onions and celery . . ."

"And cranberry sauce. How do you think we lived this long without cranberry sauce?"

"Pumpkin pie, whipped cream . . ."

"Turkey and gravy . . ."

"Those soft little rolls with poppy seeds on them."

"I'll die if I don't have Thanksgiving dinner."

Nicoletta puts her ingenuity to work and reports back that she's discovered a restaurant newly opened on Via Maffia, owned by an Italian and his American wife. The place, now called Le Scuderie Bistro, was once used as the stables *(scuderie)* for the monastery of Santo Spirito. Traveling merchants left their horses there while doing trade in Firenze.

The menu Nicoletta shows us features an Englishman dressed in formal hunting clothes, his hound running beside him as they gallop after the fleeing fox. The menu advertises "happy hours" daily at the wine bar, and a wood-burning pizza oven that produces twenty varieties of pizza, *covaccini,* and *calzoni.* The owner has promised Nicoletta that his American-born wife will have traditional Thanksgiving recipes faxed from the United States and that they will arrange an American-style, all-the-trimmings Thanksgiving dinner for our students.

It won't be cheap, Nicoletta warns us, but the students—who are already living on student loans and emergency funds wired by their parents—have shown no particular resistance to expensive entertainments. Most weekends (while we stay in Florence), they fly off to Greece or Spain or Morocco, being of the generation that takes what it can and worries later (if at all).

On Thanksgiving night, the temperature falls close to freezing, and a bitter wind is blowing. I dress myself in two skirts, three sweaters, and my down coat. I wrap a wool scarf around my head. We take the #14 bus to the station and stumble in the direction of Via Maffia by trial and error. The city seems to be arranged in triangular blocks, with streets intersecting one another (absent of logic), thwarting our plan to travel "as the crow flies"—in a straight line.

We cross the Arno (of which Mark Twain said, "They call it a river, and they honestly think it is a river, do these dark and bloody Florentines. They even help out the delusion by building bridges over it. I do not see why they are too good to wade"). The Arno surely seems a river tonight, swollen high by recent rains, careening downward from the hills and making a waterfall over the sudden drop of one of the low dams that crosses it.

Being lost has made us late; when we find the dark and narrow alley that Joe thinks will lead us to Via Maffia, we rush along, heads bowed into the wind, running over the rough road.

Somehow my foot hits a rock or a hole or an iron peg, and I feel myself take flight, upward and then down, head first, so that I am aware of the flagstones aiming themselves upward toward my eyes. In a maneuver so fast, so powerful, and so extraordinary, my husband, by the sheer will of his Superman's arm, brings me up short of the pavement by half an inch. My eyes see it happen, they are open and ready to receive rocks in them, ready to be blinded—and then I am saved.

We both stop, astonished at this feat of his strength and my salvation. We try to understand what happened, how it happened, but all we know is one thing: I didn't crack open my head when I should have, given all the laws of nature and physics. That I didn't fall seems a true miracle. My belief is strengthened by the notion that, if a miracle is bound to happen, there's no better place on earth for it than Italy.

The bright light toward which we move, as eager as moths drawn to flame on this dark and dangerous street, turns out to be the welcoming light of Le Scuderie. Inside, decorating the walls, are framed pictures from the covers of horse magazines. American music is playing from speakers overhead; bright red-plastic American-style booths line the sides of the restaurant.

Our students are already seated at two long tables and are well on their way to finishing off the first carafes of house wine. On the table are also pitchers of sangria, swirling with orange and lemon slices and chunks of banana. The students are dressed in their best, buzzing with the excitement of being together tonight in this modern, refurbished place that looks almost like a cozy coffee shop back home.

The printed menu, titled THANKSGIVING DINNER, is laid at each place setting and announces the delights to come:

Funghi ripieni di riso selvatico (Wild rice stuffed mushrooms)
Tacchino arrosto con ripieno alle erbe e salsa allo zinfandel (Roast turkey with herb stuffing and zinfandel gravy)
*Patate al gratin e polenta fritta (*Brandied potatoes gratin and fried cornbread)
Piselli (Green peas)
Torta di zucca (Pumpkin Cheesecake)

Sorbetto de mirtilli corretto alla vodka (Blueberry Sorbet with Vodka splash).

The owner himself comes out and introduces himself to our group. He speaks perfect English and assures us he has done all in his power to make us an American Thanksgiving like one we would enjoy at home.

As if to prove it, his chef, wearing a high white hat, arrives with a great heaped platter of rosettes of fried potatoes—strange soft objects, swirled like macaroon cookies, crisp on the outside, soft within (as we learn at the first delicious bite after the tray is passed around to each of us). These surely don't seem to be brandied potatoes gratin, but who cares? The owner asks our opinion of this delicacy, first Nicoletta's, since she arranged the evening, then Joe's, since he is a teacher of the group, and then mine, as the wife of the professor.

"*Perfetto,*" we say, one at a time. "*Meraviglioso!*"

There is a long pause between potatoes and stuffed mushrooms—a pause so extended that the students begin a game, the game in which someone at one end of the table invents a sentence that is whispered to the next person and the next, till at the very end the sentence is announced by the last person to hear it.

The result is cause for gales of merriment since the first sentence to result from the crooked journey of words is: "Did you wear your eggplants to the beauty shop?"

Another round is begun but is cut short as the lights suddenly go out in the restaurant. We wait in hushed expectation till a great glowing form appears, moving slowly through the darkened doorway. Two assistants in white coats materialize, carrying an enormous flaming turkey on a silver tray. Tiny flares are burning all around the edges of the platter and miniature American flags are inserted in every orifice of the bird.

Our students burst into applause and cheers. The owner comes out and takes a bow, the chef comes from the kitchen to take a bow (doffing his white cap at us), and the two helpers begin, with enormous gleaming knives, to slice the bird to bits before our eyes.

The owner himself personally arranges and delivers each plate,

Thanksgiving feast at Le Scuderie

steaming and fragrant, to our places. He is as proud of his creation as Michelangelo must have been of his.

The *tacchino* tastes like traditional roast turkey, so what does it matter if everything else has a distinctly Italian flavor? The food is delicious. And if we are not at home with our families of origin, we are at least together in our newly, if temporarily, constructed family, learning that one can feel deep connections to many varieties of "unrelated" folk.

We begin making toasts to the health and happiness of our families at home. Mrs. Pedrini toasts Nicoletta and "Mr. Joe," her two teachers, and (of course) has presents for them—large, impressive calendars of art reproductions from the Uffizi gallery. Likewise, she presents an imposing pyramid-shaped box of wrapped chocolates to one of our boys who (we had all heard) had stared down two knife-wielding thieves at the station, saving himself and the two girls with him from being robbed or worse.

Mrs. Pedrini (dressed in orange and brown silk in honor of the season) makes toasts all around, to me for navigating and surviving the many steps of Rome, to the lovers in our group who remind her "of the scrumptious joys of young love," to "Mr. Joe, who has led the class through the glories of ancient history," to Nicoletta, "who has uncurled our tongues and given them the beauty of Italian words," and in general to all things, turkeys, Chianti, pumpkins, and, not least, the beauty of the owner's daughter, a child of about eight who sits wide-eyed and smiling shyly in the corner watching us all share this strange celebration.

But wait—now the lights go out again! What is coming now, as we finish our espresso coffee and pumpkin cheesecake? The twang of a guitar turns into a few chords of fanfare, and, as the lights flash on again, Elvis Presley arrives via a wild jump into the room. Lest we not recognize him by his sideburns, his black leather pants, and the song he is playing, which sounds more or less like "Don't Be Cruel to a Heart That's True," we are allowed a big hint: his guitar is plastered with a dozen faces of Elvis, and on it, in sequins, in a rainbow of glowing letters, is written *Elvis*.

Our students scream and clap. The beautiful child in the corner is glowing with pleasure and with the privilege of being allowed to witness this adult entertainment (with her father standing just behind her, his hand resting gently on her shoulder).

Never mind that Elvis sings off-key, and that he has a missing tooth or two, and that he knows only two songs (after "Blue Suede Shoes" he moves right into "O Sole Mio")—he has a big grin on his face, and a mischievous light in his eyes.

A couple of our girls get up to dance with each other, and Mrs. Pedrini gets up to sing along with Elvis, and finally Elvis plays his closing chords, thrusting his pelvis and fist toward heaven, Elvis-style. When the wild applause dies down, he passes around a bread basket that quickly fills with lire notes (and a handful of chocolates from Mrs. Pedrini, as well).

The witching hour of midnight is approaching. If we want to catch the last bus home, we must leave at once. The students who live in *il centro* are planning the next segment of this evening—the discos are just

"Elvis"

opening up, and (for the young) the night is very young. We take our last sips of wine, bid everyone good-bye, and make our way through the doorway into the cold night air.

From the outside, Le Scuderie takes on the look of a stable once more—an ancient, crumbling building on a street of uneven stones. Joe holds my hand tightly as we walk toward the bridge. Stopping to look at the Arno, leaning against the edge of the parapet, we see the lights of Florence reflected in the black water, shimmering down the length of the lungarno. A boy and girl stand kissing in the cold wind. The towers and battlements and domes of the of the city gleam in the clear air of night. We are here now. We are more than aware—we are on fire with clarity. We look at each other and are thankful.

49

The Olive-Picking

On the second day of the olive-picking at Cornelia's house, she arranges to meet us at the last bus stop at Piazza Tolentino and drive us up the mountain so that we may witness the event. Her olives have for years been picked by the same Florentine family, which runs a small business gathering olives and pressing the oil from them. Today they will be coming back with the first day's pressing and will gather the remaining olives for the next day's.

Cornelia and her son Marlowe, tall and very thin in his adolescence and growing taller by the moment, walk us through the vineyard and olive grove behind the house. The ground is wet and spongy from the recent rains; the little stream on the property flows briskly in its gully. Though the grapes have been harvested, a few shriveled ones remain, dried and forgotten on the stalk. Marlowe leads the way across the field, careful to point out to us treacherous roots or rocks or slippery places that we must avoid.

Below, in the valley, we see a panorama of farms. Their fields are criss-crossed by patterns of planting; from this distance the light and dark squares give the appearance of a giant game board.

The quality of light is a marvel—a haze hangs over the valley and the Peretola airport in the distance, but it filters the sun in such a way as to soften and beautify whatever lies under its gentle touch. The terra-cotta-colored rooftops spread before us as far as we can see.

"You see why I love this place so much," Cornelia tells us, as if an explanation were needed. "I need it as much as I need food and water."

"Here they are," Cornelia says, as we become aware of the noise of an engine laboring up the hill. A husband and wife and their young son arrive and park their old truck near the house. The woman and her husband together carry into the house what looks like a giant wine bottle of olive oil. They hold it by the two glass ears on its sides. Once it is set over the threshold, they exchange a few words, and the husband leaves to begin his work, while his wife pulls the bottle further into the house. Cornelia and she speak in rapid Italian, having to do with the disposition of the other delivered bottles from the pressing. This one goes into the kitchen; the shed behind the house is settled on for the storage of the remaining oil.

I study the great jar of oil, greenish in color, with a slight sediment at the bottom.

"Do you really use that much oil?" I ask Cornelia, thinking of my kitchen cabinet at home with sixteen ounces of oil in it that usually last me for six months.

"Oh, we use much more than this. Last winter the pressing brought us fifty-four liters of oil, and we are down to the last few inches by this time of year. Of course, we give some away to friends, but mainly we use it ourselves."

"But you are so thin! And Italians in general are thin! How do they manage it, with all that oil in their diets?"

"We walk a lot," she says. "And, besides, olive oil is good for you. We don't worry so much like Americans do about this and that in our food." She looks out the kitchen window and beckons us to see what is happening outside.

The husband has placed a white net beneath the olive tree next to the house and is already high up in it, standing on the rungs of a ladder and hitting at the branches with a stick. His son is perched on a lower branch, shaking the smaller branches around him.

As I watch, olives begin to cascade down into the net, flowing downhill like rivers of ebony. When I look up to the very top of the tree, I see hundreds of black olives still attached, shining in the sun. Many more must be hiding among the green leaves. As the boy and his father scrape and shake the branches of the tree, the woman gathers up the olives as they fall in a large plastic bucket. Lying there, in shades of black and dark red, they look like a child's treasured marble collection.

"It seems so primitive to collect them this way, without any high-tech machinery," I say to Cornelia. "They way they do it now must be the way they did it five hundred years ago."

"And the way they press the oil from the olives between stone wheels is the same way they did it then, too. I am hoping you will taste it; there's nothing like the first day's pressing."

She brings to the table a little bowl of carrot strips, bean sprouts, and fresh mushrooms. Then she presents us each with a small saucer holding an iridescent puddle of green oil in its center.

"Now be prepared," she warns us. "It's piccante—it has a real bite to it."

I've never eaten a carrot with quite this much attention. The oil is alive with the taste of earth and sun, rich and sharp on the tongue. It coats the vegetables with a lovely sheen.

Joe agrees, it's quite wonderful.

Outside, the family is working hard, moving the net from tree to tree, the man climbing the ladder, the boy climbing the lower branches of the tree itself, his mother gathering bucket after bucket from the catch of olives in the net.

Wine from grapes, oil from olives. In Italy I am always aware of the connection of food to earth, to sky. When I buy tomatoes in Italy, the stems are still attached, and my fingers come away smelling of the tart, pungent aroma of tomato stalks and leaves. In the United States, tomatoes taste like cardboard, and cucumbers are polished with wax. All the produce at home smells of the plastic in which it is wrapped. It is no wonder Italians love their food with such passion and care for the bounty of the soil as if each fruit were a jewel.

We spend the afternoon with Cornelia, talking of books and the writers we love. Marlowe sits, long-legged in the corner, listening, and at one point says, in his fine British tongue, "I can never get my breakfast in the morning till my mother finishes her twenty pages of Dostoevsky. She doesn't let anyone sit at the table with her when she's reading. Even if it means I will be late for school."

Cornelia admits her guilt. "I can't do my day till I've read my pages. It's my only quiet time."

"I sometimes have to have a biscuit standing up in the kitchen," Marlowe accuses her.

Cornelia laughs. "I'm sorry," she says. "It's my one vice."

When I ask Marlowe whether he ever speaks Italian at home, he explains that English is the language of the house, Italian of school and of speaking with his friends.

"It's a bit of a trial," Cornelia admits. "We don't always know which country we live in. It isn't so easy for non-Florentines here. Even though Paolo and I have been married for thirty years, each year he and I must go to the government offices and sign a document that he will support me and I will not become a ward of the country. Can you imagine doing this year after year?"

"But we always go to Oxford in the summers," Marlowe adds. "My parents keep a small flat there. It's where my mother and father met. And there I speak, of course, only English."

"I don't think I could ever learn Italian as well as you," I tell Cornelia. "No matter how hard I worked at it, I'd always talk like a three-year-old. That's why it's too daunting even to try."

"It took me many years. But once you're thrust into living here, you have no choice. You just jump in and try and hope people will be patient with you."

Though we offer to take Cornelia and Marlowe to lunch in a nearby restaurant, she insists on serving us bowls of minestrone soup, pasta with garlic and basil drenched in olive oil, bread and cheese and fruit and *panforte*, that strange chewy Siennese confection she introduced me to when I first visited here.

As we eat from her hand-painted dishes, I tell Cornelia I am reminded of a story by Arturo Vivante called "The Binoculars." This reminds Cornelia that I must meet her friend, Flavia, who knew him when he was a boy.

"Her villa is just down the road. I can't take you there today, but I will call her and see if we can make a date."

"I would love to do that."

Just before Cornelia takes us down the mountain to the bus stop, she presents me with a miniature version of the great bottle of oil. In a small and delicately shaped container, with glass handle and curved spigot, with a cork at the top, she gives me a portion of the precious and glowing oil produced from her olive grove on the mountain.

50

The Artist, Her Villa, the Bombs of World War II

A calendar marking the New Year arrives in the mailbox from *Esselunga*, the largest supermarket chain in Florence, reminding me of last things: the last of the year, the last of our last few days in Florence. In less than a week, we will be packing up to go home to America.

I remember with amazement that I didn't want to leave my home, my bed, my mother, my country. Now, my fear of Italy having vanished, I most definitely don't want to leave my life here, this glorious city, my friends, the view from my roof terrace, my comforting basket-bed, and all the foods of Italy made into art on my supermarket calendar.

For even the food ads in Italy are art. The pictures representing each month of the coming year are illustrated in glowing colors: the first month, *Gennaio,* presents a scallion upside down with roots flailing like Einstein's hair. Its caption reads "Scienziato o cipolla?" (Scientist or onion?). *Febbraio* offers two arched bananas: *"Delfini o banane?"* (Dolphins or bananas?). *Marzo* shows floating upside-down red onions: *"Mongolfiere o cipolle?"* (Hot-air balloons or onions?). *Aprile* features peas and their pods shaped like dragonflies: *"Libellule o piselli?"* (Dragonflies or peas?) The rest of the months continue, "Tennis balls or grapefruit?" "Rugby or melon?" "Tulips or red peppers?" "Mouse or radish?" "Seals or eggplants?" "Hedgehog or chestnut?" and finally, for

Dicembre, a triangle of peanuts and holly berries in the shape of a tree: *"Buon Natale."*

Art and Italy are words that go together like love and marriage. To me, art is this calendar, is the view of the Arno from my window and the clouds bunched like downy thrones above the cypress trees on the hills. Art is the way the foam of milk swirls on the cup of cappuccino, the way the swallows fly from the bell towers when the bells are rung, the reflections of the Duomo in the puddles of water after a heavy rain.

Sometimes I watch the woman across the courtyard hanging her husband's shirts to dry, her way of alternating colors, arranging the collars and sleeves just so, having them face all one way so that when puffs of wind blow them outward, they are like a chorus line, dancing. There is an aesthetic at work here on every level, in nature, in architecture, in food (especially in food)—art as evident in life as it is in the paintings of the museums and the sculptures of the piazzas.

Though my kitchen utensils are very spare and utilitarian, I find in the back of a cabinet, just these few days before we leave Italy, the most beautiful hand-painted pasta bowl, brilliant with purple and yellow flowers—a capacious and elegant showcase for a pot of cooked capellini or tortellini. It's as if my countess landlady had bought it preparing for royalty. And, indeed, perhaps anyone who eats in Italy is royalty.

Art is on my mind. We now have an invitation to visit Flavia Colacicchi, Cornelia's friend, widow of the artist Giovanni Colacicchi, whose works hang in the Pitti Palace.

At age eighty-three, Cornelia tells me, Flavia is not often feeling well enough to work. Joe and I are invited to tea with her tomorrow afternoon. Cornelia will pick us up at the last stop of the #14 bus and drive us to the villa.

A large and energetic Dalmatian dog is in the yard to greet us as we drive through the stone gates and up the gravel path. A young man (quite good-looking, I can't help but notice) comes out of the house to quiet his barking.

"He is the art student who boards with her," Cornelia explains.

"Since the death of her husband, she rents a room in the villa to an art student each year. Her son—who is also an artist—and his family live in the adjoining villa, but Flavia stays mostly to herself."

"I hope she understands English," I confess. "You know how little Italian I speak."

"I think she knows a little English," Cornelia tells me. "But we always speak in Italian, so I really don't know. I may have to act as interpreter."

The villa is like so many of the houses in the hills above Florence; two floors of gray stone, green wooden shutters, and the ubiquitous terra-cotta tile roof. Cornelia has given me some little background information—that her husband, Giovanni, was the director of the Accademia delle Belle Arti, that he had many famous friends: Bernard Berenson, Mario Castelnuovo-Tedesco, and Niccolo Tuccì among them. That Flavia has always been a wonderful painter and that she has had many showings of her work. In recent years, her ill health, which has kept her from painting, has left her feeling depressed.

But now the dog's barking has brought the artist herself to the door. She is small and spry on her feet, gray-haired. She has lively eyes. She is wearing a dark sweater and a gray skirt. A polished gem on a gold chain hangs about her neck. She graciously invites us in, speaking (to my relief) excellent English. She tells me she has heard from Cornelia how much I admire the writing of Arturo Vivante and confides at once that Arturo's father saved her life, long ago in Siena, by riding a long distance to bring back a doctor on the night she was in labor with her first son.

We are off at once telling stories to one another—I describing which of Arturo's stories I love best (the one about gypsies camping on the front lawn of the villa where the narrator's mother takes in paying guests, and the one Cornelia and I discussed, about the son who goes to the Abruzzi after his mother's death to buy her the dishes she had always longed for when she was alive).

Flavia tells us how Arturo, coming to visit her here shortly after the villa was bombed during the war, climbed up on a tall ladder to nail wooden boards over her broken windows. She regrets she has not been in touch with him or kept up with his work for many years. I promise her I will try to find her a copy of his latest book, *The Tales of Arturo Vivante,* as well as a long essay about his life, which he published in an encyclopedia called *Contemporary Authors' Autobiography Series.* (I add that they have just published my autobiography, as well.)

The ice thus broken, Flavia asks whether she may serve us tea—and I ask whether I may help. We rush off, leaving Joe and Cornelia in the living room, a room that I have been too distracted to observe save for noticing the large fireplace in which a crackling fire has been set to burn.

When I admire the grand old kitchen, the wood-burning stove, the many hanging pots and baskets, Flavia shrugs her shoulders. "It was a busy place once. I do not cook much for myself now that I am alone. You know how it is."

I tell her I do know. I tell her about my widowed mother, now in a nursing home for years, unable to walk or eat.

"Getting old," she says. "It is always difficult and sad." We stand there in the kitchen for a moment of silence, thinking about the necessary losses in life. Then we do what has to be done. She puts on the pot for tea, I help her by carrying the cups and saucers into the living room, she brings in sugar and a plate of foil-wrapped chocolates.

Joe and Cornelia are admiring Giovanni's paintings on the walls of the villa. One of them, *L'Ebbrezza di Noé* (The Drunkenness of Noah), displays Noah with three young men sprawled in a meadow, all nude but for a scarf held by one of the men in such a way that it hides Noah's genitals; beside Noah on the ground is a flute. In his hand is a glass, half full of the potion that made him drunk.

Other paintings by the artist feature nude maidens, landscapes of the Italian countryside, a country house in which, Flavia tells us, they often vacationed, portraits of people dear to Giovanni, one of them his master teacher. And, of course, portraits of Flavia, in her youth, in her maturity (but none in her old age.) I ask Flavia whether I may photograph her now with my camera; I will make my own portrait of her. When she agrees, I snap a photo of her standing beside one of her portraits.

Flavia Arlotta Colacicchi beside one of her portraits

"But if you want another, let's go outside," she says. Once in the garden, she walks quickly away from me and calls back, "Take it in the dark and far away. It is the only way I can stand myself now."

We have our tea and talk as if we have all known one another for a long time. Flavia tells us the story of a secret room in the house where her family hid Jews and partisans during the war, at great risk to themselves. And how, one night, the hidden soldier in the room under the house detected a fire that had just begun and that would have destroyed the entire house had he not been hidden there.

We speak of the mysteries of life, the violence of war, the pain of loss. We recognize this rare moment—when the veil of sociability and polite chatter gives way to an urgent honesty, to truth-telling.

When Cornelia recognizes that Flavia is tiring, she suggests we all should be going home.

"First let me show you Giovanni's studio—and mine, upstairs," Flavia says. She seems reluctant to let us leave. I have the sense that she

A painting by Flavia

has few visitors these days with whom to share her life and history. The stairs are steep, the hallways are covered with hard red tile. More of Giovanni's paintings fill the hallways, and in his studio canvasses are stacked one behind the other.

Flavia shows us her bedroom, the double bed with the old brass headboard, the handsome marble-topped dresser, the photos of her grandchildren.

"I stay up here mostly," she says. "I don't go downstairs very much, only when I have to."

"May we see *your* studio?" I ask.

She ushers us into a smaller room—and there are her paintings: breathtaking portraits of young women, women in thought, women frozen with anger, women in love. There are landscapes as well, of this very house and its garden, and of haystacks in the country. Her paintings are full of personal emotion, while it seems to me her husband's carry the ideas of history and religion.

Downstairs once again, we pass a table full of photographs. "Oh, I was just looking at these," Flavia says. "See this one, of my husband with Bernard Berenson? And this one of my husband and me, in 1934, I think."

And there are Flavia and Giovanni in profile, young and beautiful at the start of their long and fascinating journey together.

"We were very good-looking," she says without vanity.

Just as we are leaving, she asks us to wait just one more moment. Leaving the room, she comes back nearly staggering under the weight of two enormous books—the collected and published artworks of her husband. She gives one to me, one to Cornelia.

"I want you to have these." On top of them, she places smaller paperback books, one of her art, one a catalog of her paintings that have been shown in public.

I don't know how to thank her enough for this invitation into her home, her life, and her heart. "I will write to you. I will send you copies of these pictures I took. I will send you Arturo's book, I will. . . ."

She smiles, but she is already withdrawing. We watch her close and lock the front door. The lights downstairs go out.

Just as Cornelia reaches the bus stop above Careggi and exclaims that we are in luck, the bus is waiting there, just as she pulls up behind it and we begin to get out of the car, the bus pulls away and accelerates down the hill.

"I'm sure he saw us!" she says. "Why didn't he wait? Shall we try to chase him?"

"No need," Joe says, "We'll just wait for the next one."

"It's getting very cold," Cornelia reminds us.

"We'll be fine."

"You could wait here in the car with me. . . ."

"No, don't worry. You just go on home."

I am having my doubts. I think we should either chase the bus or wait in the car. But Joe is clearly not remembering what I am: that endless wait for a bus in Rome one night.

"Good-bye, then," Cornelia says. "I am so glad you could meet Flavia. She is one of my dearest friends in Italy."

"It was an honor for us."

"I will try to see you again before you leave. Perhaps we can have a farewell lunch at Grande Mondo."

"Let's count on it." We hug good-bye.

After Cornelia drives away, Joe and I duck our heads against in the wind, trying to shelter against the wall. It's Saturday night; there is no knowing when or if the next bus will turn up!

By the time a bus actually arrives, we are nearly frozen statues. Winter is upon the country. Italy, in these last weeks, has been transformed into a gray and colorless land. The tourists have left in droves, the stalls of souvenir sellers have closed, the gelato shops have pulled down their iron gates, and the museums—without dozens of tour guides shouting information to their flocks—are quiet again.

Tonight only a few passengers board the bus at various stops as it makes its way down toward *il centro*. When we reach the flatlands, an enormous traffic jam is evident. Streams of cars are flowing in from every street and moving toward the center of Florence. We can only conjecture as to the cause. Joe and I concur in our guessing: a soccer match must have ended, and these are all the cars going home.

Whatever the reason, our bus moves only a foot or two every five minutes. We enter that state of suspended life, all plans and needs on hold; there will be none of the necessities of forward motion till we get out of this. A huge mental effort is required not to feel constrained, or even a little desperate. It matters not whether we are hungry, tired, or in need of a bathroom—we are imprisoned for the moment. *Be Here Now* is where we are, like it or not.

I think this would be a good time to recite to each other from memory poems we learned in our youth, but I can see this is not an idea Joe would appreciate at this moment. I try to visualize peaceful moments in an idyllic country setting, but my mind will not cooperate.

The five or six passengers still on the bus seem to be sleeping, their heads falling forward or leaning against the window. I consider studying the artworks of the Colacicchis in the books I hold on my lap, but I feel I would be doing them a disservice, using their life's work as a convenient way to pass the time while stalled in traffic and in a dim light. I will simply suffer and learn from my husband, who in his wisdom is patient and practical. "It can't last forever," he informs me.

Somewhere near the station, the bus begins to move faster. Soon, in fact, the driver is flying along at a wild speed. At this rate we will be home in no time. My spirits rise—I count the landmarks: the stop at the Duomo (where two riders get off), the short distance along the lungarno, the turn into the residential area, the tall pine tree in a parklike traffic island in the middle of the road. We're only a few miles from home!

And, suddenly, on a dark stretch of street, the bus driver pulls to a stop, opens the doors, and says something to the passengers. Those still dozing on board are roused; one man speaks to the driver, who answers brusquely. It's clear—the ride is over, we must all get off.

Get off? We are still miles from home! This is not the stop at which we intended to get off the bus.

Joe goes forward to the driver and says, *"Non continua?"*

The answer is what we feared. *Non continua* indeed. We must get off. The bus is finished with us. There is no discussion about why.

Confused, we reluctantly step off the bus we feared we might have to stay on forever. The bus pulls away, its taillights disappearing into the night.

"What was *that* all about?"

Joe is buttoning up his coat against the wind. He shrugs. There's not much point in conjecturing. Another mystery of Italy.

"Well, *I* think that he was late," I tell my husband. "The traffic jam got him off schedule, his shift was over, he didn't want to complete his route. I think he figured he'd put in his time and he wanted to get home."

"That could be it," Joe agrees. "We'll never know."

"Only in Italy," I say. "Only in Italy could this happen!"

We discuss the possibility of waiting for another bus. But we are in a deserted area of closed shops and dark streets. There may not be another bus for an hour or more. It's too cold to stand still. We begin to walk toward home. The wind chills our cheeks. We begin to laugh. In fact, freed of the constraints of the bus and the creeping movement of the bus's wheels, we find we have energy in reserve we didn't know we could call upon.

Despite the heavy art books (which Joe valiantly carries), we are light on our feet. We walk so fast we begin to run. It's cold, and the motion warms us. The fresh air wakens our senses. We laugh and hold hands, swinging them between us.

Passing the Grande Mondo, we know we are closer to home than we thought. A sense of safety and confidence returns to us. We've survived the challenge one more time. The day's events take on an aura of adventure and discovery. A visit to an elderly woman, a bus caught in traffic. At home these events would be ordinary matters, but here, in Italy, nothing is ordinary.

We are always having an "experience," something to live through now, to talk about when we return home, and to remember, no doubt, forever. That seems to be a gift we have received here, the ability, somehow, to transform the contingencies of daily life into Italian ecstasies. In one way or another, joy has been inescapable here.

51

The Christmas Mystery,
Two Big Macs

Wind rattles the windowpanes all night. Closing the wooden shutters doesn't begin to reduce the commotion. A fierce shaking like this in California would be the signal of a huge earthquake—we would be running for our lives. But tonight we are snug and secure in our basket-bed, no one can get inside our bolted door, no one can enter our shuttered windows or climb to our roof terrace. The mosquitoes, which earlier made their unwelcome visits here, are now, in the cold of winter, finally vanquished.

I feel safe in Italy. I have been healthy here, undepressed, busy, energized, living moment by moment *for* the moment, without excessive reflection upon the human condition and the certainty of death.

Even the old don't seem truly old here as they walk arm in arm along the river front, care with obvious delight for their grandchildren, and climb with their heavy packages upon the buses. Perhaps people don't die here but live forever in view of the hillsides, the cypresses and the palazzi, the racing clouds, the vast arena of hill and sky and riverbank. (And perhaps those who do die become "The Incorruptibles"—those saints whose bodies never decay but, to the contrary, continue supple and fragrant—an inspiration to faith—unto eternity.)

We had wanted to do one last thing—rent a car and drive into the country to see Lucca, Pisa, the Isle of Elba, Ischia, Bologna, Orvieto, Vallombrosa—names that roll like music on the tongue. But the weather has turned bitter, and we have much to pack up and organize for departure, so we will simply have to leave certain hillsides undiscovered, certain views unseen—until we come back again.

I already have a list of things I meant to visit and never saw: Elizabeth Browning's apartment near the Pitti Palace and *La Specola,* the museum of medical wonders that features—in wax—the human body and all its organs, with special attention given to the more diseased and grotesque formations. In pictures I have seen of the wax models, they are all beautiful, full-size sculptures of men and women lying on their backs, with forms and faces as beautiful as Michelangelo's creations, yet each one of them is split open from neck to pelvis and his (or her) insides are revealed to show the reproductive or the skeletal or the circulatory system and disease processes within.

I have other regrets: that I never climbed to the top of the Duomo, never visited the ostensible home of Dante, never went into the Palazzo Vecchio or to the Casa Buonarroti, owned by Michelangelo. I missed the Bargello and the Medici Palace. In fact, what was I doing all these months? Did I see anything at all?

I appeal to my husband. If there is one more thing we can see— what shall it be?

We decide on a practical course of action—tomorrow afternoon we will go to a Christmas concert at the American Church, where our student Marta is singing a solo. The American Church is another place I meant to visit, especially its thrift shop, but I never got to it. Millie Materassi had told me it was an excellent place to find bargains as well as babysitters, a bake shop, an exchange place where one might locate a partner with whom to practice Italian (while the partner practices English), and a place where an Alcoholics Anonymous group meets on a weekly basis.

Not being in need of any of these services at the moment, we still would like to see where Americans who live in Florence gather for social and religious events. St. James Episcopal Church, as it is formally named, is located on Via Bernardo Rucellai, not far from the station, and also close to Le Scuderie, where our group met for Thanksgiving dinner. By checking the map, we determine that it will be a simple matter to get to the church: bus #14 to the station, and, because it's Sunday, there will be no crowds to battle.

The bus, to our delight, is empty when we board it. Within two stops, however, it is standing room only, and, within four, people are pressing in the doors with the crushing weight of a steamroller.

What could be going on?

We start our old guessing game. A soccer match to which everyone is going? (But wasn't there one just yesterday?) A festival we haven't heard about? A parade? An exodus from Florence because the river is about to overflow its banks as it did in 1966? We have no clue. When there is absolutely no more room for even one person on the bus, the driver stops, the doors open, and fifteen more get on. People are now nearly sitting in our laps. I begin to feel claustrophobic. I gasp for air. I don't understand this hellish crush, and no one is about to enlighten us.

"Let's see if we can get off at the next stop," I tell Joe.

He concurs, but the possibility is academic—there is no way we can exit the bus till fifty other people get off first.

I try my various methods of panic control. I unbutton my jacket and breathe deeply of air that was trapped inside it from the vicinity of our apartment, my theory being that it is fresher air than the exhaled carbon dioxide in the atmosphere around me. I try visualization: a peaceful seashore idyll, where I trail my toes in the delicately unfurling waves.

"God, I *have* to get off!" I cry to my husband. I leap up from my seat, step on the toes of whomever is in my way, and begin to claw my way toward an exit. Fortunately, the bus has just reached a designated stop, and I and a hundred others have the same idea: we shove and push and dig our way to the bottleneck and then pop out through the door.

We find ourselves downtown, at the stop just before the station. Whereas on all other Sundays the shops are closed and the streets deserted, today every shop door is open, every sign is lit, every window is draped with merchandise. Music is playing in the streets, the vendors are selling roasted chestnuts, the gelato shops are open for business, and the pizzerias are crowded to their doorjambs.

"Am I missing something?" I ask my husband, once I have had the good fortune to locate him in the crowd.

Just then we pass a large downtown department store (another place I haven't visited in Florence) and are pushed inside by the crowds behind us. People are milling about like sheep, examining the merchandise, looking at the price tags (making copious notes on slips of paper!), trying on hats, scarves, gloves, smelling perfume samples, holding sweaters against their bosoms, as well as dresses still on their hangers—but not many people seem to be buying anything. The cash registers are silent; the clerks who staff them are idle or chatting with other salespersons.

When we manage to escape back to the street, there are even more people milling around than before. There is an air of almost wild hysteria, high spirits; the store with sports equipment is full of young men picking up rugby shirts and checking their labels or examining soccer shoes; the store with handbags is filled with women counting the compartments in the purses, trying the zippers, clicking the latches. I think I have found myself in a dream.

"Let's go in and look at handbags," I tell Joe. "I think it's an Italian custom."

He takes my arm, kindly but firmly. "I think we'd better get to the church if we want to see Marta's concert."

In the entry of the church is a bulletin board where a small sign is tacked up beside the photo of a beautiful young woman with long dark curls. Joe and I both step closer to read the message:

My name is Caterina Fellini, I am twenty-two years old, I am Catholic and I live in Florence with my family, we are active in our church.

I can speak and write English very good, that was given by the help of intensive courses at the British Institute and by periods of permanence in England where I had the possibility of working as a babysitter, too.

I can speak and write German very good, that was given by long periods of permanence in Germany where I worked as a cat sitter.

I can speak and write French quite good, that was given by long periods of permanence in France, where I cared for dogs. My only desire is to continue specialising English not to forget it by making conversations with old dames or handsome males and helping them at home.

Joe studies the announcement.

"Too bad we're leaving. I could have practiced Italian with her, and she could have improved her skills with me."

"Which likely would have resulted in long periods of permanence in Italy for you . . . without me." It is both a joke and not a joke. It has not been easy for me to live in Florence among the Botticelli maidens so plentiful here. But Joe—though hardly blind to the boundless female beauty in this city—has been prudent and tactful in his appreciation of it. Even now, he takes my hand in order to end my teasing, reassure me, and lead me toward the chapel.

Inside the church, the concert has already begun. We are handed a program with forty-two songs listed on it, all of them Christmas songs, nearly all of them familiar to us. Our student, Marta, is listed as the very last performer on the program. Up front, a choir of six-year-old angels is singing "O Little Town of Bethlehem"—with a noticeably out-of-tune piano accompaniment.

Though it's bone-cold in the church, an ingenious electric heater is installed in the pew just under the Bible rack in front of us. All we need to do is push a button and the wires in front of our seat turn red and warm our hands and knees. In a very short time, however, the air becomes hot and stuffy, so the device must be turned off. On and off, hot then cold, I am kept busy operating the heating system.

We sit through eight songs: between each one a group of children must march off the stage, the next group of children must march on. I begin to make a little paper boat of my program. Fold the paper in half, fold the edges down into triangles, fold the bottom edges up—and I have a paper hat. Now, open the bottom of the hat, fold again. Pinch the sides and pull the ends and voila, a little boat. Now I need somewhere to sail it.

Joe sits listening respectfully to "Jingle Bells," "Deck the Halls," and, once again, "O Little Town of Bethlehem." I wonder if it would be rude to stretch out and lie down in the pew. I am suddenly very hungry.

I notice that many of the families attending this concert look astonishingly American—a sight I have not seen in some time. In fact, their faces appear weak to me and without character. I am not ready to confront America or Americans yet. If I am in Italy, forced to witness a Christmas concert, it should be of Italian songs, all sung in Italian. Pavarotti and Bartoli should be up there.

"Do you think we could leave in a little while?" I whisper to Joe.

"What about Marta's solo?"

"It's thirty songs away!"

"Maybe we can go out and then come back later."

"Yes, good idea!"

"Maybe get something to eat."

"Wonderful."

At a convenient moment between numbers, we tiptoe out of the pew and march up the aisle. Once outside, in the night air, we rush along the street toward the lights of downtown. Joe says, "I think we have time for a quick dinner and still can be back for Marta's song."

"Where shall we eat?"

"How about McDonald's? They just opened a new one in the station. It's nearby and bound to be faster than anywhere else."

"We can begin our decompression there. We have to start making the transition to home in some fashion. The Golden Arches are as good a way as any, I suppose."

The shops in the underground corridors leading into the train station are just as busy as the shops on the city streets. The crowds are not quite as thick, but there's a lively flow around the merchandise, yet I don't see people carrying parcels or bags.

At McDonald's we have a decadent dinner of Big Macs and large fries and medium Cokes. This time, American style, they offer plenty of free ketchup packets. As I watch Joe remove the pickles from under his bun as he always does at home, I realize we have begun the long initiation to becoming American again.

When dinner is over and the paper cups and cardboard wrappers have been tossed, we emerge from the station refreshed, rested, and ready for more punishment. Back at the American Church, we observe that Marta is still ten slots away from singing her song. But we are patient, blood sugar restored, mellow now in the certainty of an end in sight. As the world turns, Marta will sing, the concert will end, we will take the bus home, we will sleep, still in Italy, still in our Italian bed, safe from our own country for yet another few days.

When Riccardo comes the next evening—his last time—to practice English with Joe, our good Italian friend solves the mystery for us: "In Florence, on the Sunday three weeks before Christmas, all the stores open and stay open late. Every Florentine rushes into the city to look at the merchandise and choose the Christmas presents he wants to buy for others. (He also makes note of some things he hopes to receive and where his family can find them.) He may not buy things right away— there are other stores to look at, prices to compare. But, yes, that's why you were caught in such a crowd. And perhaps why you didn't see anyone buying things in the first hour or two."

While Riccardo and Joe retire to the living room to converse in Italian (and to make plans for us to have dinner together so that we can meet Riccardo's betrothed, Angela), I take the suitcases out of the bedroom wardrobe and begin to contemplate how I might arrange our belongings for departure. How will I possibly fit so much volume into so little space? This is something akin to imagining how I can gather all my experience of Florence into a small area of my brain known as "memory" and cart it off to America without having to leave some precious things behind.

52

L'Ultimo Addio, Last Views of the Ponte Vecchio

Ice crystals creep across the window hours before dawn on our last night in Florence. Rain has been forecast, but the night is clear and icy. The alarm has just waked us at 2 A.M.; we must be outside with all our luggage, the apartment vacated, by 3 A.M., when the taxi will arrive at the gate to take us to the meeting place on the lungarno where the bus from Rome first dispatched us into our Italian lives.

Flung out of sleep into groggy awareness, we stumble about, getting our balance and trying to accept the fact that we have come to the end of our grand adventure. For the past two days, we have been making our good-byes.

Professor Materassi and his wife held a tea to bid us farewell, inviting an illustrious Italian publisher (who promised to consider my work for publication in Italy), the son of an American writer who was visiting in Florence, and Riccardo and the young woman, Angela, to whom he is engaged to be married. Angela, a shy, pretty woman, managed to communicate to me that she wished her English were better. I confessed that my Italian was just as lacking, and we both laughed. We clasped hands, liking one another at once.

Millie Materassi served us slices of delicious *panettone,* cream-filled delicacies, fruit tarts on lacey paper circles. Professor Materassi,

Professor Mario Materassi, Millie, Luisa, and Figaro

Our landlady, Rina

handsome and professorial in his beard, sipped his tea and told us last-minute tales of Florence and its wonders. The Materassis' soulful-eyed cat, Figaro, perched on the piano bench, the curve of his back a question mark. *How can you leave here?* was the question.

Yesterday, Cornelia and I had our parting luncheon at the Grande Mondo Ristorante Cinese. We hugged good-bye over a table of plum wine, Dragon chips, and *primavera* rolls. We promised to write to each other.

Later in the afternoon, our landlady, Rina, stopped by to settle our phone bill and to offer us a bottle of their lovely wine from the farm. We had to decline, pleading lack of space and too much weight in our bags. She thanked me, amused, for all the packages of pasta and jars of tomato sauce I was leaving behind for her.

Finally, we shared our last supper with Riccardo and Angela, who gave us as a parting gift a book—of the same gargantuan size as the Giovanni Colacicchi artworks—containing magnificent aerial views of Tuscany. We toasted all the simple and fine things: our last pizza, our last bottle of Chianti Classico, our last noisy, smoky, passionate pizzeria.

283

Now, in this last dawn, our small bedroom is emptied of all objects but our suitcases, which lie open, packed to their brims, waiting for one last and desperate compression to get them closed.

We dress in haste, pack up our toothbrushes, toss away the last of the soap and shampoo, focus on removing the dust and debris of our occupancy as well as we can. Last, fast, things must be done: coffee made in the *due tazze* espresso maker, the last lighting of the stove with the *accendigas,* a bite or two of packaged sugared buns, and a brief regret for the foods to be left behind for Rina: the bags of potatoes and onions, the full jar of Nutella hazelnut chocolate creme, the frozen gelato, the sealed bottles of *succo di pomodoro,* the too many packages of pasta I bought in the zeal and hope of making pasta here for eternities to come.

All these decisions are wrenching; this is not a sentimental parting, this is surgery! Joe and I are silent in our preparations to leave, each counting his own duties, his own losses. I feel, with the force of blows on my back, what I will no longer have.

Time is going faster than we imagined; we are nearly breathless with our little jobs; taking the garbage down, scrubbing the surfaces of the stove, sink, and table, checking the closets and the drawers, stripping the basket-bed of its heavy linens, looking once more from each window, memorizing how the lights on the hills look to the east, west, and south but having no time to climb to the roof terrace to look north to Fiesole and Mount Morello.

This is it. In a final choreographed and practiced move, I sit hard on the suitcases—one after the other—and Joe pulls the zippers closed. Pure will and conjuring force the objects within to bend and shrink to the size we require of them (except for one bulky bathrobe of Joe's and one heavy shirt of mine. These we leave behind with a note of apology to Rina).

We roll and pull our bags into the hallway, leaving them in front of the *ascensore,* then going back for a check of the apartment. Silence and emptiness, all the life of the past three months pressed into suitcases, the genie back in the jar, not a crumb of evidence left behind to prove that from one window we saw a woman put a Picasso in the dustbin, from another we watched a storm raise the level of the Arno high enough to create a rushing silver torrent, and from still another observed the weekly arrival of Riccardo as he parked his motor scooter, took off his helmet, looked up to see us at the window.

Whoever will inhabit this apartment next will never know what we knew here. If this is sentimental, well—I allow myself this much.

It's nearly 3 A.M. One of us must go down and stand in the cold lest the taxi driver arrive, find no one there, and leave. Or he may not come at all. If we lock ourselves out of the apartment, leaving the keys within, and then no taxi comes, what then?

I suddenly have no patience with *what ifs* and *what thens*. I've played that game long enough to last me through eternity. Here we are—having survived Italy, all manner of travel, mishaps, confusion, having overcome exhaustion, disappointment, an overload of art, the misery of public transportation—and we are nevertheless glowing with love for this country and heartbroken to have to leave it.

We ride down with our belongings. Piece by piece, we drag our luggage out of the elevator, through the hallway, past the mailboxes, out the inner door and the outer door, and through the gate. Joe goes up to make one more quick check and to leave the keys on the oilcloth-covered kitchen table.

Ungrateful Florence, said Byron. *Magnanimous Florence,* said Twain. It would take a book, a thousand books, to describe what Florence is. Joe slams the door of the apartment—I can hear the finality of it from the foot of the staircase.

Ciao, Florence! Addio. Arrivederci, Firenze!

The waiting bus casts a huge shadow on the river wall. Our students are clustered at the edge of the Arno, sobbing and clinging to one another. Nicoletta, concerned that they will wake everyone in the apartments overlooking the lungarno, makes a futile effort to bring order. But the kids are not to be quieted or consoled. They burst out in fresh waves of tears, embracing one another, moving through the crowd, flinging their arms about everyone and anyone. We are not spared. The girls weep on my shoulder, dampen the front of Joe's coat. Mrs. Pedrini is busy passing out chocolates to sweeten the moment.

"How can I bear it?" says one of our girls in the darkness. Bundled up as she is in a hat and scarf, I can't even tell who it is. "I'll die if I don't come back."

"Look at the Duomo, just *look* at it!" cries another.

And I look. There, across the river, in the cold still night, is the looming dome of the great cathedral, Santa Maria del Fiore, Saint Mary of the Flower. Brunelleschi's dome glows like an otherworldly shape, perhaps a crown, or the cap of God. Its lantern, its warm colors, its consoling supporting white struts, is a living countenance and seems to offer the reassuring gaze of a kind mother. The dome has been our compass, our point of reference, our guiding light during these past months.

"I'm going to come back and spend my life here," vows Maria. "I can babysit while I go to school."

"And I'm going to work at home for a year to get enough money to come back and study here." Pledges, vows, and promises are announced to the river, to the sky, and to the stars above the Arno.

Several Italian young men have gathered valiantly with us in the predawn cold; Mai Jing's friend Massimo is here to ride to Rome with her on the bus, as are the three young men who first took three of our girls out into the countryside in their van to give them bags of clothes. The six of them have become inseparable friends, and the girls have become like daughters to the young men's families.

Natalie's suitor, the handsome Cesare, whom she met at the Full-Up Disco, is here, in his black leather jacket, a mournful look on his face. In fact, the two of them have just walked off alone a short distance toward the Ponte Vecchio.

"Oh, my God," says one of the girls. "Is he going to? Is he? Is he?"

Everyone turns to watch Natalie and Cesare.

"My God, I think he is."

The tall young man has lifted Natalie up to sit on the parapet, and now he is kneeling before her.

"Oh, he must be asking her! He's asking her right now!!"

Even Nicoletta has paused in directing the organization of the luggage in the compartments under the coach to watch the events transpiring on the river wall.

Beyond the couple, the familiar three arches of the Ponte Vecchio glow in the light of the street lamps, its shops closed, the corridor that runs above it from the Uffizi to the Pitti Palace a dim strip, its circular windows looking like closed eyes.

"I'm going to die of excitement," say Maria. "To think we're actually seeing it happen."

"No, I think they're just taking a picture," says Marta, matter-of-factly. And, yes, now in the dimness, it seems that Cesare is aiming upward from his kneeling position to take a picture of Natalie with the Florentine skyline behind her.

"I was certain he was proposing," says Maria, in a new burst of tears.

"He already has, but don't breathe a word of it," Marta whispers. "I know they've made a plan to be together. She's going to finish the school year at home and then come back to marry him."

"Oh, how lucky she is," sobs Maria. "If only it had happened to me."

I suspect we all would like to be proposed to in the glow of the Duomo. Who wouldn't want to fall in love in Florence?

I feel Joe's hand press my shoulder briefly, for which I return a grateful glance.

The bus driver revs his motor. Nicoletta announces that the headcount is complete, the luggage is loaded, everyone needs to get on the bus, it's time to go. We have a three-hour trip to Rome and then hours of checking through customs before we board the plane.

"*Andiamo,*" Nicoletta calls to the students, but she says it gently, almost like a prayer.

Our kids board the bus as if beginning a life sentence in prison. Their heads are down, they are moaning. Only Phil and Sara get on the bus briskly, holding hands, a couple from home who can stay coupled if they choose to. Cesare remains on the bank of the Arno, his face impassive, his bearing military, like the King of Italy on his horse. Natalie takes the window seat behind me; tears are flowing down her cheeks. I offer her a tissue over the seat, but her forehead is pressed to the window glass, her eyes soldered to her young man's gaze. The bus driver closes the doors; he begins to move out slowly from the curb.

I think the sounds of sobbing must be audible in the tombs of Santa Croce as the bus lumbers along the narrow streets, makes a right turn, crosses Ponte Alle Grazie, and moves east along the opposite lungarno.

To my astonishment, I see that the bus is returning to our neighborhood, that the driver, on his way to the *autostrada* and Rome, has just turned into the street that passes our apartment house on Via Venosta. I look up to our windows, half expecting to see Joe and myself moving about in our warmly lit kitchen. I want to call out to everyone, *Oh look, that's our house—that window is our bedroom, that one our living room.*

But the rooms are dark. Like black mirrors, the windowpanes reflect the river lights back to the river. I breathe in this new reality. The bus turns south, and the city disappears behind us. The sobbing in the bus modulates to sighing, then to silence. The driver turns off the interior lights so that we may contemplate the dark landscape flying by.

I feel the speed of departure as surely as if Botticelli's God of Wind were blowing us homeward. If I look closely, I can see him hovering over the fields, his wings shimmering, his blue cape billowing, his cheeks puffed with the force of his intention.

He is telling us that we no longer live in Florence. Now Florence lives in us.